BST

FRIENDS
OF ACPL

P9-CML-489

NOLO *Your Legal Companion*

"In Nolo you can trust." —**THE NEW YORK TIMES**

OUR MISSION
*Make the law as simple as
possible, saving you time,
money and headaches.*

Whether you have a simple question or a complex problem, turn to us at:

NOLO.COM

Your all-in-one legal resource

Need quick information about wills, patents, adoptions, starting a business—or anything else that's affected by the law? **Nolo.com** features free articles in our Nolopedia, legal updates, resources and all of our books, software, forrms and online applications.

NOLO NOW

Make your legal documents online

Creating a legal document has never been easier or more cost-effective! Create an online will or trust, form an LLC, or file a Provisional Patent Application!
Check it out at **http://nolonow.nolo.com**.

NOLO'S LAWYER DIRECTORY

Meet your new attorney

If you want advice from a qualified attorney, turn to Nolo's Lawyer Directory—the only directory that lets you see hundreds of in-depth attorney profiles so you can pick the one that's right for you. Find it at **http://lawyers.nolo.com**.

ALWAYS UP TO DATE

Sign up for NOLO'S **LEGAL UPDATER**

Old law is bad law. We'll email you when we publish an updated edition of this book—sign up for this free service at **nolo.com/ legalupdater**.

Find the latest updates at NOLO.COM

Recognizing that the law can change, we post legal updates during the life of this edition at **nolo.com/updates**.

Is this edition the newest? ASK US!

To make sure that this is the most recent edition available, just give us a call at **800-728-3555**.

(Please note that we cannot offer legal advice.)

Please note

We believe accurate, plain-English legal information should help you solve many of your own legal problems. But this text is not a substitute for personalized advice from a knowledgeable lawyer. If you want the help of a trained professional—and we'll always point out situations in which we think that's a good idea— consult an attorney licensed to practice in your state.

1st edition

Nolo's Essential Retirement Tax Guide

Your Health, Home, Investments & More

**By Twila Slesnick, Ph.D., Enrolled Agent
& Attorney John C. Suttle, CPA**

FIRST EDITION	NOVEMBER 2008
Editor	LISA GUERIN
Cover Design	SUSAN PUTNEY
Proofreading	ROBERT WELLS
Index	THÉRÈSE SHERE
Printing	CONSOLIDATED PRINTERS, INC.

Slesnick, Twila.
  Nolo's essential retirement tax guide : your health, home, investments & more
/ by Twila Slesnick and John C. Suttle. -- 1st ed.
      p. cm.
    ISBN-13: 978-1-4133-0912-6 (pbk.)
    ISBN-10: 1-4133-0912-7 (pbk.)
    1. Individual retirement accounts--Law and legislation--United States--Popular
works. 2. Old age pensions--Taxation--Law and legislation--United States--
Popular works. I. Suttle, John C. II. Title. III. Title: Essential retirement tax guide.
    KF6425.S54 2008
    332.024'0145--dc22

                                2008022977

Copyright © 2008 by Nolo
ALL RIGHTS RESERVED. PRINTED IN THE U.S.A.

No part of this publication may be reproduced, stored in a retrieval system, or transmitted
in any form or by any means, electronic, mechanical, photocopying, recording, or otherwise,
without prior written permission. Reproduction prohibitions do not apply to the forms
contained in this product when reproduced for personal use.

Quantity sales: For information on bulk purchases or corporate premium sales, please contact
the Special Sales Department. For academic sales or textbook adoptions, ask for Academic
Sales. Call 800-955-4775 or write to Nolo, 950 Parker Street, Berkeley, CA 94710.

Dedication

This book is dedicated to Damien Arthur Suttle, 1981–2008.

Acknowledgments

Thanks to Nolo editor Lisa Guerin for using her keen intellect and sharp eye to help make this book the best that it can be, and to Acquisitions Editor Marcia Stewart for her hard work in helping us develop and organize the project. Thanks to Terri Hearsh for her attention to detail and for making the book look great.

Thanks also to Durf for always being interested in what comes next; and to Mojdeh for her patience.

Table of Contents

Your Retirement Tax Companion

4 Your Health

5 Charitable Contributions and Volunteer Work

11 Gifts, Inheritances, and Surviving Your Spouse

Index

Your Retirement Tax Companion

There was a time when the word "retirement" meant more or less the same thing to everyone: Quitting your job and taking it easy. Simplifying your life and your finances. Signing up for Social Security and Medicare. In this simpler world, financial decisions would be a snap, even those involving your taxes. You could fire your accountant and file Form 1040-EZ. Or maybe you wouldn't even have to file a tax return.

My, how things have changed. Because we are living longer, healthier lives, many of us have plenty of time and energy to spare after we leave the workaday world. Today, retirement might mean starting a new career, moving to a dream locale, or traveling the world. Some people quit their corporate jobs only to turn a long-time hobby into a money-making home business. Some choose not to pay off their mortgages, instead using excess cash to buy a vacation home in Florida, a getaway condominium in San Francisco, or a two-week time-share in Hawaii.

Life after retirement isn't as simple as it used to be. Nor is the tax code. Even though you won't be getting a paycheck, you'll have other income—and expenses—to deal with. Retirement often brings with it a number of new tax issues, with accompanying IRS forms. You might be analyzing financial transactions you've never thought much about before, like purchasing your own health or long-term care insurance, funding a grandchild's education, drawing down your IRA, or stepping up your charitable giving. Are your insurance premiums deductible? If you buy a second home, are any of the expenses deductible? What sort of tax benefits are available if you start a little business or give your children or grandchildren some financial help?

Like the rest of your life, your tax situation will likely be different after retirement, but not necessarily simpler. The good news is that plenty of tax benefits are available to retirees; you just have to know where to look. That's where this book comes in: It will help you take advantage of the credits, deductions, and exemptions that are most likely to apply in retirement, with an eye to those issues that are more likely to come up for you in the years after you've left your nine-to-five job, finished rearing your children, and moved on to new adventures.

Each chapter explains the tax ramifications of a particular issue or decision after retirement, such as your health, your family, or your investments. You'll find tax tips and strategies to help you save money, as well as checklists you can use to make sure you haven't missed important deductions and credits. Whether you're starting a business, selling or renting out the family home, passing your wealth on to your kids, doing volunteer work for favorite causes, or facing health challenges, this book will help you find new (and old) tax benefits available to you as you embark on this exciting new stage of your life.

Some Tax Basics

Once you retire, your financial picture changes. The most obvious change, of course, is that you no longer receive a paycheck; instead, you must live off other sources of income, such as retirement accounts or other investments, Social Security, pensions, or rental income. Your expenses probably will also change, especially if you are facing health problems or making lifestyle adjustments, such as selling your home or starting a business.

When your income and expenses change, so do your taxes. This book explains the tax benefits that apply to common retirement scenarios, from paying for a grandchild's education to purchasing long-term care insurance, buying a second home, or turning a favorite hobby into a profitable side business. Before you can take advantage of these benefits, however, you'll need a basic understanding of how taxes work.

At the simplest level, of course, you must pay tax on your income. But what counts as income for tax purposes? How do deductions, exemptions, and credits work? And are you going to have to worry about the alternative minimum tax? This chapter will help you answer those questions, so you can better understand the tax benefits associated with retirement issues and activities. Those tax benefits are described in detail in the rest of the book.

Income

It's pretty common for recent retirees to be nervous about outliving their nest eggs. If you are like many retirees, you will receive Social Security benefits for life, but those benefits are unlikely to sustain you in the style to which you have become accustomed. Hopefully, you also have some investments that generate additional income in the form of interest, dividends, or maybe rental income, and that you can sell if and when you need extra cash.

If you have such investments, one of your tasks during retirement will be to manage that portfolio so it isn't gone before you are. Fortunately, you have a lot of control. You can decide when to take money out of your accounts and when to sell assets, factoring in how your timing will affect your tax liability. For example, you might find that it makes more sense to wait until January to sell some stock (rather than selling in December) because you expect your income to be lower next year.

This section briefly covers some of the most common sources of retirement income.

Social Security

Most people who work in the corporate world contribute to Social Security through payroll taxes. If you are one of them and have paid into the system for the required time period, you may begin collecting Social Security benefits when you retire, as long as you are at least age 62. The amount you receive depends on a variety of factors, including how long you've been contributing to Social Security, how much money you earned over the years, and how old you are when you start receiving benefits.

If you did not contribute to Social Security during your lifetime, but your spouse did, you might be able to collect benefits based on your spouse's work record, even if you and your spouse are divorced. If your spouse has died, you may be entitled to survivor's benefits based on your spouse's Social Security contributions.

Social Security benefits are not subject to income tax if your total income is below $32,000 if you are married filing jointly, or $25,000 if you are single. (To determine whether or not your income is under the threshold, you must total all of your other taxable income and add to it certain tax-exempt income plus half of your Social Security benefits.)

Once your income exceeds the threshold amounts, the portion of your Social Security benefits that is subject to income tax increases as your income increases. However, you can never be taxed on more than 85% of your benefits. For more information about calculating the amount of Social Security that is subject to tax, see IRS

Publication 915, *Social Security and Equivalent Railroad Retirement Benefits.*

Social Security benefits are paid to you for life, so you don't have to worry about outliving these funds. However, regardless of how much Social Security you receive, it probably won't cover all of your expenses during retirement.

Retirement Plans and Pensions

Another benefit of having worked in the corporate world might be a retirement nest egg that you accumulated through contributions you and your employer made to a retirement plan, such as a 401(k). Perhaps you are one of the lucky retirees who will receive a monthly pension from a former employer.

If you were self-employed, you might have established and contributed to your own retirement plan—a SEP, perhaps, or a 401(k) of your own. And, whether working for another employer or for yourself, you might also have contributed to a traditional IRA or a Roth IRA.

Now, during your retirement, you will likely be using these plan assets for living expenses. Most of the funds you receive, whether in the form of pension payments or withdrawals you make from your retirement plan or traditional IRA, will be fully taxable in the year you receive them. (Note, however, that Roth IRA distributions generally will not be taxable. And, if you made nondeductible contributions to any of the plans, those contributions generally will not be taxed a second time when you withdraw them.)

 RESOURCE

Want more information on withdrawing money from retirement accounts? Take a look at *IRAs, 401(k)s & Other Retirement Plans: Taking Your Money Out,* by Twila Slesnick and John C. Suttle (Nolo), which explains the rules governing retirement plan distributions. You'll learn how to avoid penalties and minimize your tax liability while making the most of your retirement investments.

Investments

If you inherited the thrifty gene from an ancestor, you might also have accumulated a portfolio of investments separate from your various retirement accounts—at a bank or brokerage firm, for example. Those assets might include cash and stocks and bonds that throw off interest and dividends on which you pay tax each year.

During retirement, there will probably be times when you need more money than your interest and dividends provide. In that case, you might have to sell some of your securities or other investment assets. If the asset has appreciated since you bought it, you might have a capital gain on which you must pay tax. If the asset has not appreciated, you might have a capital loss to claim against other income, thereby lowering your tax liability. See "Selling Assets," below, for more information on calculating capital gains and losses.

Rental Income

Some people enter the retirement phase of their lives with a rental property or two. Often, the property was acquired specifically for the purpose of providing extra income during retirement, or perhaps with an eye to selling the property when cash is tight.

Owning rental property comes with a lot of tax benefits. Although you generally have to declare the rent you receive as income, you may deduct the expenses you pay as a landlord (such as the cost of maintenance, utilities, and insurance). You may also claim depreciation: an additional deduction that might run to thousands of dollars a year. (You'll find more information on the tax benefits associated with rental property in Chapter 8.)

If you sell rental property during your lifetime, you might face a big gain if you've held the property for a long time. See "Selling Assets," below, for more information on calculating capital gains and losses.

Business Income

Many retirees take on small or part-time jobs during retirement. Some even start their own businesses, whether to pursue a passion, keep busy, or put a little extra money in their pockets. The compensation you earn will be subject to income tax, just as it was during your preretirement years. (If you start your own business, you can offset your income with the expenses you incur.)

As long as you earn income from a job or business, you will also pay Social Security and Medicare taxes either through your employer's payroll taxes or through self-employment taxes you must pay when you have net income from your own business. See Chapter 3 for more information on the tax issues associated with running a business.

Bear in mind that earning income from a job or business might affect your Social Security benefits, both in terms of how much you receive and how much will be subject to income tax. For more information about Social Security benefits, go to the Social Security Administration's website, www.ssa.gov.

Selling Assets

At some point during your retirement, you may decide to sell an asset, whether it's rental property; artwork, antiques, or other valuable personal property; stocks and bonds; or even your home. Perhaps you need more money than your retirement investments are generating. Or, it might just be time to make a change. You might be tired of being a landlord, for example, or feel ready to move to a smaller home.

Whenever you sell an asset, you must calculate your gain or loss. If you have a gain, you might owe tax on it; if you have a loss, you might be able to use it to offset other income.

For tax purposes, your gain or loss is the difference between the sales proceeds and your adjusted basis in the asset. Beware, however: Sales proceeds are not necessarily the price the buyer paid you for the asset, nor is the adjusted basis necessarily what you paid initially to purchase it.

Sales Proceeds

When you sell an asset, the buyer pays you a certain amount to purchase it. In some cases, however, you won't get to pocket every dollar of the purchase price; some of it will go toward the expenses of the sale (such as a transaction fee, broker's fee, or commission). To come up with the sales proceeds—the figure you have to use to calculate your capital gain or loss—you subtract your expenses from the sales price.

Adjusted Basis

If you talk taxes with an accountant, you might notice that the word "cost" isn't used very often. Instead, accountants talk about the "basis" or "adjusted basis" of an asset, which is a more nuanced concept. (Accountants often use the terms basis and adjusted basis interchangeably, and we follow that practice in this book.)

Whenever you sell an asset, whether stocks, bonds, a rental property, or even your own home, you need to determine your adjusted basis to calculate your gain or loss. Adjusted basis is essentially what you originally paid for the asset, minus any cost recovery you were entitled to claim (such as depreciation), plus any additional capital expenditures you made. For example, if you own rental property, your adjusted basis is your original purchase price, plus the cost of improvements you have made, less the depreciation you were entitled to claim on your tax return. In the case of securities that you purchase and sell through a broker, your adjusted basis is typically your original cost plus any commissions you pay.

If you inherit property, your adjusted basis when you inherit it is usually the property's fair market value on the owner's date of death (the date you inherit it). Of course, your adjusted basis will change if you later make improvements to the property or recover any of your cost through depreciation.

Tax Strategy: Should You Sell Appreciated Property?

If you own property that has appreciated significantly over the years, it might make sense not to sell the property at all, as long as you have other resources to fall back on. If you hold the property until your death, your beneficiaries will get the benefit of a stepped-up basis. Their basis will be the fair market value of the property at the time of your death. Tax liability for the gain (the property's appreciation during your lifetime) evaporates.

This rule applies to many capital assets, such as rental property and stocks and bonds that are held outside of retirement accounts. (There is no step-up for assets that are held inside a retirement account, such as an IRA or 401(k) plan.) It can be especially beneficial for rental property. You must subtract your depreciation deductions—often thousands of dollars a year—to calculate your basis. This means that your basis in rental property that you've held a long time is often quite low (and your gain high). If you allow your heirs to inherit that property rather than selling it during your lifetime, their basis will be stepped up to its fair market value at your death, and all of the depreciation benefits you enjoyed won't have to be repaid. See Chapter 11 for more information about inherited assets generally; rental property is covered in Chapter 8.

3 1833 05620 2499

If you receive property as a gift, your adjusted basis when you receive it depends on whether the property appreciated while the donor owned it. If so, your adjusted basis when you receive it is the same as the donor's adjusted basis when he or she gave it to you.

If the property's fair market value when you receive it is *less* than the donor's adjusted basis, then your basis is calculated in one of two ways. For purposes of determining whether you have a loss when you later sell the property, your basis is the property's fair market value on the date of the gift. To determine whether you have a gain, your basis is the donor's adjusted basis on the date of the gift. If you sell the property at a price that falls somewhere in between its fair market value and the donor's adjusted basis at the time of the gift, you have no gain and no loss.

> **EXAMPLE:** Your uncle gave you 100 shares of XYZ stock, which he originally bought for $5,000. On the date he gave you the stock, it was worth $4,000. You later sell the stock for $6,000. Because you have a gain from the sale, you use your uncle's basis of $5,000 to calculate your gain. Your gain is $1,000.
>
> If you sell the stock for $3,000, you have a loss on the sale. In this situation, you use the stock's fair market value on the date of the gift ($4,000) to calculate your loss. Your loss is $1,000.
>
> If you sell the stock for an amount that is between your uncle's basis ($5,000) and the fair market value at the date of the gift ($4,000), you are deemed to have no gain and no loss.

Deductions

Once you've tallied up your income, you get to subtract your deductions. Generally, deductions represent money you've spent for certain items that Congress has decided you shouldn't have to pay tax on. Examples of deductible expenses are interest you pay on a mortgage, medical bills, operating costs for an ongoing business, and gifts you make to charity.

Not all deductions are created equal, however. Some deductions offset income dollar for dollar, so every deductible dollar you spend is a dollar on which you don't have to pay tax. Other expenses are not deductible until they exceed a certain dollar amount or a percentage of your gross income. And some deductions must be used to offset specific types of income (for example, business expenses are claimed against business income, and rental expenses against rental income).

There are several different types of deductions: itemized deductions, the standard deduction, and "above-the-line" deductions. Let's sort these out.

Itemized Deductions

When calculating your taxable income, you are permitted to claim certain personal (nonbusiness) deductions. You subtract these deductions from your income to determine how much of your income is subject to tax. Like exemptions (described below), deductions help to ensure that your tax liability is commensurate with your income. If your income is relatively low, you should pay little or no income tax, with the help of deductions and exemptions.

To take advantage of many of these personal deductions, you must separately list, or "itemize," deductions on Schedule A, an IRS form that you must submit with your income tax return.

With only a few exceptions, the law allows you to claim the same deductions after retirement that you were permitted to claim before retirement. However, once you retire, you are likely to spend your money differently—perhaps more on health care and less on business expenses, more on travel and less on a mortgage.

After you retire, you might even discover that you have very few qualified expenses to claim on Schedule A. Perhaps it hardly seems worth the trouble to wade through the receipts you have accumulated during the year. If you do not want to spend your time tallying receipts, or if the totals seem too paltry to bother with, you might choose to claim the standard deduction instead of itemizing your deductions. (See "Standard Deduction," below.)

Common Itemized Deductions

Looking at the list of possible deductions on Schedule A will help you decide if itemizing is worth your while. Commonly claimed itemized deductions include:

- mortgage interest
- property tax
- state income tax
- charitable contributions
- medical expenses (but only to the extent they exceed 7.5% of your adjusted gross income)
- investment fees, and
- tax preparation fees.

CAUTION

Itemized deductions are limited in 2008 and 2009 for high-income taxpayers. If your income is high, you might not be able to claim all of your itemized deductions. For 2008, most of your itemized deductions (but not your medical expense deduction or investment interest expense) will be reduced by 1% of the amount by which your adjusted gross income exceeds $159,950 (this amount may increase for 2009). Even if your itemized deductions exceed the standard deduction, this rule could bring your itemized deductions below the standard deduction, which isn't subject to this reduction. Beginning in 2010, there will no longer be a reduction in itemized deductions for high-income taxpayers.

Standard Deduction

You don't have to itemize your deductions and file Schedule A with your income tax return. If you prefer, or if it saves taxes, you may simply claim the standard deduction, a fixed dollar amount that increases each year for inflation.

Although it is to your advantage to complete and file Schedule A when your itemized deductions exceed the standard deduction, you would not be alone if you decided it was just too much trouble. Maybe you have more important things to do, like playing golf or going skiing.

> CAUTION
>
> **Don't be too quick to forgo itemizing your deductions.** If you have a mortgage or you paid a significant amount of state income taxes, itemizing will almost certainly be more beneficial. And, because the standard deduction amount is adjusted each year for inflation, you will need to calculate your itemized deductions every year anyway, to see which provides a greater benefit.

The actual dollar amount of the standard deduction depends on your filing status. If you are married filing a joint return, your standard deduction is larger than it is for single filers. Also, if you are at least 65 years old or you are blind, you are eligible for a higher standard deduction.

For 2008, the standard deduction amounts are as follows:

Single	$ 5,450
Married filing jointly	$10,900
Married filing separately	$ 5,450
Head of Household	$ 8,000
Additional amount if over age 65 or blind (if single)	$ 1,350
Additional amount if over age 65 or blind (if married)	$ 1,050

You are entitled to claim your full standard deduction no matter how high your income is. Unlike other tax benefits, the standard deduction is not phased out as your income increases. (See Chapter 4 for more detailed information about claiming the standard deduction.)

Above-the-Line Deductions

When claiming itemized deductions or the standard deduction, you first calculate your adjusted gross income (AGI). Then, you subtract your deductions (and exemptions—see below) from your AGI to come up with your taxable income.

Above-the-line deductions are different: They are subtracted from your income to arrive at your AGI. The "line" is essentially your AGI. This distinction might seem insignificant, but in fact, above-the-line deductions can be much more valuable. Like other deductions, they directly reduce the amount of your income that is subject to income tax. But above-the-line deductions also reduce your AGI. A lower AGI is often to your advantage because AGI is used as a measuring stick for phasing out or even eliminating certain tax benefits:

- The amount of your Social Security benefits that are subject to tax depends on your AGI. If your AGI falls below a certain level, none of your benefits are taxable. As your AGI increases, more and more of your benefits are subject to tax. (However, no more than 85% of your Social Security benefits are ever subject to tax, regardless of how high your AGI is.)
- Until 2010, your itemized deductions and exemptions are subject to a phase-out once your AGI exceeds a certain threshold amount.
- Until 2010, you are not permitted to convert a traditional IRA to a Roth IRA if your AGI exceeds $100,000.
- If you have rental property that is operating at a loss, the amount of the loss you may claim in the current year is reduced and eventually eliminated as your AGI increases. (You'll find more information on rental property in Chapter 8.)
- Many education benefits, such as the Hope and Lifetime Learning credit, are eliminated when your AGI exceeds a certain threshold. (See Chapter 6 for more on these education credits.)

- Your eligibility to make a Roth IRA contribution or claim a saver's credit for a retirement plan contribution depends on your AGI. (Chapter 3 covers IRAs and the saver's credit.)

These are just a sampling of tax benefits that are tied to AGI. Because the potential savings can be significant, above-the-line deductions are the most valuable kind. Deductions you can take above the line include:

- rental expenses
- business expenses
- student loan interest
- alimony paid
- deductible contributions to an IRA or other retirement plan
- moving expenses related to a job
- self-employed health insurance premiums
- health savings account contributions, and
- higher education expenses.

Deductions Tied to Particular Types of Income

Even during retirement, you might incur expenses related to a particular money-making activity, such as running a business or renting out property. Many of those expenses are also deductible. In fact, they are considered above-the-line deductions because you claim them to arrive at your AGI. However, you report the income—and claim the deductions—on a separate form. You then transfer the total to Form 1040 and attach the separate form to the rest of your tax return.

For example, if you own rental real estate, you pay real estate taxes on the property. You probably also pay insurance premiums related to that property. You might have cleaning and maintenance expenses. You can claim all of those expenses to offset the rental income you receive. Both the income and the expenses are reported on a separate tax form, Schedule E, *Supplemental Income and Loss*.

You don't claim any of the expenses as an itemized deduction on Schedule A. (For more information about rental income and expenses, see Chapter 8.)

The same principle applies if you run a business as a sole proprietor. You report the income and the expenses related to the business on Schedule C, *Profit or Loss From Business*, rather than claiming the expenses as itemized deductions on Schedule A. (Business expenses are covered in Chapter 3.)

Exemptions

With a few exceptions (for example, those who are dependents of another taxpayer), every person may claim a personal exemption on his or her tax return. If you and your spouse file a joint return, you may each claim a personal exemption.

The personal exemption is a set dollar amount that you can subtract from your taxable income. The purpose of the personal exemption is similar to that of the standard deduction: to help ensure that your tax liability is commensurate with your income.

If you are supporting others, you might be able to claim a dependency exemption for one or more of them, in addition to your own personal exemption. This benefit provides some additional tax relief to those who are supporting families.

Like the standard deduction, personal exemptions are increased annually for inflation. However, there is an important difference between the standard deduction and personal exemptions: All personal exemptions you claim on your tax return, including dependency exemptions, are subject to a phase-out as your income increases. This phase-out rule will remain in place until 2010, when you will once again be able to claim the full amount of your exemptions. (For more information about personal exemptions, see Chapter 10.)

Credits

Although deductions reduce the amount of income that is subject to tax, credits reduce your actual tax liability dollar-for-dollar, which makes credits potentially much more valuable than deductions.

> **EXAMPLE:** You are single. During 2008, you paid $750 in foreign taxes as a result of some foreign investments you own. You will be itemizing your deductions and you qualify to claim the $750 as either an itemized deduction or a tax credit. Your taxable income before claiming either the credit or the deduction is $60,000.
>
> If you claim a deduction, you calculate your tax liability as follows:
>
> | | |
> |---|---|
> | Taxable income before deduction: | $ 60,000 |
> | Deduction for foreign taxes paid: | $ (750) |
> | Taxable income: | $ 59,250 |
> | Total income tax due: | $ 11,156 |
>
> If you claim a tax credit instead of a deduction, you calculate your tax liability like this:
>
> | | |
> |---|---|
> | Taxable income: | $ 60,000 |
> | Income tax before credit: | $ 11,344 |
> | Less credit: | $ (750) |
> | Total income tax due: | $ 10,594 |

Claiming a credit rather than a deduction saves you more than $500. (See Chapter 7 for more information about the foreign tax credit.)

Some of the tax credits that might be available to you as a retiree include:

- foreign tax credit
- credit for the elderly and disabled
- hybrid vehicle credit

- dependent care credit
- education credits
- earned income credit, and
- saver's credit.

Alternative Minimum Tax (AMT)

Once you add up your income and subtract all of your deductions and exemptions, you calculate your tax, claim any credits you qualify for, and send your money to the IRS. All done for the year, right? Not quite. You might have to worry about the alternative minimum tax.

It comes as a surprise to many taxpayers that they must actually perform two tax calculations: one to compute their regular income tax, and the second to compute their alternative minimum tax (AMT). Then, they must pay whichever is higher. The AMT is a completely separate tax with its own definitions of taxable income and its own set of deductions, some of which overlap with the regular tax and some of which do not.

The original purpose of the AMT was to ensure that everyone pays his or her fair share of taxes. In 1969, Congress targeted a handful of wealthy individuals who, through the use of arcane tax shelters, managed to rake in substantial income and pay little or no tax on it. The AMT was originally enacted to make sure at least some of that income was subject to tax. Although all taxpayers were required to calculate their regular income tax and AMT, in the good old days, only the wealthy would have seen their liability go up. But Congress's failure to update the AMT has caused vast numbers of middle income taxpayers to be caught in its web, as well.

When you calculate your AMT liability, you must include some income that is excluded for regular tax purposes. In addition, some items that are deductible for regular tax purposes are not deductible for AMT purposes. Also, the AMT calculation does not take into account personal or dependency exemptions, but instead has its own exemption amount (which is phased out as your income increases). You can't take the standard deduction, nor can you take certain credits that would otherwise be available.

You are probably already familiar with most of the forms that you must complete when calculating your regular tax liability (Form 1040, Schedules A, B, and so on). When calculating your AMT liability, you must complete Form 6251, *Alternative Minimum Tax— Individuals*. If you work through the form and discover that you are not subject to AMT (in other words, your regular tax liability is higher than your AMT liability), you are not required to submit Form 6251 with your income tax. If you discover you are subject to AMT, you must include the form with your other tax forms and include an AMT version of some of the regular tax forms.

> CAUTION
>
> **If you're subject to the AMT, you won't be able to take advantage of all the tax benefits covered here.** This book is about regular tax deductions and credits. Consequently, some of the deductions and credits described in this book will not be available to you if you are subject to the AMT. Also some calculations will be different. For example, if you are subject to the AMT, you might need to use different figures to calculate your depreciation deduction than you would for regular tax purposes.

Most people can make a reasonably good guess about whether they will be subject to the AMT by looking at certain income items and expenses. Here are some of the circumstances you might encounter—even during retirement—that could require you to pay the AMT:

- **A high state income tax bill.** If you paid an extraordinary amount of state income taxes during the year, it increases the chance that you will be subject to the AMT. State income taxes are not deductible for AMT purposes. Not only are the state income taxes you paid disallowed, but real estate taxes, personal property taxes, sales taxes, and other taxes typically deductible on Schedule A are also disallowed for AMT purposes. (Note, however, that you may still claim taxes as rental expenses on Schedule E or as business expenses on Schedule C: It is only the taxes you claim on Schedule A that are not deductible.) If, for example, you have an unusually high income year in 2010 and pay a big state income tax bill in April of 2011, the big payment will increase the likelihood that you will be subject to the AMT in 2011.

- **Significant interest paid on home equity debt.** If you have a home equity loan (one secured by your first or second home that you didn't use to purchase or improve the home), the interest on that debt is not deductible for AMT purposes.

- **Capital gains.** If your income from the sale of stocks you have held long term (longer than one year) is large relative to your ordinary income, you might find yourself caught in the AMT.

- **Large amount of miscellaneous itemized deductions.** Miscellaneous itemized deductions, such as investment expenses, tax planning, and other items you claim on Schedule A under "miscellaneous deductions," are not deductible for AMT purposes. If those expenses happen to be especially high (perhaps you have a large investment portfolio and you pay your investment advisor big bucks to manage it), you might find yourself subject to the AMT.

- **High medical expenses.** Although medical expenses are deductible for both AMT and regular tax purposes, the deduction is limited. For regular tax purposes, you may deduct your medical expenses only to the extent the expenses exceed 7.5% of your adjusted gross income (AGI). For AMT purposes, medical expenses are deductible only to the extent they exceed 10% of your AGI. If you have extraordinary medical expenses in a given year, those expenses might well determine whether you will be subject to the AMT.

Your Home

Tax Benefits in This Chapter

☐ **Do you own your home?**
- You may deduct interest you pay on your mortgage and home equity loans, up to a limit.
- You may deduct your real estate taxes.

☐ **Did you recently obtain a loan to buy a home?**
- You might be able to deduct any points you paid for the loan.

☐ **Are you remodeling your home?**
- If you took out a loan secured by the house, you may deduct the interest you pay on the loan, up to a limit.
- Keep track of what you spend on improvements; you may use them to reduce your taxable gain (if any) when you sell the house.
- You may claim a tax credit for energy-saving improvements made in 2006, 2007, or 2009.
- You may claim a tax credit for solar energy systems you purchase before the year 2017.

☐ **Are you building a home?**
- The interest on your construction loan might be deductible as mortgage interest.
- Do you need cash?
- You might look into a home equity loan; the interest and points on the loan may be deductible, no matter how you spend the money.
- Consider a reverse mortgage, a loan that pays you a portion of your equity in the home.

☐ **Is your mortgage interest too high?**
- Consider refinancing, but be sure you know the rules for deducting interest on a refinanced mortgage.
- If you paid points, you may amortize them—deduct a portion of them each year over the life of the loan.

☐ **Did your home suffer storm damage?**
- You may be able to claim a casualty loss.

☐ **Did you recently sell your home?**
- You may deduct interest and property taxes you pay for the final year when you own the home.
- You may subtract certain costs of sale, including commissions, inspection fees, escrow fees, and so on, from the final sales price to reduce your taxable gain.

I f you are like most retired homeowners, your home represents a large chunk of your net worth. You may have spent years saving enough money to make a down payment. Once you made the purchase, you almost certainly continued to spend plenty of money and time making the house a home. A haven. A place to welcome friends and family.

Because owning a home occupies such a prominent place in the "American Dream," we have come to expect that the government will encourage—and even subsidize—homeownership. And it does: Tax deductions associated with home ownership, such as mortgage interest and real estate taxes, are virtually sacrosanct (as unsuspecting legislators have discovered only after trying to tinker with these benefits).

Over the years, additional deductions and credits have come and gone, but the staples of mortgage interest and property tax deductions have endured. Although these deductions have changed over time, they have never disappeared entirely. And, in most years, there are a variety of other tax benefits homeowners might enjoy.

Some of these benefits are particularly helpful once you enter retirement, when you are likely to make some changes in your living situation. Perhaps you are planning to remodel your home for better accessibility, to make room for grandchildren, or simply to better accommodate your changing interests. Maybe you will buy a second home, a vacation getaway, or an RV. Or, you might be planning to sell your home and find something that better suits your lifestyle. No matter what changes you plan to make, you are likely to find that the tax code offers some valuable deductions and credits.

TIP

Where is your principal residence? As far as the tax code is concerned, not all houses are created equal. If you own more than one home, each entitles you to different benefits under the tax code, and your principal residence is generally eligible for more and better tax benefits than the rest. Unfortunately, you may not simply designate one of your residences as your principal residence. It must be the place where you actually spend most of your time. Your principal residence doesn't have to be a house; it can be a condominium, a co-op apartment, a mobile home, an RV (house trailer), or even a boat, as long as you actually live in it and it has sleeping space, a toilet, and cooking facilities. This chapter focuses on your principal residence; the rules that apply to second homes, vacation homes, rental property, and investment property are covered in Chapter 8.

Loans Secured by Your Home

You might obtain a loan secured by your home for a number of reasons: to purchase the home in the first place, pay for a remodeling project, or simply generate some cash to spend as you wish. No matter how you use the money, you'll probably be able to deduct at least some of the interest you pay, as explained below.

If you obtain a loan to build a home, a different set of rules will apply. The deductions associated with construction loans are explained below as well.

Some seniors are house-rich and cash-poor: They might own most or all of their home free and clear, but lack spending money to live as comfortably as they would like. If this is your situation, you might consider a reverse mortgage. If you qualify for a reverse mortgage, the bank makes monthly payments to you (or gives you a lump sum) in exchange for an interest in your home. The deductions associated with this type of loan are also explained below.

Mortgage Interest

Generally, you may deduct the interest you pay on your mortgage if the loan is secured by your principal residence, as long as the debt does not exceed certain limits. A secured loan is one that gives the lender the right to take back the property if the borrower doesn't pay. So, if your lender has the right to foreclose on your home if you default on the mortgage, your loan is secured by your home, and you may generally deduct your interest payments.

You may also deduct mortgage interest you pay on a loan secured by a second home, although, again, your deduction might be limited. (For more information about deductions associated with owning a second home, see Chapter 8.)

There are essentially two types of mortgages, or debt, you might have on your home: acquisition debt and home equity debt. The interest on both types of debt is deductible, up to a limit.

Acquisition Debt

Acquisition debt is money you borrow to construct, purchase, or improve your principal residence or second home. For example, if you obtain a loan of $200,000 to purchase your new home, the interest you pay on that $200,000 is tax deductible each year, as long as the loan is secured by your home. If you decide, after living in the home for a few years, to borrow $20,000 to remodel your kitchen, the interest on that loan is also tax deductible, but again, only if the debt is secured by your home.

There is a cap on how much acquisition debt you may have, however. You may deduct all of the interest you pay only if all of your debt for buying, building, or improving your home (and a second home, if you have one) does not exceed $1 million. If your total acquisition debt is more than $1 million, then the interest attributable to the excess is not deductible. You may deduct only the interest you pay on the first $1 million of acquisition debt.

> CAUTION
>
> **Interest paid for a third home is not deductible.** The $1 million limit applies to the total debt on your principal residence and second home, if you have one. If you have three homes in which you reside for some part of the year, your principal residence generally must be the one in which you live most of the time. You may choose which of the remaining two to designate as your second home. Be careful when you make the choice, however, because mortgage interest on your third home generally won't be deductible.

If your acquisition debt exceeds $1 million, you must use IRS guidelines to determine how much of the interest you pay each year is deductible mortgage interest and how much is nondeductible personal interest. The IRS provides a worksheet to help you make the calculation. (You'll find instructions for completing the worksheet in "Combined Limit on Acquisition and Home Equity Debt," below.)

Special Rules for Older Mortgages

If you acquired the mortgage on your home before October 14, 1987, interest on that debt is not subject to the $1 million limit. These older loans are considered "grandfathered debt," and all of the interest you pay on them is fully deductible.

This exception applies even if you refinance the grandfathered debt, as long as you refinance for no more than the amount remaining on the loan. The interest on the new loan will be fully deductible, just as if you had not refinanced. If the refinanced debt is greater than the remaining grandfathered amount, however, the excess is not grandfathered.

Although interest paid on grandfathered debt is fully deductible, that debt reduces the $1 million limit on total acquisition debt. For example, if you have a $400,000 grandfathered debt on your principal residence, and you want to buy a second home for your retirement years, your deductible acquisition debt on the second home will be limited to $600,000 ($1 million less the grandfathered debt).

Home Equity Debt

Home equity debt is simply any debt that is secured by your principal residence or second home and is used for any purpose other than buying, constructing, or improving the home. In other words, home equity debt is mortgage debt other than acquisition debt.

You may use your home equity loan proceeds any way you choose, and deduct the interest, as long as all of the following are true:

- The debt is secured by your principal residence or second home.
- The debt does not exceed your equity in the home—the fair market value of the home, less your current acquisition debt and any grandfathered (pre-October 14, 1987) debt on the home.
- The total of all your home equity debt does not exceed $100,000.

EXAMPLE: You purchased your home in 1986 with a 30-year mortgage for $300,000. The remaining principal on the original loan is $150,000. In 1999, you borrowed $50,000, with the house as security, to remodel the kitchen and finish the basement. You still owe $40,000 on that loan. Your home is currently valued at $400,000. You would like to obtain a home equity loan of $60,000 to buy a handsome boat to play with during your retirement. You are hoping the interest on the home equity loan will be fully deductible. To find out, you follow these steps:

Fair market value of your home:		$ 400,000
Less pre-October 14, 1987 acquisition debt	–	150,000
Less post-October 13, 1987 acquisition debt	–	40,000
Your equity in the home	=	$ 210,000

The interest on your home equity loan of $60,000 will be fully deductible because the loan satisfies the three conditions listed above: (1) the debt is secured by your home; (2) the debt does not exceed $210,000, your current equity in the home; and (3) your total home equity debt does not exceed $100,000.

Tax Strategy: How Can You Make the Most of Your Home Equity Debt Allowance?

If you use your home equity loan to pay for something you can deduct under another provision of the tax code, you might be able to deduct interest on more than $100,000 of home equity debt.

EXAMPLE: You obtain a home equity loan of $100,000. You use $90,000 to buy a new Ferrari and $10,000 to purchase computer equipment for your business. Because the computer equipment is a business expense, you can characterize that portion of the home equity debt as a business loan, and deduct the interest as a business expense. (See Chapter 3 for more on business deductions.) You can now borrow an additional $10,000 of home equity debt to use for personal expenses and deduct the interest as home equity mortgage interest. Because you recharacterized $10,000 of your original debt as a business debt, your total home equity debt does not exceed $100,000.

Combined Limit on Acquisition and Home Equity Debt

As long as your total acquisition debt does not exceed $1 million and your total home equity debt does not exceed $100,000, you may deduct all of the mortgage interest you pay. If either type of debt exceeds the limit, however, you must calculate how much of your mortgage interest you may deduct. IRS Publication 936, *Home Mortgage Interest Deduction*, contains a worksheet designed to help you wade through the math; we've reproduced a sample below.

CAUTION

You can't combine your debt limits. In its publications and worksheet, the IRS suggests that if you have no home equity debt, you may add the $100,000 home equity limit to your acquisition debt limit for a total acquisition debt limit of $1.1 million. Unfortunately, however, the tax court doesn't agree, and has ruled that the debt limits may not be combined. And, in spite of what its publications and worksheet indicate, the IRS appears to be following the tax court ruling. To make the worksheet conform to the tax court's interpretation, enter on line 7 of the worksheet the average balance of all of your home equity debt, but no more than $100,000. If you have no home equity debt, enter zero on line 7.

Before you start plugging numbers into the worksheet, you will need to gather the following information about your various loans:

1. The amount of your grandfathered debt, if any.
2. The average balance of all of your home acquisition debt.
3. The average balance of your home equity debt.
4. The total amount of interest you paid during the year (on your acquisition debt and home equity debt combined).

Tax Strategy: How Should You Calculate Your Average Debt Balance?

There are a number of different ways to calculate your average debt balance for home acquisition and home equity debt. You are permitted to use the highest balance for simplicity, but that won't give you the best result. If you are over either of the limits, the lower your average balance the better; a lower average will bring you closer to the $1 million and $100,000 limits, and you'll be able to deduct more interest. Consider one of these alternate methods:

- If your lender can provide you with an average balance, you may use that number.
- You may take the principal balance at the beginning of the year, add to it the principal balance at the end of the year, and divide the result by two to obtain an average. However, you may use this method only if you made regular payments during the year and did not borrow additional money.
- You may divide the total interest you paid during the year by the interest rate on your loan. If the interest rate changed during the year, use the lowest rate. You may use this method only if you made paid interest at least monthly.

The sample worksheet, below, shows the calculations for Karen, who wants to know how much of her mortgage interest is deductible. Karen has only one home, and she still has her original mortgage (acquisition debt). Her house has appreciated dramatically and is now worth three times what she paid for it, so in August she tapped into the equity and obtained a home equity loan to improve her cash flow and take a trip to Borneo in March. In February, she begins working on her tax return so that she can finish it before she leaves on her trip.

Karen has gathered the following information in preparation for completing the IRS worksheet:

- She has no grandfathered debt because she purchased her home after 1987.
- The average balance of her home acquisition debt for the just-completed tax year was $1,200,000.
- The average balance of her home equity debt was $150,000.
- The total amount of mortgage interest she paid during the year was $57,000.

After running the numbers, Karen concludes that she can deduct $46,455 of her mortgage interest; the remaining $10,545 is not deductible. Karen's worksheet looks like the one shown below.

How to Deduct Mortgage Interest

Claim your deductible mortgage interest on Schedule A, in the "Interest You Paid" section.

Points

When you purchase a home, you pay a variety of fees as part of the transaction. Those fees are known as "closing costs" or "settlement costs." The costs, which are generally itemized on a settlement statement, vary from transaction to transaction. They also vary by jurisdiction—county by county, and state by state. Although most of the costs that appear on a settlement statement, such as title

Part I	**Qualified Loan Limit**		
1. Enter the average balance of all your grandfathered debt. See line 1 instructions . .	1.		*0*
2. Enter the average balance of all your home acquisition debt. See line 2 instructions	2.		*$1,200,000*
3. Enter $1,000,000 ($500,000 if married filing separately)	3.		*$1,000,000*
4. Enter the larger of the amount on line 1 or the amount on line 3	4.		*$1,000,000*
5. Add the amounts on lines 1 and 2. Enter the total here	5.		*$1,200,000*
6. Enter the smaller of the amount on line 4 or the amount on line 5	6.		*$1,000,000*
7. Enter $100,000 ($50,000 if married filing separately). See the line 7 instructions for a limit that may apply.	7.		*$ 100,000*
8. Add the amounts on lines 6 and 7. Enter the total. This is your qualified loan limit.	8.		*$1,100,000*

Part II	**Deductible Home Mortgage Interest**		
9. Enter the total of the average balances of all mortgages on all qualified homes. See line 9 instructions	9.		*$1,350,000*
• If line 8 is less than line 9, go on to line 10. • If line 8 is equal to or more than line 9, stop here. All of your interest on all the mortgages included on line 9 is deductible as home mortgage interest on Schedule A (Form 1040).			
10. Enter the total amount of interest that you paid. See line 10 instructions	10.		*$ 57,000*
11. Divide the amount on line 8 by the amount on line 9. Enter the result as a decimal amount (rounded to three places).	11.		*× 0. 815*
12. Multiply the amount on line 10 by the decimal amount on line 11. Enter the result. This is your deductible home mortgage interest. Enter this amount on Schedule A (Form 1040)	12.		*$ 46,455*
13. Subtract the amount on line 12 from the amount on line 10. Enter the result. This is not home mortgage interest. See line 13 instructions	13.		*$ 10,545*

insurance, transfer taxes, notary fees, and recording fees, are not deductible, some are. For example, you might pay some mortgage interest or real estate taxes as part of the settlement; these will appear on the statement. In addition, you can deduct any points you pay for your loan.

What Are Points?

Points, also known as "loan origination fees" or "loan discount fees," are fees you pay up front to obtain a lower interest rate on your mortgage. The IRS considers such fees to be a type of prepaid mortgage interest and, therefore, allows you to deduct them.

Points are computed as a percentage of the loan amount, which makes them easy to identify. For example, one point would be 1% of the loan amount. If you paid two and a half points, that means you paid 2½% of the loan. If the loan fees on your settlement statement are a payment for services a broker provides, however, those fees are not points and are not deductible.

> **EXAMPLE:** You purchase a home for $350,000. You put down $70,000 as a down payment and obtain a loan for the remaining $280,000. In order to obtain an interest rate of 6% for the mortgage, you agree to pay two points. Those points amount to $5,600 (2% x $280,000), which you can deduct as mortgage interest. The points are identified on your settlement papers as a "loan origination fee."

CROSS REFERENCE

Deducting points paid for a second home. Points you pay when purchasing a principal residence are treated differently from points you pay when purchasing real estate that will be used for another purpose. See Chapter 8 for more information about points associated with second homes and rental real estate.

Tax Strategy: Should You Amortize Your Points or Deduct Them All at Once?

Here's a quirky rule that might provide a bit of a tax benefit. If you purchase a principal residence and pay points, but your itemized deductions in the year of the transaction don't exceed the standard deduction, you may amortize the points. When you amortize points, you spread your deduction out over time by deducting a portion of the points each year for the entire term of the loan. If you choose to use this rule, you begin amortizing the points in the second year (the year after you buy the house). Of course, the amortized points will provide a tax benefit only if you are able to itemize your deductions in future years.

EXAMPLE: Charles is single. He purchases a new home on December 15, 2008. He obtains a 30-year mortgage for $150,000 and pays two points in order to bring the interest rate down. His total deduction for points is $3,000 (2% x $150,000). At tax time, Charles adds up his itemized deductions and discovers that the total, including points, is only $4,630. Because the standard deduction for 2008 is $5,450, he will claim the standard deduction instead of itemizing deductions on Schedule A.

Because he was not able to claim a deduction for the points he paid in 2008, Charles elects to amortize the points over 30 years (the life of the loan). He may deduct $100 ($3,000 in points divided by 30 years) on Schedule A each year, beginning in 2009. Because Charles will be paying interest on his $150,000 mortgage, as well as property tax for his new home, his itemized deductions in future years will almost certainly exceed the standard deduction, so he will obtain a tax benefit by amortizing his points.

Points Paid by the Seller

If you're a savvy negotiator, you might be able to convince the person selling you your home to pay the points on your new mortgage. By helping you obtain a loan with a lower interest rate, the seller sweetens the deal and makes it more likely that you will complete the purchase. This is one of the many bargaining chips that might come into play during the sales transaction.

You may deduct seller-paid points even though you didn't actually pay them yourself. The IRS treats the transaction as though the seller gave you the money and then you paid the points.

Although you are permitted to deduct seller-paid points on your tax return for the year in which you purchase the home, you are required to reduce the basis of the home by the amount of those points. (After all, the seller gave you the money to pay the points, in effect reducing the cost of the house.) If and when you sell the house, your gain will be your sales proceeds (the selling price of the house minus your expenses of sale) minus your basis (the price you originally paid for the house, plus the cost of any improvements you made, minus the points paid by the *seller* back when you first bought the home, which represent a reduction of your original purchase price).

> **EXAMPLE:** You bought your house ten years ago for $250,000. Additional expenses related to that purchase totaled $2,000. The person who sold you the home paid $1,500 in points on your behalf, and you deducted those points on Schedule A for the tax year in which you bought the home.
>
> You made no improvements to the house while you lived in it. This year, you sold the home for $350,000. Expenses related to the sale, including broker commissions, totaled $20,000. You calculate your gain as follows:

Step 1:   Amount realized from the sale:

Sales price:	$ 350,000
Less expenses of sale:	(20,000)
Sales Proceeds:	$ 330,000

Step 2:   Adjusted basis of home:

Original cost:	$ 250,000
Plus expenses related to purchase:	2,000
Less seller-paid points:	(1,500)
Adjusted Basis:	$ 250,500

Step 3:   Gain:

Amount realized:	$ 330,000
Less adjusted basis:	(250,500)
Gain:	$ 79,500

You must reduce your basis by seller-paid points even if you did not claim a deduction for those points—or a deduction for the amortized points—on your tax return. In other words, the IRS will treat you as if you deducted the points, whether or not you took advantage of the benefit. This rule does not apply if you purchased your home after December 31, 1990 and before April 4, 1994, however. Homeowners who purchased during this window must reduce their basis by the amount of seller-paid points only if they actually deducted those points. (Before 1991, seller-paid points were not deductible.)

How to Claim a Deduction for Points

If you are deducting the full amount of the points you paid, claim them on Schedule A, in the "Interest You Paid" section. If you are amortizing points, you must compute the amount you are permitted to deduct in the current year and claim that amount on Schedule A, in the "Interest You Paid" section, on the line "Points not reported to you on Form 1098."

Interest on Home Construction Loans

Life becomes complicated when you decide to build your own home, and it's not just because of battles with your contractor, architectural gaffes, and rain delays. When it comes time to recoup some portion of the enormous cost of building your dream house, you'll need to follow a different set of rules to figure out whether your mortgage interest is deductible.

If you obtain a loan to build a home, the mortgage interest is deductible as acquisition debt only if (1) the loan is secured by the lot and any property to be constructed on it, and (2) the home you build will be your principal residence or second home when it is completed. The amount you may deduct depends on when you incur the debt and what you use the money for:

- **Debt incurred before construction is complete.** If you obtain a loan before construction on your new residence is complete, you may deduct interest on loan proceeds that you use to pay construction expenses incurred up to 24 months before you obtained the loan.

  EXAMPLE: You began constructing your dream home on June 1, 2008. You spent $60,000 of your own money, but couldn't afford to finish the job. On August 1, 2009, you obtained a loan for $50,000. The house was finished in November 2009; happily, you had to use only $10,000 of the $50,000 loan proceeds to complete work. Can you treat the entire loan as acquisition debt and deduct all of your interest payments?

  Yes. Interest on the entire $50,000 loan proceeds will be deductible mortgage interest, because you may "reimburse" yourself out of the loan proceeds for construction expenses you incurred for up to 24 months before you obtained the loan.

- **Debt incurred after construction is complete.** If you obtain a loan within 90 days after your home is completed, you may deduct interest on loan proceeds you use to pay (or reimburse yourself for) expenses you incurred to construct the home up to 24 months before construction was complete and up to the date you obtain the loan.

EXAMPLE: You began building your home on October 1, 2008. You finished construction and moved in on June 1, 2010, after spending $550,000 of your own money on the construction. On August 1, 2010, you obtain a loan secured by the home in the amount of $550,000. You may treat the loan as acquisition debt because you obtained it within 90 days after construction was complete and used it to reimburse yourself for expenses you incurred within 24 months before construction was complete. All of the interest on the loan will be deductible as mortgage interest.

TIP
You don't have to actually receive your loan proceeds within 90 days after you finish your house. As long as you file your loan application within 90 days, you may deduct the interest you pay on proceeds used for home construction costs during the 24 months before the house was complete and up to the date of your loan application. However, the funds must be distributed to you within a reasonable time (usually, 30 days after your application is approved). If the lender rejects your application, you will be given a little extra time to submit an application elsewhere.

- **Debt incurred to purchase land.** The interest you pay on debt used to buy the land on which your house will be built is deductible only after construction begins, not before. However, if you obtain a loan within 90 days after construction is complete, you may use that money to reimburse yourself for the cost of the land and deduct the applicable loan interest, even if you purchased the land more than 24 months before construction was complete.

EXAMPLE: On January 15, 2007, you paid $40,000 to purchase some land on which you intended to build your new home. Construction on the home began August 1, 2008 and was finished July 1, 2010 at a cost to you of $300,000. On September 1, 2010, you obtain a loan for $340,000, secured by the new home. The entire loan is considered acquisition debt because the construction expenses were incurred within 24 months before the home was completed, and because the cost of the land may be included even though you bought the land more than 24 months before construction was complete. All of the interest on the $340,000 loan will be deductible as home mortgage interest.

CROSS REFERENCE

Deducting interest on a loan to buy land. Although the interest you pay on a loan to buy land is not deductible as mortgage interest until you actually begin construction, you might be able to deduct the interest as an investment interest expense. See Chapter 7 for more information.

How to Claim a Deduction for Mortgage Interest on a Home Construction Loan

To the extent your construction loan interest qualifies as mortgage interest, you may claim the deduction on Schedule A, in the "Interest You Paid" section.

Refinancing

When you refinance, you obtain a new loan to replace your existing loan. You might do so to obtain a more favorable interest rate. If you need a little extra money, you might replace your existing loan with a larger loan to convert some of your equity to cash. When you refinance, the rules for deducting points and interest on the new loan are a bit different.

Interest

Unfortunately, it is not safe to assume that the interest on the entire amount of the refinanced debt will be deductible. The amount you may deduct depends on the size of the new debt relative to your old debt.

If you refinance for the precise amount of the remaining acquisition debt on your home, the new loan will continue to be treated as acquisition debt and the interest will be fully deductible, as long as your total acquisition debt does not exceed $1 million.

Remember that when you refinance your acquisition debt, the remaining debt is generally less than it was when you first bought your home. Your acquisition debt is the amount remaining, not the original amount of your mortgage.

> **EXAMPLE:** You purchased your home with a $25,000 cash down payment and a mortgage of $200,000. Now, some years later, you want to refinance the debt to obtain a lower interest rate on your mortgage. Your loan balance is currently $150,000. If you refinance, the amount of the new loan that will be treated as acquisition debt is only $150,000 because that is the remaining amount of your acquisition debt.

If the refinanced loan is greater than your remaining acquisition debt on the home, the interest on the excess is treated as deductible mortgage interest if:

- you use the additional loan amount to improve the home and the total debt does not exceed $1 million, or
- you use the additional loan amount for a purpose other than building or improving the home, and the total excess combined with any other home equity debt you have does not exceed $100,000.

> **EXAMPLE:** You still owe $150,000 on the original mortgage you obtained to buy your home. You refinance with a new loan for $200,000 because you are finally going to buy that

fishing boat you've had your eye on. It's a bargain at $50,000. The interest on $150,000 of the new loan is deductible as interest on acquisition debt. The interest on the remaining $50,000 is deductible as interest on home equity debt.

Points

If you pay points when you refinance, you may deduct them all at once only if you use all of the loan proceeds to improve your home. If you use the loan to pay off your previous acquisition debt, or for purposes unrelated to your home, then you may deduct only a portion of the points every year for the entire term of the loan. In other words, the loan points are "amortized" over the life of the loan.

> **EXAMPLE:** You refinanced the mortgage you used to purchase your home with a new 30-year loan. You paid $2,000 in points to obtain a lower interest rate. To determine the amount you may deduct each year, you divide $2,000 by 30 (the term of the loan). You come up with $66.67, which can be rounded to $67. So you may deduct $67 in points each year until you have deducted the entire $2,000. For the first year, you must prorate the points you claim as a deduction. Therefore, if you refinance on July 1, you may deduct only $33 (half of the annual deductible amount) for the first year.

If you spend half of the loan on improving your home and the rest on things unrelated to the house, then you may deduct half of the points in the year you refinance. You must amortize the other half over the life of the loan.

A special rule applies if you refinance a loan that you've already refinanced once. If you refinance again, and you've been amortizing the refinance points on the previous loan, you may deduct all of the remaining points from the previous refinance loan in the year you pay off that loan. However, this rule applies only if you refinance with a different bank. If you use the same bank for your second refinance, you must combine the points remaining on your old loan with the points you pay on the new loan and amortize the total over the life of the new loan.

> **EXAMPLE:** You refinanced your mortgage ten years ago and have been amortizing the $2,000 you paid in refinance points at the rate of $67 per year. You have deducted $670 so far. In 2008, you refinance again to reduce your interest rate. If you refinance with a different bank, you may claim a deduction on your 2008 tax return for all of the unamortized points from the earlier refinance: $1,330. If you refinance with the same bank, however, you must add your $1,330 in unamortized points to any points you pay for the new loan, then amortize the total over the life of the new loan. If you pay another $2,000 in points for a new 30-year loan, for example, you may deduct $111 each year ($1,330 in unamortized points from the previous loan plus $2,000 in new points divided by 30 years).

How to Deduct Interest and Points on Refinancing

To the extent your refinanced loan qualifies as acquisition debt or home equity debt and doesn't exceed the limits described above, you may claim the mortgage interest on Schedule A, in the "Interest You Paid" section. If you pay points on the refinance and you are permitted to deduct the full amount of the points you paid, you claim them in the same place. If you are amortizing points, you must first compute the amount you are permitted to deduct in the current year, and then claim that amount on Schedule A, in the "Interest You Paid" section, on the line "Points not reported to you on Form 1098."

Reverse Mortgages

It's not uncommon for seniors to be cash poor, yet living in a beautiful, mortgage-free home. More than 80% of homeowners who are older than 75 own their homes outright. But seniors who need money to live as they would like (or even just to pay their bills) are understandably hesitant to sell their homes to get at that equity.

Out of this dilemma was born the "reverse mortgage," a vehicle designed to allow seniors to tap the equity in their homes. Not all lenders offer reverse mortgages, and those that do generally restrict eligibility to homeowners who are at least age 62 and have a significant amount of equity in their homes. Although your mortgage might not need to be completely paid off, the smaller the mortgage, the more money you will receive.

If your application for a reverse mortgage is approved, the lender will generally give you cash equal to a certain percentage of the current value of your home—often 70%. You might receive the cash in a lump sum or in monthly payments. If you opt for a lump sum, many lenders will put a ceiling on the total amount you can receive.

Sadly, the reverse mortgage is not simply a gift of cash from your friendly neighborhood banker. Technically, you are borrowing those funds, much as you do with a standard mortgage. Unlike a standard mortgage, however, a reverse mortgage does not require you to make mortgage payments. Instead, the interest you owe is simply added to the lump sum that you borrowed. The entire amount—principal and interest—is due to the lender when you eventually sell the house, or when you die.

You aren't allowed to deduct the interest that accrues on a reverse mortgage because you aren't actually paying it. If you sell the house and pay off the entire debt—principal and interest—you may claim a deduction for all of the interest in the year you pay off the debt.

A reverse mortgage is a good strategy for some seniors. Before you take the plunge, however, you should be aware of some of the drawbacks. First, the closing costs on reverse mortgages can be quite high—in line with what you might pay to buy or sell your home. Costs might include service fees, loan origination fees, and insurance costs (to protect the lender from loss and to protect you if the lender goes out of business).

Second, if you keep the house until your death, chances are good that it will go to the bank, unless your heirs are prepared to pony up enough cash to pay off the reverse mortgage.

Third, if you decide to sell the property during your lifetime and use the proceeds to buy a new, perhaps smaller, home, you will have to come up with enough cash from the sale to both retire the reverse mortgage debt and have enough left over to buy another house. This might be easier said than done, especially when you consider the interest that's been accumulating since you originally acquired the reverse mortgage.

Tax Strategy: Does a Reverse Mortgage Make Sense?

If you plan to sell your home, you might not want a reverse mortgage. If you sell your home after obtaining a reverse mortgage, you could very well come out of the deal with little or no cash to pay for a new home (if you want to downsize, for example). Although the law ensures that the amount you will owe on your reverse mortgage when you sell will not exceed the total value of the house (unless the house has declined in value), you still have to pay back the entire amount of the reverse mortgage plus interest. More often than not, you will be left decidedly short of cash.

Even if you know you don't want to downsize—and instead plan to live the rest of your days in your large and lovely home—a reverse mortgage might make it impossible to pass the house on to your heirs. When you die, they will have to come up with a lump sum payment to retire the reverse mortgage, if they want to keep the house. Otherwise, the bank could require the house to be sold to recover the debt.

On the other hand, if your heirs are forced to sell the house, they are likely to owe little or no capital gains tax on the sale because the basis of the house is "stepped up" when you die. This means that your heirs' basis in your home is deemed to be the fair market value of the house on the date of your death. When they sell the house, they will owe tax only on the difference between the fair market value of the house on the date of your death and what they sell it for. If they sell the house shortly after you die, there will likely be no taxable gain at all.

Real Estate Taxes

Real estate taxes that you pay on just about any piece of real property you own—including your principal residence, your second home, and your investment property—are deductible in the year you pay them.

 CROSS REFERENCE

You may be able to deduct taxes you pay on other types of property. Real estate taxes are a type of property tax. Property taxes are imposed on owners of certain types of property based on the value of the property. In addition to real estate taxes, you might pay property taxes on your car (to your state's Department of Motor Vehicles, for example) or your boat. To find out about deductions for other types of property taxes, see Chapter 9.

Most people pay their real estate taxes in one of two ways. Some write a check directly to the county tax collector. Others pay their taxes through the bank that holds their mortgage. The bank collects a little extra from you each month and puts it into an "impound" account from which it pays real estate taxes each year on your behalf.

If you use the latter method to pay your real estate taxes, then you will receive a report from your bank each year, showing how much real estate tax you paid during the year. (This statement will also tell you how much you paid for mortgage interest.)

If you write the checks yourself, then it is up to you to keep track of how much you paid during the year so that you can claim the appropriate deduction on your tax return.

CAUTION

Deducting property tax for rental property. If you own rental property, you must report your rental income and expenses—including property tax payments—on Schedule E, *Supplemental Income and Loss*, not on Schedule A, *Itemized Deductions*. And you certainly shouldn't try to deduct them on both schedules.

If You Buy or Sell Property

If you sell your home or another piece of property during the year, you and the buyer will each pay part of the real estate taxes for that year. You will be responsible for the real estate taxes through the day before the date of sale, and the buyer will be responsible for real estate taxes beginning on the actual day of the sale.

Often, you will pay your share of the real estate taxes as part of the purchase or sales transaction. If you buy property, you might pay these taxes with your down payment or as part of your closing costs. If you sell, the taxes may be taken out of your proceeds from the sale. If you have a real estate transaction during the year, be sure to check the settlement papers for real estate taxes you might have paid, because they will be deductible on your tax return. Also check to see whether you received a credit for real estate taxes—taxes that the other party in the transaction owes for the days he or she owned the property. If you did receive a credit, you must reduce the amount of real estate taxes you claim as a deduction by the amount of the credit you received.

In certain—very specific—circumstances, you might be able to deduct real estate taxes even if you didn't pay them. A special provision of the tax code allows you to deduct the portion of real estate taxes allocated to you as part of a sale, regardless of whether you or the other party actually paid the tax. For example, if you are selling your house and the buyer offers to pay your share of the prorated real estate taxes for the year, you may deduct your share even though the buyer actually pays it.

This rule applies only to a purchase or sale transaction. In virtually all other cases, you may deduct only real estate taxes for which you are liable and which you have actually paid.

CAUTION

Tax payments can affect your basis in the property. If you did not actually pay the real estate taxes allocated to you in a purchase or sale of real estate, your cost basis for the property (if you were the buyer) or your sales proceeds (if you were the seller) will be affected. See "Calculate Your Gain" under "Selling Your Home," below, for more information.

Assessments

Occasionally—or maybe even regularly—your real estate tax bill will include assessments: additional charges over and above your basic property tax to pay for services, construction, repairs, and so on. The reason for the assessment—that is, what the assessment will pay for—determines whether you can deduct it.

You may not deduct payments for various services, such as municipal water, sanitation, title registration, or sewage. For example, if your bill includes payments for garbage pickup services, you may not deduct that portion. You also may not deduct payments on assessments for new construction or improvements (construction that increases the value of the property rather than returning it to its original condition). For example, if the assessment is to pay for new streets and sidewalks in your neighborhood, you may not deduct that portion of your payment. However, you may add the amount of your payments for these charges to the basis of your house. This will reduce your taxable gain when you eventually sell the property.

You may deduct fees for maintenance or repairs, such as a repair of streets, sidewalks, and water or sewage systems. Also, if part of your real estate tax bill includes interest on a loan to pay for such repairs, the interest is deductible as part of your real estate taxes.

Homeowners' Dues and Assessments

Homeowners' dues are not deductible, nor are assessments by home-owners' associations to raise money for repairs, to pay for safety or recreation, or to maintain common areas. If the assessments are to raise funds for improvements, again, you may not deduct them. You can, however, add them to the basis of your home, thereby reducing your gain when you sell the property.

How to Deduct Real Estate Taxes

You claim a deduction for real estate taxes you pay on Schedule A, in the section "Taxes You Paid." If you do not itemize your deductions, then for tax years 2008 and 2009 only, you may claim real estate taxes you could have claimed on Schedule A, up to a maximum of $500 if you are filing as an individual or $1,000 if you are married filing a joint return, as an addition to your standard deduction. For example, if you are married and filing a joint return in 2008, the standard deduction is $10,900. However, if you don't itemize your deductions, and you paid at least $1,000 in real estate taxes that you could have claimed on Schedule A, you may increase your standard deduction to $11,900 for tax year 2008.

Home Improvements

Most improvements that you make to your home do not provide any immediate tax benefit. You can't deduct the cost of remodeling your kitchen or bathroom, for example. Instead, you add these expenses to the basis of your home. The higher your basis, the lower your gain when you sell—and the less likely you are to owe capital gains taxes. (For more information, see "Selling Your Home," below.)

If you make repairs rather than improvements, those expenses are not deductible nor do they contribute to the basis of your home. A repair simply returns the property to its original condition, while an improvement increases its value. If you pay a plumber to fix a leaky pipe, for example, that would be a repair; if you pay to have all of your plumbing upgraded to copper pipe, that would be an improvement.

CROSS REFERENCE

Energy-saving home improvements provide an immediate tax benefit. Although most improvements cannot be deducted, changes that make your home more energy efficient are an exception to the rule. For more information, see "Energy Credit," below.

If you borrow money to improve your home, the loan will be treated as acquisition debt. That means the interest you pay on the loan is fully deductible, as long as your total acquisition debt (including the home improvement loan amount) does not exceed $1 million.

Energy Credit

For tax years 2006 and 2007, homeowners could claim a tax credit for certain energy-saving improvements made to their principal residences. The credits are not available for 2008, but will be reinstated in 2009 for one year only. If you made eligible improvements during 2006 or 2007 and did not claim a tax credit, you generally have until April 15, 2010 (for tax year 2006) or April 15, 2011 (for tax year 2007) to file an amended federal tax return and claim any credit to which you were entitled.

If you made eligible improvements in 2006, 2007 and 2009, you may claim a credit for each year. However, your total combined credit cannot exceed $500.

Improvements that might qualify include installing certain types of windows and doors, water heaters, furnaces, air conditioners, and metal roofs, among other items. If you made energy efficient improvements, ask the manufacturer whether they qualify for the credit. Many manufacturers will provide you with a certificate stating that your improvement qualifies. You can also go to the Energy Star website (a joint program run by the U.S. Department of Energy and Environmental Protection Agency), at www.energystar.gov, for more detail than you are ever likely to need about the standards each improvement must meet.

Although the total energy credit you can claim is subject to a $500 cap, additional restrictions apply to some improvements. For many improvements, the credit is limited to 10% of the cost. For example, if you install qualified energy efficient windows, your credit for that particular improvement is limited to 10% of the cost or $200, whichever is less. If you purchase a qualified furnace, your credit is limited to the lesser of the cost of the furnace or $150.

How to Claim the Energy Credit

Claim your unclaimed Residential Energy Credit for years 2006 or 2007 (or both) on the credit line of the "Tax Liability" section of the respective Form 1040X, *Amended U.S. Individual Income Tax Return*. You must also complete and attach Form 5695, *Residential Energy Credits*, to show how you arrived at your credit amount. For 2009, complete Form 5695, attach it to your tax return, and enter the credit amount on the second page of Form 1040, in the "Tax and Credits" section.

Solar Energy Credit

In addition to the energy credit described above, you may claim a separate credit for the cost and installation of certain solar electric or solar water heating systems that you install in one of your residences (it need not be your principal residence) from 2006 through 2016.

For tax years through 2008, you may claim 30% of the cost of the solar energy system (such as panels), up to a maximum credit of $2,000 for each year you make a purchase. Beginning in 2009, the $2,000 limit will be lifted, but only for solar energy property used to generate electricity in your house. The credit for solar energy systems that are used to heat water will remain capped at $2,000 for each year you make a purchase.

You will need to obtain a certificate verifying that your solar energy system qualifies for the credit. It must be certified by the Solar Rating Certification Corporation or a similar organization endorsed by your state. The company that installs your solar property should be able to provide you with this certification.

How to Claim the Solar Energy Credit

Calculate the solar energy credit on Form 5695, *Residential Energy Credits*, and attach the completed form to your tax return. Enter the credit amount on the second page of Form 1040, in the "Tax and Credits" section.

Casualty and Theft Losses

Most people are unlikely to make it through life without experiencing the wrath of nature in some form, whether it's a hail storm that punches holes in a new roof, an earthquake that brings the back porch into the living room, or a hurricane that takes the garage with it.

Even worse, some people lose their property not through acts of nature but at the hands of others, through theft.

In both cases, there is some relief in the tax code, although perhaps not as much as you might wish. The tax laws don't permit you to deduct the value of every item stolen or the cost of every repair necessitated by storm damage. Instead, the casualty and theft loss rules are designed primarily to help out in the event of a devastating catastrophe.

Casualty Losses

To claim a casualty loss, you must first prove that the damage was in fact caused by a casualty—a "sudden, unexpected and unusual event." (Insurance companies are still apt to call them "acts of God.") Hurricanes, earthquakes, hail storms, and fires are all considered sudden, unexpected, and unusual events, or casualties.

Much to the frustration of affected taxpayers, casualty losses do not include damage caused by termites, dry rot, carpet beetles, and similar problems. Such damage typically occurs over a long period of time (rather than suddenly). Also, the IRS likes to see an element of chance in the devastation, as there is with a storm (apologies to meteorologists everywhere).

It's not always easy to tell what types of catastrophes will qualify your loss as a casualty loss in the eyes of the IRS. However, a little research should turn up a raft of examples of losses similar to yours that will or will not pass muster. One place to start is with IRS Publication 547, *Casualties, Disasters and Thefts*, or with the instructions for Form 4684, *Casualties and Thefts* (on which you report a casualty loss).

You should also be prepared to prove that the damage you sustained was in fact caused by the casualty. If the IRS asks for such proof, the best evidence will probably be before and after photos. You might also want to save some news reports about the event, to prove that it occurred and to provide evidence of its devastation. Because it will be difficult for you to take *before* photos *after* the casualty, it might be a good idea to take photos of your property on a regular basis—say, every year—just in case you suffer a casualty loss in the future.

Calculating the Deductible Loss

Once you determine that you have a casualty loss, you must calculate the deductible amount of your loss. These are the rules you must take into account:

- Your loss is the decline in the fair market value of your property. In calculating the damage to your house, you should include any damage to the land and the landscape. Attorneys fees that you incur to claim recovery of your loss are also deductible as part of the casualty loss. You may not include appraisal fees, however; those are deductible only as miscellaneous itemized deductions.
- Temporary housing and other personal expenses incurred while you are displaced are not deductible. In fact, if your insurance company reimburses you for those living expenses, you must include that amount as income on your tax return.
- Your loss cannot be greater than the basis of your house. (Remember, the basis is what you spent for the house, plus

improvements, and then reduced by any cost recovery, such as depreciation. See Chapter 1 for a detailed discussion of basis.)

- You may not deduct the entire amount of your loss. To compute the deductible amount, you must reduce the loss as follows:
  - First reduce the loss by $100.
  - From that amount, subtract 10% of your adjusted gross income for the year you are claiming the loss deduction.
  - Finally, subtract any amount of your loss that you have recovered, including the amount you have received or expect to receive from your insurance company.

CAUTION

You might owe tax on your insurance reimbursement. If your insurance recovery exceeds the amount of your loss, you might have to pay tax on some of the insurance proceeds. For more information, see IRS Publication 547, *Casualties, Disasters and Thefts.*

If your loss is covered, in whole or in part, by insurance, you must file a claim in order to deduct a casualty loss on your tax return. If you expect to be reimbursed by the insurance company, you may not claim a deduction for the amount of the reimbursement, even if you haven't yet received the funds. If the insurance company never coughs up the money, you may deduct your loss in the year the insurance company denies your claim.

After you claim a casualty loss deduction, you will have a new basis for your property. The new basis is the original basis (before the casualty) reduced by any casualty loss deductions you claimed, and reduced further by any insurance or other reimbursement you receive.

The IRS most often disallows casualty loss deductions because the taxpayer fails either to establish the property's decline in value or to supply adequate proof of the property's basis. A professional appraisal of the fair market value before and after the casualty will strengthen your case. However, you can also use the cost of cleanup and repairs to establish the loss, as long as the repairs are actually done. Bear in mind that you may not deduct more for repairs than your property was worth before it was damaged.

When to Claim a Casualty Loss

As a rule, the IRS is strict about allowing loss deductions only in the year you actually incurred the loss. That's bad news if you just happen to have a big chunk of income in the year of a casualty. (Remember, you have to subtract 10% of your AGI from your casualty loss to figure out how much you can deduct. The higher your AGI, the lower your deduction.)

There are a couple of exceptions to this rule, however. As mentioned above, you might have a pending insurance claim that could determine when you claim the loss. However, don't wait too long to claim the casualty loss. If the insurance company is moving slowly on processing your claim and you are running out of time to file your tax return, you should claim your casualty loss deduction based on what you expect to recover from the insurance company. If you eventually receive more from the insurance company than you expected, you include the additional recovery in income on your tax return for the year of the recovery. However, you should not report the additional income if you did not claim a casualty loss deduction for at least that amount in an earlier year.

If you receive less than you expected from the insurance company, you may claim the difference as a casualty loss on your tax return for the year the claim is finally settled.

You may also be able to postpone the deduction if you can prove that the amount of the loss was not ascertainable in the year of the casualty. (If you try a postponement, however, remember that you are at the mercy of the court's definition of "ascertainable.")

Special Rules for Disaster Losses

You have a bit more leeway if your property is in a location that has been declared a disaster area by the president of the United States. In that case, you may elect to take the loss in the year preceding the disaster. You make this election by claiming the loss on a tax return or an amended tax return (if you already filed for that year) for the year *before* the disaster. The tax return or amended tax return must be filed by the later of:

- the due date (not including extensions) for filing your original return (generally April 15) for the year in which the disaster occurred; or
- the due date including extensions for filing your original return for the year before the disaster.

In addition, you must attach to the tax return (or amended return) for the prior year a signed statement indicating that you elect to deduct the loss in the year preceding the disaster. The statement should provide the date of the disaster as well as the city, county, and state where the damaged property is located.

Tax Strategy: In Which Year Should You Claim a Disaster Loss?

As long as you watch the calendar and don't miss any deadlines, you will have the option to claim a disaster loss on your tax return for either the year of the disaster or the year before the disaster. You'll have to do some calculations to find out which option will yield the tax larger benefit.

EXAMPLE 1: You suffered a disaster loss in August that resulted in a $20,000 decline in the fair market value of your home. You had to quit your job and devote all of your time and energy—and a great deal of your savings—to putting your life and property back together. Your AGI for the year was $40,000, which, after deductions, puts you in a 15% tax bracket. Your deductible loss is:

Amount of loss	$20,000
Less $100	(100)
Less 10% of AGI	(4,000)
	$ 15,900

Tax Strategy: In Which Year Should You Claim a Disaster Loss? (continued)

You can deduct—and, therefore, won't have to pay tax on—$15,900. Because you are in a 15% tax bracket, your tax savings will be 15% x $15,900, or $2,385. In the year before the disaster, your AGI was $110,000. If you claim the loss in the previous year, the deductible loss is:

Amount of loss	$ 20,000
Less $100	(100)
Less 10% of AGI	(11,000)
	$ 18,900

Because you were in a 28% bracket last year, your tax savings would be $2,492 (.28 x $8,900), a bit better than claiming the loss in the current year. But slightly different numbers might change your decision:

EXAMPLE 2: If your AGI for the prior year was $150,000 instead of $110,000, then your deduction is figured as follows:

Amount of loss	$ 20,000
Less $100	(100)
Less 10% of AGI	(15,000)
	$ 4,900

Because you were in a 28% bracket last year, your tax savings would be $1,372. Although you were in a higher tax bracket, the 10% AGI threshold reduced the deductible loss so much that the current year deduction is more valuable.

If you find that the tax savings are roughly the same for both years, you might want to claim the loss on your prior year return simply to speed up delivery of your refund. You can request a refund for the prior year by immediately filing a tax return or an amended tax return for the prior year. On the other hand, if you claim the loss for the current year, you will have to wait until the tax filing deadline to claim the deduction.

Theft Losses

When your property is stolen, your loss is the lower of your basis or the fair market value of the property. For example, if you purchased a Rolex watch in 1945 for $250 and it is now worth $15,000, the loss from the theft of the watch is $250, not $15,000.

You might be able to add other expenses to the amount of your loss, such as the cost of an investigator to recover the property or legal fees you incur for the recovery.

Like casualty losses, theft losses are deductible only to the extent the fair market value (or the basis, if it is less) of the stolen property, less $100, exceeds 10% of your adjusted gross income.

In addition, you must prove that the missing item or items were in fact stolen, not simply misplaced or lost through your own carelessness. You should file a police report. A statement from someone who witnessed the theft would, of course, be ideal, but might be too much to hope for. Even if you have no witnesses and no real proof, the IRS might be convinced that your property was stolen if the facts point in that direction. For example, the IRS allowed a theft loss when a stand of trees disappeared from a taxpayer's property.

How to Claim Casualty and Theft Losses

Claim your casualty and theft losses on Schedule A, on the line designated for them. You must complete Form 4684, *Casualties and Thefts*, to show how you calculated your deductible loss.

Selling Your Home

Although some retirees look forward to staying in the family home and then passing it on to their children or other worthy heirs, many choose to sell their homes and move—maybe to a single-story home, a home without an acre of lawn to mow, a house with less square footage to clean and heat, or a home with a smaller kitchen (so you won't be expected to cook big dinners any more).

If you decide to downsize, you're probably wondering about the tax consequences of selling your home. Once upon a time, long long ago, it was possible to defer paying tax on the gain from selling a home as long as you kept "buying up." When you sold your home, you could simply purchase another, more expensive, home within two years and put off paying tax on the gain. In fact, you could keep doing that throughout your life until you decided it was time to downsize. Then, as long as you were older than age 55, you could take advantage of a once-in-a-lifetime opportunity to exclude up to $125,000 of the gain.

Much to the amazement of many taxpayers, this rule has been gone for decades. Under the "new" rules (which are not so new anymore), you can't defer paying tax on gains from the sale of your home. Instead, each home sale now stands alone. When you sell your home, you compute your gain (if any), figure out how much of the gain you can exclude from tax liability (if you are eligible), and pay tax on the rest. When you buy a new home, the process starts all over again.

Review the Settlement Statement

When you sell your home, the entire transaction is usually summarized on a "Settlement Statement," typically consisting of one or two sheets of paper generated by the company (such as a title company) or individual (such as a lawyer) handling the transaction for you. On those pages you will find most, if not all, of your expenses related to the sale. Some of those expenses are deductible on your tax return, some are considered expenses of sale (and therefore, reduce your taxable gain, if any), and others are simply expenses with no tax benefit.

Deductions

When you sell a home, deductible items include interest and real estate taxes, both typically prorated for the time you own the home. You won't have points to claim because you are not acquiring a mortgage for the property. If you pay loan points on behalf of the buyer, you may not deduct them. Instead, they are considered selling expenses and reduce the amount you receive from the sale (and, therefore, your gain).

Expenses of Sale

Other expenses listed on the settlement statement are not deductible but are costs of the transaction itself. When you sell your home, these expenses reduce your proceeds, and ultimately reduce your taxable gain, if any. (For more about how the costs of selling a home can reduce your tax liability, see "Calculate Your Gain," below.)

Personal Expenses

Some of the expenses on your settlement statement are neither deductible nor do they affect your basis or gain calculation. Instead, they are simply considered personal expenses. These expenses have no tax consequences or benefits. Among the more common are prorated fees charged by homeowners' associations or fees associated with paying off your loan.

Calculate Your Gain

When you sell your home, you will compute your gain: the difference between the "amount realized" (your selling price less selling expenses) and your "adjusted basis" (your original cost, adjusted by such things as improvements, settlement fees at the time of purchase, and so on).

Amount Realized From Sale

When you sell your home, you and the buyer will negotiate a sales price. You will also incur expenses related to the sale of the house. The agreed sales price reduced by all the expenses of sale is called the "amount realized."

Sales expenses include most of the nondeductible closing costs that appear on your settlement statement. The largest item is usually the sales commission you pay to one or more real estate brokers. Also included are legal fees related to the transaction, title fees, and title insurance.

 TIP

Keep track of what you spend to get the house ready to sell. Costs you incur to fix up your home for sale are considered expenses of sale and will reduce your proceeds. These might include painting inside and out, decorating, doing repairs, and even staging the home. Such expenses would be nondeductible personal expenses that have no effect on the basis of your home if you incurred them while living there. However, when associated with the sale of your home, they can be treated as part of the cost of selling the home and thereby reduce your gain.

Expenses of sale also include loan points you pay on behalf of the buyer of your property. (Those points are not deductible by you, but are deductible by the buyer, even though you pay them.) Similarly, if you pay real estate taxes on behalf of the buyer, you should add that cost to your expenses of sale.

Adjusted Basis

To determine your basis on the sale of your house, you must start with your original cost—in other words, what you paid for it. That's not the end of the story, however. A number of items increase your basis and reduce your taxable gain. There are also items that reduce your basis, thereby possibly increasing your taxable gain.

Additions to Basis

You can add the cost of improvements, such as putting in a new roof, remodeling the kitchen, or adding a third story to the house, to your original purchase price. All of those improvements add to the basis of your home. Repairs, on the other hand, do not add to basis because such expenses are meant to maintain the current value of the home rather than increasing its value.

You should also include costs related to your original purchase. Most of those costs appear on your settlement papers (for the original purchase), as described above. Such costs might include title fees, title insurance, transfer taxes, legal fees (perhaps for preparing a contract of sale or for preparing and recording a deed), and escrow fees charged by the title company.

If you paid any expenses on behalf of the seller when you purchased your home, those expenses typically increase your basis, as well. For example, let's say you agreed to pay real estate taxes owed by the seller when you originally purchased your home. You may not deduct them as taxes on your own income tax return, because the taxes were legally the seller's liability, not yours. However, you may add these costs to your basis when you sell the house, because they effectively increased the cost of buying the house in the first place.

Subtractions From Basis

Just as some items increase your adjusted basis, others decrease it. For example, if the seller paid your share of real estate taxes for the year when you bought the house, you must subtract from your basis what the seller paid on your behalf. In effect, the seller reduced the cost of purchasing the house by paying those taxes.

If you claimed a casualty loss while you lived in the house, you must subtract that amount from your basis (because you already claimed the tax benefit).

Also, if you ever claimed any depreciation on the house or part of the house (if you rented it out or used part of it as an office, for example), you will have to subtract the amount of depreciation you claimed from your basis. (For more about depreciation related to renting your home, see Chapter 8.)

 CAUTION

If you've taken depreciation, the math gets more complicated. This is a book about tax deductions, not about gain or loss from the sale of your home. If you have ever used your home or part of your home as anything other than your own principal residence, the calculation of gain is different from that described above. For example, if you have rented out your home or part of your home, or if you have used part of the home as a home office, you will have to figure in the depreciation you've already claimed on the house when calculating your gain. See *Every Landlord's Tax Deduction Guide* or *Home Business Tax Deductions*, both written by Stephen Fishman and published by Nolo, for more information.

Exclusion of Gain

Generally, you and your spouse will be able to exclude up to $500,000 of gain when you sell your home, as long as you and your spouse have owned and lived in the home for at least two out of the last five years. If you are single, your exclusion is limited to $250,000. There are many nuances to determining how much of an exclusion you may claim. For more information about selling your home and computing the gain, see IRS Publication 523, *Selling Your Home.*

Tax Strategy: Would It Be Better Not to Sell Your House?

If you are ambivalent about whether or not to sell your house, here's a situation in which it is wiser, from a tax standpoint, not to sell the house. If your gain from the sale will be more than the amount you are permitted to exclude from your income ($250,000 if you are single), then it might make more sense to keep the house. If you stay in the house until you die, the basis of the house is deemed to be the fair market value of the house on your date of death. (This is called a "step up" in basis.) If the house were sold immediately, there would be no gain from the sale.

A similar rule applies to married couples, who generally have a $500,000 exclusion available. However, in some states, the step up in basis applies only to the deceased spouse's interest. In other states (community property states), the step up applies to both spouses' interest (in other words, to the entire house), even though only one spouse has died. For more information about the basis of inherited property, see IRS Publication 559, *Survivors, Executors, and Administrators.*

How to Report Deductions and Gain From Your Home Sale

If you have deductions to claim from the sale of your home, you claim these deductions just as you would if you were still living in the home. For example, you deduct property taxes on Schedule A, in the "Taxes You Paid" section, and interest payments on Schedule A, in the "Interest You Paid" section.

You are required to report the sale of your principal residence on your tax return only if you have a taxable gain on the sale. If you go through the gain calculation and discover that you have no taxable gain (after including all expenses related to the transaction and excluding gain, if you are eligible), then you are not required to report the transaction on your tax return. If you do have a taxable gain, you report the transaction on Schedule D, *Capital Gains and Losses* (the same form on which you report gains from the sale of stocks and other securities).

Your Business

Tax Benefits in This Chapter

☐ **Did you spend money on your business before it was up and running?**
- You might be able to deduct or amortize start-up expenses, even if the business never gets off the ground.

☐ **Does your business have day-to-day operating expenses?**
- Keep track of all of the expenses you incur for the business; most will be deductible.

☐ **Do you travel for your business?**
- You may deduct the costs of transportation.
- If you stay out of town overnight, you may deduct the cost of lodging and half your meal expenses.

☐ **Do you entertain clients for your business?**
- You may deduct half the cost of business-related meals and entertainment.

☐ **Have you purchased assets for your business, like office furniture or a computer?**
- You may depreciate the asset—deduct a portion of the cost for each year of its useful life—or, in some cases, you may deduct the whole cost in the year you buy the asset.

☐ **Can you establish a retirement plan for your business?**
- If your business makes money, you may establish some type of retirement plan for the business and claim a deduction for your contribution.
- If you are older than 70½, you may contribute to some types of retirement plans but not others. But you must also take money out of those plans.

☐ **Do you have a home office?**
- If you use it exclusively for business, you might be able to deduct the expenses of maintaining that office, including part of what you pay to maintain the whole house, such as mortgage interest, real estate taxes, utilities, and depreciation.

☐ **Is your business losing money?**
- You might be able to claim the loss on your tax return. If you can't use the entire loss in the current year, you might be able to use it in an earlier year or a future year.

☐ **Is your business profitable, but just barely?**
- You might qualify for the earned income credit, a tax benefit designed to help those struggling to live on low earnings.

Some people use their retirement to catapult themselves out of the corporate world and into their own business. It's become more and more common for retirees to forgo a life of leisure for a new business venture, at least for a while. Maybe it's time to start your own hot air balloon charter service. Perhaps you should launch the gardening newsletter you've been writing in your head all these years. Or, you might want to turn what was once a hobby—such as buying and selling used books, knitting, making fishing lures, or taking photographs—into a money-making enterprise.

If you decide to start your own postretirement business, you will discover that most of your expenses will be deductible. Although you and the IRS might not see eye to eye on every cent you spend, you will almost certainly find more deductible business expenses than you ever expected.

Of course, burdens come along with the tax benefits. As a self-employed person, you must report your business income and expenses each year, and pay tax on your net income. If your business suffers a loss, you generally may use it to offset other taxable income on your tax return. (But beware: If your business regularly fails to make money, the IRS might decide that you are actually just indulging in a hobby—and might disallow your loss. See "Business or Hobby?" below, for more information.)

If the business is profitable, you will usually be required to pay self-employment tax (for Social Security and Medicare), as well. When you worked for someone else, your employer paid half of these taxes (called FICA and Medicare taxes) and withheld the other half from your paycheck. When you are self-employed, you have to foot the whole bill, although you may deduct half of the self-employment taxes you pay.

This chapter explains the tax consequences of starting and running your own business. Although starting a business certainly adds a new level of complexity to your tax return, it also provides a rich source of deductible expenses. As a result, many retirees find that they can deduct many of the costs of pursuing an activity that they love—and perhaps, earn some good money in the bargain.

> ## Business Entities
>
> Most people who start a business during retirement run the business as a sole proprietorship. This means there is only one owner of the business, who reports business income and expenses on Schedule C of his or her individual income tax return.
>
> A sole proprietorship is arguably the simplest form of business, but it won't work for every business. For example, a sole proprietorship can have only one owner. If you want to start a business with someone else, you will need to form a different type of business entity, such as a partnership. Or, if you are concerned about liability issues, you might want to form a corporation or a limited liability company (LLC).
>
> In this chapter, we assume that you will run your business as a sole proprietorship. However, you might want to research the alternatives to find out which type of business entity best fits your situation. You can read up on the pros and cons of different business entities in *The Small Business Start-Up Kit*, by Peri Pakroo (Nolo), which will also help you determine whether you need an expert to advise you and help you with the paperwork.

Business or Hobby?

This chapter covers the income you must report—and the deductions you may claim—when running a business. You will discover that the tax code is fairly generous with tax benefits for business. On the other hand, Congress is not interested in subsidizing your hobby. But what makes an activity a business, rather than a hobby?

You probably won't be surprised to learn that the IRS has given this some thought. Perhaps most important, the IRS wants to see evidence of a profit motive. The taxpayer who tries to claim business tax reductions for a hobby, claiming losses year after year with no apparent need or desire to make a profit, might as well be waving a red flag.

If you are in fact running a business, you may claim all of your business deductions even if it means claiming a loss on your tax return. If your "business" is actually a hobby, you are not permitted to claim a loss. Instead, you must report the hobby income, and you may claim expenses only to offset that income. Once you have used enough hobby expenses to reduce your hobby income to zero, all remaining expenses are disregarded—you may not deduct them or carry them over to a future year.

Of course, a business looks more like a business if it's making money. Sometimes, however, it takes a while for a business to turn a profit. And some businesses never do.

The IRS recognizes this problem. Even if you don't make a profit, you may claim a loss for your business if you can show you have a profit motive—that is, if you act in ways that demonstrate that you want to make a profit. But the IRS will want some proof—and, generally, it's up to you to provide it.

If you make a profit in three out of five years, you are deemed to have a profit motive and the burden of proof shifts to the IRS. If you never show a profit, it is more difficult to prove that you have a profit motive. After all, why would you stick with it if you aren't making any money?

The IRS will consider a variety of facts and circumstances to decide whether you are really running a business. For example, if you are wealthy and don't need the income from the business to support you, the IRS might question your profit motive. Or, if your business activity looks more like recreation than work, the IRS might look askance. That doesn't mean your goose is cooked, however. Just be prepared to defend your position.

Here are some steps you can take to help make your activity look like a business:

- Conduct the activity like a business, keeping accurate records of revenue and expenses and producing the occasional profit and loss statement or balance sheet.
- Don't mix business funds with personal funds. Keep a separate bank account for your business.

- Start a business in a field in which you have some long-standing expertise.
- Devote significant time and effort to the business (and keep the records necessary to prove it).
- Make capital investments in your business, by purchasing equipment or machinery, for example.

RESOURCE

Want more information on the hobby loss rule? You can find out more about how the IRS distinguishes a business from a hobby in IRS Publication 535, *Business Expenses.* You'll find more on the hobby loss rule, including ways to show the IRS that you're trying to earn a profit, in *Deduct It! Lower Your Small Business Taxes*, by Stephen Fishman (Nolo).

Start-Up Expenses

You don't have deductible business expenses until you are actually running a business. Generally, if you haven't yet opened for business or offered your services to the public, then you aren't yet in business and the expenses you incur are not business expenses.

Of course, it can be difficult to get a business off the ground without spending some money. For example, suppose you need to do some market research. Maybe you need to scout out some office space and put down a deposit. Maybe you do a little advertising to see if anybody out there is interested in what you have to offer before you take the big plunge.

Expenses that you incur for your business before you are actually open for business are called start-up expenses. Start-up expenses are those that would be deductible as business expenses if your business were up and running. (See "Operating Expenses," below.) As long as your business eventually opens, you may deduct at least some of your start-up expenses. Even if the business never gets off the ground, you might be able to recover some of your costs.

Deducting Start-Up Expenses

You may deduct up to $5,000 of start-up expenses that you incurred before your business officially began. However, you must wait and deduct them on your return for the year your business actually begins. Even if it takes several years to get your business off the ground, you may not deduct any of your costs until the first year your business is up and running.

If you spend more than $5,000 to get your business going, the excess is not lost. You may amortize the rest over the next 180 months (15 years), beginning with the month your business began.

> **EXAMPLE:** You opened your new batik T-shirt business on July 1 of the current year. Your start-up expenses total $8,600. You may deduct $5,000 of those start-up expenses in the current year. You must amortize the remaining $3,600 over 180 months, which means you may claim a deduction for $20 per month ($3,600 ÷ 180), beginning July 1 of the current year.
>
> In the current year, your total deduction is $5,000 plus $120 ($20 per month x six months of business), or $5,120. You may continue to deduct $20 per month until you have deducted all of your start-up expenses.

Those with very high start-up expenses are subject to a phase-out. If your start-up expenses exceed $50,000, you may not deduct $5,000 of them in your first year of business. Instead, the $5,000 must be reduced, dollar for dollar, by the amount by which your start-up expenses exceed $50,000. If you have start-up expenses of $55,000 or more, you won't be able to claim any part of the $5,000 deduction for the first year. You can still recover your start-up expenses (including any part of the $5,000 you can't claim in the first year), but you must do so by amortizing the expenses over 180 months.

Electing to Claim Start-Up Expenses

To claim start-up expenses as a deduction, you must make an election to do so, which you then submit with your tax return. This election is a written statement that you attach to your income tax return for the year business begins.

The statement must declare that you are making an election under Section 195 of the tax code. It must also include all of the following:

- a statement that you elect to deduct the first $5,000 of start-up expenses
- a statement that you are electing to amortize the remaining expenses (if any) over 180 months beginning in the month business began, and
- a list of your start-up expenses, including a description, dollar amount, and date for each expense incurred.

 CAUTION

Don't miss the deadline to claim start-up expenses. Generally, you must make your Section 195 election when you file your income tax return for the year your new business begins. If you request an extension of time to file your return, you may submit the election with the return by the extended due date. But even if you don't make the election with the appropriate return, you have a six-month grace period to file an amended return and make the election. The six-month period begins on the due date of your return (*not* including extensions). If you don't file an amended return within the six-month grace period, you may not deduct your start-up expenses.

When Does Business Begin?

Because you may not deduct any start-up expenses until your business actually begins, you'll need to know when the IRS believes that moment has arrived. By IRS measures, a business begins when it starts to function as a going concern and perform the activities for which it was organized. The start date is not measured by when you bring in your first dollar of revenue.

In the case of a retail operation, business begins when you offer items for sale. If you are providing a service, business begins when you offer that service. If you purchase another business that is already a going concern, you are deemed to be in business from the moment you become the new owner. If you are a writer, you are deemed to be in business from the moment you begin writing, not when you submit your finished product to a publisher.

What If Your Business Never Begins?

One of the reasons you might spend time and money before actually starting a business is to determine whether or not your business idea is viable. Spending a little money up front might save you more money and heartache later.

Because start-up expenses are deductible only after business begins, expenses for a business that never gets off the ground will never be deductible. A couple of important exceptions might allow you to recover some of your costs, however.

- Start-up expenses related to a specific business—as opposed to a general search for an unspecified new business—might be deductible as a capital loss (reported on Schedule D). For example, assume you were hoping to sell batik T-shirts to boomers galore. You paid market research fees and put down a nonrefundable rental deposit on a store front. When you discovered that you were hopelessly inept as a batik artist, you gave up on your plan. Although your attempt to start a new business was unsuccessful and you never opened shop, the IRS is likely to allow you to claim a loss because you attempted to start a specific business.
- If you purchase assets for a business that never opens its doors, you may recover those costs if and when you sell the assets. At that time, you will add your costs to the basis of the property,

which will reduce your taxable gain or increase your loss when the assets are sold.

What If You Close the Business After a Few Years?

Suppose your business opens its doors, but eventually shuts them again. This is fairly common: After all, half of all businesses fail in the first five years. Even if your business is wildly successful, you might decide to get out. Perhaps you've decided to move on to the more leisurely phase of your retirement.

No matter why you decide to close your business, you might have unclaimed start-up expenses. Perhaps you were amortizing some of those expenses over 180 months and closed your business before 15 years had passed. Fortunately, the IRS allows you to recover all of your remaining start-up expenses in the year you close your business.

How to Claim Start-Up Expenses

You calculate your current year deduction for start-up expenses on Form 4562, *Depreciation and Amortization*. You then claim the deduction on Schedule C, *Profit or Loss From Business*, under "Other Expenses." In addition, you must attach your Section 195 election (see "Electing to Claim Start-Up Expenses," above) to your tax return for the year you start your new business.

Operating Expenses

Once your business is up and running, most of what you pay to operate it is deductible. For the most part, these expenses are easy to identify. The IRS's Schedule C, on which you report your income and expenses, provides a helpful guide. Some of the most common categories of expenses include:

- advertising
- commissions and fees
- contract labor

- employee benefits, such as health care premiums you pay for employees (but not for yourself); contributions to a retirement plan fall into a separate category
- insurance (other than health), such as business liability insurance or business property insurance
- interest on business loans
- fees for legal or other professional services
- office expenses, such as janitorial service, telephone answering service, coffee or water delivery service, or window washing
- retirement plan benefit (this includes contributions for employees but not for you)
- rent you pay for business equipment or office space
- repairs and maintenance
- supplies
- taxes and licenses, including business taxes or license fees you might be required to pay to the city in which you do business
- travel
- meals and entertainment (these are not deductible in full; see "Meals and Entertainment," below)
- utilities (include this expense if you have an office outside the home and pay the utilities for the office)
- wages you pay employees, and
- other expenses, such as postage, Internet access fees, or telephone expenses.

Some business expenses require special treatment. For example, if you purchase equipment or other assets, you might be required to depreciate them (see "Depreciating Assets," below). Home office expenses are also subject to certain restrictions (see "Home Office Deduction," below). This section covers a few additional categories of expenses for which you might need to follow special rules: continuing education, meals and entertainment, business gifts, and travel.

Continuing Education

Unfortunately, the IRS is not willing to subsidize a career move by allowing you to deduct training or education in a new field. Suppose you have just retired from your job as a software engineer and now you want to sell real estate. You may need to take some courses to prepare for your new career. Those expenses are not deductible as business expenses, because you are acquiring the basic skills necessary to enter a new profession.

On the other hand, you are permitted to deduct the cost of business-related education that helps you maintain or improve skills that you already have and that are required for your existing business. If you are legally required to take courses to maintain a professional license, for example, those education expenses are deductible.

You may also deduct the cost of conventions, seminars, or professional meetings related to your business activity. Other deductible expenses include tuition, fees, books or other materials, and travel expenses.

Meals and Entertainment

If you take a client out to dinner, take customers to a ball game or concert, or host a company holiday party, you probably have incurred costs for business-related meals and entertainment. As long as you engage in these activities for the purpose of pursuing new business or reinforcing the goodwill and loyalty of existing customers, you may deduct the expenses.

Perhaps because it can be difficult to separate business from pleasure, the law limits your deduction to half of your business-related meals and entertainment expenses. In order to claim any deduction at all, the activity (dining or other entertainment) must clearly be business-related and you must be able to substantiate that fact along with the expenses themselves.

It can be difficult to show that meals and entertainment are business-related, and unfortunately the burden of proof is on your shoulders. Although the IRS provides guidance, it can be somewhat murky. For a portion of the cost to be deductible, your meal or entertainment activity should satisfy one of these two tests:

- You must conduct or discuss business before, during, or after the meal or entertainment activity.
- The activity itself must be directly related to conducting business or must occur in a clear business setting. For example, you might pay for a catered lunch for prospective clients at your place of business, so you can display the batik T-shirts you want to sell.

As with any expense that could be either personal or business-related, you must keep detailed records of your meal and entertainment expenses, the purpose of the activity, and the nature of the business you discussed.

Business Gifts

A gift might be a business expense if the purpose of making the gift is to promote your business or perhaps to thank a customer for continued loyalty. You may deduct business gifts, but your deduction is limited to $25 per person, per year (even if you spend much more).

The rules are a little fuzzier when you give to employees. For example, suppose you give your sole employee a bonus at the end of the year. If you treat the bonus as compensation, then it is fully deductible, along with the wages you pay. If you give your employee a $200 fruit basket, it looks like a gift, and you might have to work a little harder to convince the IRS that you intended it to be part of your employee's compensation. If you cannot convince the IRS it is compensation, your deduction will be limited to $25 even though you spent $200. Bear in mind that items treated as compensation will be subject to all of the usual compensation-related rules, such as payroll tax requirements.

Also potentially confusing is the treatment of event tickets. Suppose you purchase opera tickets to give to a customer. You might consider them a business entertainment expense, rather than a gift. But how do you know for sure? The IRS says that if you accompany your client to the opera, the tickets are an entertainment expense. If you do not, then you may choose to treat the expense as either entertainment or a gift.

Bear in mind that entertainment expenses are limited to 50% of your cost. Gifts, on the other hand, are limited to $25 per person. So your best course of action might depend on how much you spend. But beware of this additional limit: If you give a customer two tickets—so the customer can bring along a spouse or friend, for example—you are deemed to have given only one gift, and your deduction is limited to $25.

Auto and Travel

Your business travel expenses are treated differently for tax purposes depending on whether you are traveling locally or you are traveling out of town and will be gone overnight.

Local travel

When you travel around town to take care of business or to meet with a customer or client, the cost of your local travel is deductible. However, you may not deduct the cost of your meals when you're away from your office or other business location. Meals (and lodging) are deductible only if you must be away from home overnight.

Local travel expenses might include the cost of a bus, taxi, or similar transportation. Those costs are fully deductible when the travel is for business. When you use your car for such travel, however, calculating your deductible expense becomes quite a bit more complicated. There are two ways to calculate your travel expense from use of your own car:

Option 1: Actual expenses. Your first option is to track your actual expenses. Any expenses that are directly related to your business—such as the cost of parking at your office or tolls paid when you drive to call on clients—are fully deductible. For expenses that you must pay to maintain and service your car (such as insurance, repairs, gas, and registration fees), you must calculate the portion of those costs that are attributable to your business use of the car. To do this, you must determine how much you use the car for business as opposed to personal use. Typically, you will allocate by mileage. For example, if you drove 10,000 miles during the year and you put 2,000 of those miles on the car while driving to and from your hot-air balloon launching site, then the expenses of operating and maintaining the car would be allocated 20% to your business and 80% to personal use (which is not deductible).

Option 2: **Standard mileage rate**. If you don't want to bother with extensive record keeping, you can use the standard mileage rate. Although the actual expense method often yields a larger deduction, it also requires you to keep meticulous records of all of your car expenses and mileage. If you choose to use the standard mileage rate to compute your deduction, you need only keep track of the miles you travel for business. Each year, the IRS provides the amount you may deduct for each business mile traveled. (For 2008, it's 50.5 cents per mile for the first half of the year and 58.5 cents for the second half of the year.) In addition, you may deduct expenses for business parking and tolls, personal property taxes you pay on the value of your car, and the business portion of your car loan (if any); these costs are not included in the standard mileage rate.

As long as you elect to use the standard mileage rate in the first year you use your car for business, you may choose whichever method gives you the larger deduction in all subsequent years. However, if you chose to use the actual expense method in the first year, you must continue to use it for as long as you use that car in your business.

- Also, you may not use the standard mileage rate if you have ever claimed depreciation on the car and used a depreciation method other than straight line (see "Depreciating Assets," below, for more information). There are a few other situations in which you may not use the standard mileage rate; see IRS Publication 463, *Travel, Entertainment, Gift, and Car Expenses*, for more information.

Out-of-Town Travel

If you travel out of town for business, you may deduct the full cost of your travel and lodging, and half of what you spend on meals. However, you may not deduct your travel expenses if the primary purpose of your trip is personal. For example, suppose you go to Montana with your spouse to spend a week on a dude ranch, learning how to ride and getting away from it all. If you just happen to have a customer nearby and take a day to go visit him, you can't deduct the entire trip. If you actually conduct business with your customer, however, you may deduct the cost of your side trip to meet with him.

If the primary purpose of your trip is business, but you spend more than 25% of your time on personal activities, you must allocate your travel expenses (including meals and lodging) between business and pleasure.

Depreciating Assets

Many of the items you purchase for your business can be deducted in the year you buy them. For example, you can deduct the cost of supplies (such as paper, packaging materials, or business cards) as a business expense.

The rules are different for property that has a longer life, such as computers, office furniture, cameras, a copier, or a vehicle. These types of property generally must be deducted over time, using a process called "depreciation." In some cases you might be able to claim a deduction for the entire cost of this type of property in the year you buy it: This is called "first-year expensing" (or sometimes, a "Section 179 deduction," after the part of the tax code that allows it).

The rules on depreciation and first-year expensing are complicated. For example, when you depreciate property, you must figure out how much you can deduct each year, over how long a time period, and what to do if you sell or replace the property during its useful life. In the case of first-year expensing, you'll need to know which property qualifies, what the limits are, and what happens when you dispose of the property. Luckily, the tax benefits make it worth your while to learn the basics: These deductions can easily save you thousands of dollars in taxes.

First-Year Expensing Deduction

Although you generally have to depreciate long-lived assets, you may use first-year expensing to deduct the full cost (up to a dollar limit) of certain business assets that you acquire during the tax year. You may use first-year expensing only for property you purchase during the year to use for your business. You may not expense the cost of property you bought in a previous year or the cost of property you purchased for personal use then started using in your business.

Property Subject to First-Year Expensing

You may claim a first-year expensing deduction for tangible personal property such as office equipment, furniture, machinery, computer equipment, and cars used for business. You may deduct the cost of all qualifying property as long as your total deduction does not exceed the limit (see "How Much You May Expense," below).

As long as you use the property more than 50% of the time for business and it otherwise qualifies, you may claim a first-year expensing deduction. You may deduct only the business portion of your cost. For example, if you pay $2,000 for a computer and use it 75% of the time for your business and 25% of the time for personal email, Web surfing, and photo storage, you may deduct only 75% of the cost ($1,500). (If the asset is a vehicle, the deduction might be subject to additional limits. See "Special Depreciation Rules for Cars," below.)

You may not claim a first-year expensing deduction for:

- real property, such as buildings and structural components of such buildings (such as air conditioning and heating units)
- landscaping
- personal assets you have converted to business use
- property that you use less than 50% of the time for business
- property you received from a relative or spouse, or
- property you acquired by gift or inheritance.

If you have property that doesn't qualify for the first-year expensing deduction, you may be able to depreciate it (see "Depreciation," below).

How Much You May Expense

You may expense a total of $250,000 (for tax year 2008 only). Note that the limit is a total; it doesn't apply per item of property. This limit is scheduled to drop down to $128,000 in 2009. If you spend more than the limit, you may claim the rest of your costs using depreciation (see "Depreciation," below).

> CAUTION
>
> **Exceptions and restrictions may apply.** Section 179 is rife with special rules—and exceptions to those rules. For example, if your business is located in an "enterprise zone," your Section 179 limit might be higher. If you are using Section 179 for a car you use for business, the deduction is severely limited (see "Special Depreciation Rules for Cars," below). If you drive an SUV for business, the expensing limit may be $25,000. And, if the total cost of all of your qualifying purchases is more than $800,000 (for 2008), you must reduce the $250,000 limit by the amount of the excess. For more information about these special situations, see IRS Publication 946, *How to Depreciate Property.*

If your business is operating at a loss, you might not be able to claim an expensing deduction. The deduction is limited to your net income from the business. If you have a loss before claiming any expensing deduction, then you must use depreciation on the full cost of the asset. If you have some income but not enough to cover the asset's full cost, you may claim the expensing deduction to the extent you have income and then carry over the excess and claim it in the following year (provided your net income in that year will cover the remainder).

Tax Strategy: Should You Expense Only Part of the Cost of an Asset?

If you elect first-year expensing for an asset, you are not required to claim a deduction for the entire cost. Instead, you may expense part of the cost and depreciate the rest. For example, suppose you purchase office furniture for $15,000. You might elect to expense only $5,000 and recover the remaining $10,000 over the expected life of the furniture, using depreciation.

This strategy makes the most sense if your net income from the business is not high enough to claim an expensing deduction for the full $15,000, and you do not expect to have enough income in the next few years to cover your remaining $10,000 expense. Because you are permitted to claim a regular depreciation deduction even if you have a net loss from the business (which is not the case for Section 179 deductions), it might make sense to begin claiming your depreciation deduction right away rather than carrying over the entire amount until you are able to expense some or all of it.

If You Sell an Asset During Its Useful Life: Recapture

The first-year expensing deduction allows you to recover the cost of your business assets more rapidly than if you had used regular depreciation and recovered the cost over the expected life of the asset. But if you sell the property before the end of its useful life, you will be doubling up on your benefits—claiming the full cost as a tax deduction but also getting some of that cost back as proceeds from the sale. Not surprisingly, the tax code covers this situation. When you sell a business asset or stop using it in your business, you might have to give back, or "recapture," some of the first-year deduction you claimed. This means you must report, as ordinary income, the extra deduction you claimed in the year you purchased the asset.

To determine whether you have any recapture to report, you must calculate your gain on the sale of the asset. Your gain is the sales proceeds reduced by your basis. Basis is generally your original cost reduced by any cost recovery (such as depreciation or first-year expensing). If you have gain, you must recapture—report as ordinary income—the lesser of the gain or the sum of the expensing deduction and depreciation you claimed. This is only fair, because your original expensing and depreciation deductions were used to offset ordinary income in the year you claimed them.

> **EXAMPLE:** Last year, you bought a new computer that you use only for your business. You paid $2,000 for it and claimed a $2,000 expensing deduction on your return. This year you sold the computer for $1,500. You calculate your gain as follows:
>
> | Basis of computer: | |
> |---|---|
> | Original cost | $ 2,000 |
> | Less expensing deduction | (2,000) |
> | Basis of computer | $ 0 |
> | | |
> | Gain from sale: | |
> | Proceeds from sale | $ 1,500 |
> | Less basis | (0) |
> | Gain | $ 1,500 |

Because you have gain from the sale of the computer, you must recapture your expensing deduction to the extent you have gain. That means you must recapture $1,500 and report it as ordinary income on your tax return.

You might also be required to recapture some of your first-year expensing deduction if your business use of an asset drops to 50% or less. (Remember, you may claim an expensing deduction only if you use an asset more than 50% of the time for business in the year you purchase it.) The amount of the expensing deduction you must recapture is the amount by which your expensing deduction exceeds what you could have claimed through depreciation.

> **EXAMPLE:** You paid $2,000 for a computer for your business in 2007. Because you were using the computer exclusively for business, you expensed the entire cost in 2007. You continued to use the computer 100% for business until 2009, when you began using the computer 60% of the time for personal activities. For the 2009 tax year, you must recapture some of the expensing deduction you claimed in 2007. The recapture amount is the amount by which $2,000 exceeds the total of the regular depreciation you would have claimed by the end of 2009 if you had not elected to expense the cost of the computer in 2007. You compute the recapture amount as follows:
>
> What you could have claimed using regular depreciation:
>
> | | |
> |---|---:|
> | 2007 (100% business use) | $ 200 |
> | 2008 (100% business use) | 400 |
> | 2009 (40% business use) | 160 |
> | Total | $ 760 |
> | Expensed amount | $2,000 |
>
> Recapture amount: $2,000 − $760 = $1,240

Depreciation

If you can't—or decide not to—use first-year expensing to recover the cost of an asset, you may depreciate it. Depreciation allows taxpayers to deduct the cost of business property over the "expected life" of the property itself, deducting a portion each year until the cost has been recovered. To determine how much you can claim as a depreciation deduction, you must first determine the expected life of the property, then figure out what formula, or depreciation method, to use to calculate your deduction each year.

For tax year 2008 only, you might be able to claim some additional depreciation (sometimes called "bonus" depreciation) on certain types of property. To qualify, generally the property must be new and you must be the original owner. For more information about this bonus depreciation, see IRS Publication 946.

Expected Life

Technically, expected life is a measure of wear and tear, exhaustion, or obsolescence of an asset. It is a bit of a murky concept, which is, according to the IRS, unrelated to the value of the asset itself.

You are not permitted to use your own good judgment in coming up with an estimate of an asset's expected, or "useful" life. Instead, the tax code and the IRS provide guidelines to help you determine the useful life of the most common types of depreciable property. Here are some of the categories that often apply to small businesses (you can find the whole list in IRS Publication 946):

5 years

Computers and peripheral equipment

Most office equipment (such as copiers and typewriters)

Cars

7 years

Office furniture

Safes

File cabinets

Cell phones

Fax machines

Uncategorized property (this is a catch-all for property that has not been assigned to another category)

39 years

Nonresidential real property, which would include an office used for business, if you own the property, or your home office if you do business out of your home.

Depreciation Methods

There are three formulas (called depreciation methods) you can use to calculate how much you can claim as a depreciation deduction each year. The simplest, called "straight-line depreciation," allows you to deduct a set amount for each year of the item's useful life (prorated for partial years). The other two methods, called the "double-declining balance" method and the "declining balance" method, allow you to take larger deductions in the early years of the item's useful life.

Although you will sometimes be required to use a particular depreciation method, often you will be able to choose whichever of the three methods makes the most sense for your business.

CAUTION

If you are subject to the alternative minimum tax (AMT), depreciation rules and methods might be different. See Chapter 1 for more information about the AMT, or see IRS Instructions for Form 6251, *Alternative Minimum Tax.*

Method 1: Straight-Line Depreciation

Using straight-line depreciation, you take the same deduction for each year of the item's useful life. However, your deductions in the first and last years will be smaller, to reflect the date you bought the property or started using it in your business.

Generally, you may choose whether or not to use straight-line depreciation. However, you are required to use straight-line depreciation for:

- **Nonresidential real estate and improvements.** You are required to use straight-line depreciation for business real estate, such as office space (whether in your home or elsewhere), as well as improvements you make to the property. When computing your depreciation deduction for such property, you must exclude the cost of the land, which is not eligible for depreciation.

- **Listed property.** Listed property is property that could easily be used either for business or for personal use. The most common items of listed property are cars, computers, and mobile phones. If you are using listed property less than 50% of the time for business, then you must use straight-line depreciation. For example, if you use your cell phone 20% of the time for business and 80% of the time for personal calls, you must recover the business portion of the cost using straight-line depreciation.

When computing straight-line depreciation, you simply divide the depreciable basis of property by its expected life. In most circumstances, the IRS requires you to assume that you first purchased or started using the property for business halfway through the year (this assumption is called the "half-year convention"). In the first and last years of the property's useful life, you may therefore claim only half the normal amount.

> **EXAMPLE:** You spent $560 on a new fax machine for your business. You elect to recover the cost using straight-line depreciation. According to IRS guidelines, the expected life of the fax machine is seven years. Your depreciation deductions will be as follows:
>
> | | |
> |---|---|
> | Year 1: | $40 |
> | Year 2: | $80 |
> | Year 3: | $80 |
> | Year 4: | $80 |
> | Year 5: | $80 |
> | Year 6: | $80 |
> | Year 7: | $80 |
> | Year 8: | $40 |

As you can see, you may take a deduction in each of eight years, even though the expected life of the fax machine is only seven years. That's because of the half-year convention, which presumes that you used the machine for only half of year one and half of year eight.

> **! CAUTION**
>
> **If you buy property late in the year, you must use a different calculation.** A special rule applies if more than 40% of the total value of property you purchased (or started using in your business) for the year was purchased or first used in the last quarter of the year. In that case, you must use special (and less favorable) tables provided by the IRS. This is called the "midquarter convention." (Publication 946 contains tables you may use to calculate your deduction if you are required to use this convention.) The midquarter convention does not apply to real estate, so you need not include the cost of your office space when applying the 40% rule.

Method 2: Double-Declining Balance

The double-declining balance method also requires you to claim depreciation over the useful life of the property, but instead of claiming equal amounts each year, you may skew the cost recovery so that your deduction is larger in the earlier years and lower in later years.

As is the case with straight line depreciation, either the half-year or midquarter convention will apply. If the half-year convention applies, you can calculate your depreciation deduction using the chart below. (If the midquarter convention applies, see IRS Publication 946 to figure out your deduction amounts.)

	200% Declining Balance Depreciation Method Convention: Half-Year					
	If the recovery period is:					
Year	3-year	5-year	7-year	10-year	15-year	20-year
1	33.33%	20.00%	14.29%	10.00%	5.00%	3.750%
2	44.45%	32.00%	24.49%	18.00%	9.50%	7.219%
3	14.81%	19.20%	17.49%	14.40%	8.55%	6.677%
4	7.41%	11.52%	12.49%	11.52%	7.70%	6.177%
5		11.52%	8.93%	9.22%	6.93%	5.713%
6		5.76%	8.92%	7.37%	6.23%	5.285%
7			8.93%	6.55%	5.90%	4.888%
8			4.46%	6.55%	5.90%	4.522%
9				6.56%	5.91%	4.462%
10				6.55%	5.90%	4.461%
11				3.28%	5.91%	4.462%
12					5.90%	4.461%
13					5.91%	4.462%
14					5.90%	4.461%
15					5.91%	4.462%
16					2.95%	4.461%
17						4.462%
18						4.461%
19						4.462%
20						4.461%
21						2.231%

EXAMPLE: In February of this year, you spent $1,200 for a new copier for your business. A copier has an expected life of five years. On your tax return for the year, you may claim a deduction of $1,200 x 20%, or $240. For next year, you may claim a deduction of $1,200 x 32%, or $384. You continue using the above chart through year six, after which you will have recovered the entire cost of the copier.

Method 3: Declining Balance

The declining balance method is similar to the double-declining balance method, but for some classes of property, the deductions in the early years are smaller than they would be if you used the double-declining balance method. (And consequently, the deduction is larger in later years.) If the half-year convention applies, use the chart below to calculate how much you may deduct each year. (Again, see IRS Publication 946 if you have to use the midquarter convention.)

150% Declining Balance Depreciation Method Convention: Half-Year							
If the recovery period is:							
Year	3-year	5-year	7-year	10-year	12-year	15-year	20-year
1	25.00%	15.00%	10.71%	7.50%	6.25%	5.00%	3.750%
2	37.50%	25.50%	19.13%	13.88%	11.72%	9.50%	7.219%
3	25.00%	17.85%	15.03%	11.79%	10.25%	8.55%	6.677%
4	12.50%	16.66%	12.25%	10.02%	8.97%	7.70%	6.177%
5		16.66%	12.25%	8.74%	7.85%	6.93%	5.713%
6		8.33%	12.25%	8.74%	7.33%	6.23%	5.285%
7			12.25%	8.74%	7.33%	5.90%	4.888%
8			6.13%	8.74%	7.33%	5.90%	4.522%
9				8.74%	7.33%	5.91%	4.462%
10				4.37%	7.32%	5.90%	4.461%
11					7.33%	5.91%	4.462%
12					3.66%	5.90%	4.461%
13						5.91%	4.462%
14						5.90%	4.461%
15						5.91%	4.462%
16						2.95%	4.461%
17							4.462%
18							4.461%

> TIP
>
> **Consider your total tax picture when choosing a depreciation method.** Many taxpayers assume that they should choose the depreciation method that allows them to recover their costs most quickly—in other words, the double-declining balance method. However, this isn't necessarily the best strategy. You might prefer to use a less aggressive method if the depreciation deduction is likely to be more valuable to you in later years (if, for example, you expect to be in a higher tax bracket or have more business income in a later year).

Special Depreciation Rules for Cars

In some ways, the rules for depreciating cars are the same as the rules for depreciating other types of property. For example, if you use the car for personal trips as well as business, you may depreciate only the portion of your basis in the car that is attributable to business use. And, you often have the choice of the three depreciation methods described above, unless you don't use your car more than 50% of the time for business. Cars are listed property, so you must use straight-line depreciation if you use the car 50% of the time or less for your business.

Once you settle on a method and calculate the depreciation according to the usual rules, however, the law slaps another limit on the amount of depreciation you may claim for your car in any given year as shown below.

Maximum Deprecation for Cars				
Year car placed in service	1st Year	2nd Year	3rd Year	4th year and later
2008*	$2,960/$10,960	$4,800	$2,850	$1,775
2007	$3,060	$4,900	$2,850	$1,775
2006	$2,960	$4,800	$2,850	$1,775
2005	$2,960	$4,700	$2,850	$1,775

* Note: For tax year 2008 only, the first-year depreciation limit has been increased by $8,000 for certain passenger autos. Your car will generally qualify for the higher limit if you purchased it new during 2008 and placed it in service in the same year.

Keep in mind that these limits apply if you use the car 100% for business. If your business use is less than 100% (which is often the case), then you must apply your business use percentage to the above dollar limits, as well. For example, if you began using the car in 2006, but you used it only 50% of the time for business, the maximum deduction you would be able to claim for the first year, no matter which depreciation method you use, is $1,480 (50% of $2,960).

> **EXAMPLE:** You began using your car for business in January 2007. In 2008, you used your car 15% of the time for business. The depreciable basis of your car is $25,000. Because the car was not used more than 50% of the time for business, you must use straight-line depreciation. On your 2008 tax return, you compute your deduction as follows:
>
> **Step 1:** Straight-line depreciation for year two of the car (which has an expected life of five years) is $25,000 divided by five years, or $5,000.
>
> **Step 2:** Because the car was used only 15% for business, the amount of depreciation allocated to business is $5,000 x 15%, or $750.
>
> **Step 3:** According to the chart above, the maximum you can depreciate for a car that was placed in service in 2007 and is in its second year of business use is $4,900. However, because the car was used only 15% of the time for business, the ceiling is limited to $4,900 x 15%, or $735.
>
> Therefore, your auto depreciation deduction for 2008 is limited to $735.

Although most cars are subject to the additional depreciation limits described above, an exception has been carved out for certain trucks, vans, and SUVs that weigh less than 6,000 pounds. If you have such a vehicle, see IRS Publication 946 to see whether your vehicle qualifies for an exception.

Amortization

Amortization is similar to depreciation in that you recover the cost of an asset over its expected life. Depreciation applies only to tangible property, however, while amortization generally applies to intangible property. Intangible assets are those that are not physical in nature, such as copyrights, patents, and computer software.

When you amortize the cost of a business asset, you recover it evenly over the asset's expected life. The business costs you are most likely to amortize are computer software and perhaps business start-up expenses, such as organizational costs.

Special Rules for Computer Software

Computer software is an intangible asset that is subject to amortization over a 15-year expected life. However, there are some exceptions to this rule that might allow you to recover the cost of software more quickly.

- If the software has a useful life of one year or less (for example, if you replace the software every year), you may deduct the full cost as a business expense in the year you buy it.
- If you purchase "off-the-shelf" software in any tax year after 2002 and before 2011, you may choose to expense the cost (under Section 179) or to depreciate it over 36 months. For this purpose, "off-the-shelf" software is software that meets all of the following requirements:
  - The software is available to the general public.
  - You do not have an exclusive license to use the software.
  - You have not substantially modified the software for use in your business.

Home Office Deduction

Many people who qualify for a home office deduction choose not to take it because they fear it's a "red flag" that will lead to an IRS audit. And indeed, the IRS probably is more inclined to scrutinize a return that claims a home office deduction than one that does not. But there's a good reason for the IRS's concern: Many people claim the deduction even though they are not entitled to it.

Qualifying for the Deduction

To claim a home office deduction, you must use the space exclusively for business. And, you must use it for that purpose on a regular basis, not just occasionally. The "exclusive use" requirement is often the deal-breaker. For example, a room that you use as an office in the morning and a family room in the afternoon or evening does not qualify, unless you can show that the portion of the room that houses your office is not used as part of the family room.

If the home office is actually inside your home (rather than a separate structure on your property, such as a studio or garage), you must also satisfy one of these two tests:

The office is a place of business where you meet with clients or customers on a regular basis.

The office in your home is your principal place of business. This means that you spend most of your work time in that office and conduct the bulk of your management and administrative activities from there. If you have another office outside the home, be prepared to prove that you do most of your money-making activities and administrative work at the home office.

If your office is a separate structure on your property, you do not need to satisfy either of the tests above. In other words, the office does not have to be a place where you meet customers, nor does it have to be your principal place of business. However, you must still use the separate structure exclusively as an office, and on a regular basis.

Calculating Your Deduction

If you have a space in your home that qualifies as a home office, you may deduct all of your expenses for maintaining that office, including a portion of the cost of maintaining your entire home.

Home Maintenance Expenses

Part of your overall home maintenance costs will be deductible as home office expenses. Generally, you use the square footage of your home office relative to the rest of the home to calculate the proportion of house expenses that are deductible as a home office expense. For example, if your office constitutes 10% of the square footage of your home, then you would be able to claim 10% of the expenses of operating and maintaining the home.

As an alternative to the square footage method, you may allocate expenses based on the total number of rooms in your home. However, you may use this method only if all of the rooms are about the same size. For example, if you have eight equal-sized rooms in your house, one of which is your office, you may allocate ⅛ of the expenses of operating and maintaining the house to the home office. Because most homes have rooms of different sizes, however, you will most likely need to use the square footage method.

Some of the house expenses you may allocate proportionately to your home office and deduct as home office expenses include:

- real estate taxes
- mortgage interest
- rent (if you are renting your home)
- utilities
- painting the exterior of the home
- repairs that affect the entire home, such as to the furnace, sewer, or water systems
- alarm system
- homeowner's association fees
- homeowner's insurance, and
- depreciation for the portion of the home used as an office.

Depreciating a Home Office

If you own your home and claim a home office deduction, you may claim a depreciation deduction for the cost of the office portion. When you claim the depreciation deduction, the following rules apply:

- The depreciable amount is the lower of your adjusted basis or the fair market value of the property (the office portion) when you begin using it for business.
- You may claim depreciation only for the building, not the land on which it sits.
- You must use straight-line depreciation.
- The expected life of the property is 39 years.

The following table from IRS Publication 946 provides the percentages you must use to compute your depreciation deduction. The percentage varies according to the month in which you began using the office for business.

Nonresidential Real Propery Straight-Line Method			
Midmonth Convention—39 Years			
Month First Used for Business	Percentage to Use in Year:		
	1	2–39	40
1	2.461%	2.564%	0.107%
2	2.247	2.564	0.321
3	2.033	2.564	0.535
4	1.819	2.564	0.749
5	1.605	2.564	0.963
6	1.391	2.564	1.177
7	1.177	2.564	1.391
8	0.963	2.564	1.605
9	0.749	2.564	1.819
10	0.535	2.564	2.033
11	0.321	2.564	2.247
12	0.107	2.564	2.461

EXAMPLE: You paid $500,000 for your home and, fortunately, the current fair market value is much higher. When you bought the home, the land was valued at $100,000 and the building (the house itself) was valued at $400,000. In March of this year, you began using one of the rooms in your home exclusively as a home office for your business. That room constitutes 10% of the square footage of your home. Therefore, the depreciable basis of your home office is 10% of $400,000, or $40,000.

For the current year, you compute depreciation for your home office as follows:

Depreciable basis	$40,000
Percentage for March (the third month)	2.033%
Depreciation deduction for the current year ($40,000 x 2.033%)	$ 813
The annual depreciation deduction for each of the next 38 years ($40,000 x 2.564%)	$ 1,026
Your deduction in the final year ($40,000 x 0.535%)	$ 214

IRS Form 8829, *Expenses for Business Use of Your Home,* will help you calculate your depreciation deduction.

Direct Expenses

The expenses discussed above are called "indirect expenses" because they are expenses of running the entire home and are therefore allocated between personal use and business use of the home.

Direct expenses, on the other hand, are those you incur solely for your business. For example, the costs of painting and decorating only the office, or making repairs to the office space would be considered direct expenses. You may deduct 100% of your direct expenses.

Nondeductible Expenses

Some household expenses are unrelated to maintaining your home office and consequently are not deductible as a home office expenses. Typical nondeductible expenses include:

- gardening
- landscaping, and
- repairs and maintenance on areas other than the home office, such as painting a bedroom or replacing a kitchen floor.

Home Office Deduction Limit

If you have a net loss from your business, your home office deduction may be limited. You are required to claim your home office expenses in a particular order, as follows:

- First, you claim the home office portion of real estate taxes, mortgage interest, and any casualty loss to your home (if you experienced a casualty, such as an earthquake, fire, or hurricane, during the year).
- Next, you claim other expenses of operating the home that are allocable to your home office, such as utilities, insurance, rent (if you do not own your home), repairs, and maintenance.
- Depreciation of the home office portion of your home is always deducted last.

You may claim expenses in the first category regardless of your net income from the business. That's because those expenses would be deductible in full even if you did not have a home office. However, the expenses in categories two and three are allowed only if you have net income from the business to offset the expenses. If you don't have enough net income, the excess expenses are disallowed for the current year and must be carried over to the next year. You may deduct them in the next year, but again, only if you have net income from your business.

To calculate your allowable home office deduction for the current year, follow these steps:

Step 1: Calculate your net income or loss from your business without taking into account any home office deduction.

Step 2: Subtract the home office portion of your real estate taxes, mortgage interest, and casualty loss (if any). If the result is zero or less, your home office deduction is limited to the home office portion of those expenses.

Step 3: If the result from Step 2 is a positive number (meaning you have net income from the business after subtracting the home office portion of real estate taxes, mortgage interest, and any casualty loss), then you may deduct your remaining operating expenses, but only to the extent they bring your net income to zero. Any excess operating expenses must be carried over to the next tax year.

Step 4: If you still have net income from the business after Step 3, you may deduct depreciation for the office portion of your home. Again, you may deduct depreciation only to the extent it reduces your net business income to zero (after taking into account the deductions in Steps 2 and 3). Any excess depreciation must be carried over to next year.

If you carry over part of your home office deduction to future years, you must deduct home office expenses in the following order:

- The current year's home office portion of real estate taxes, mortgage interest, and casualty losses.
- Any remaining operating expenses for the current year, plus any carryover operating expenses from prior years, plus any carryover depreciation deduction.
- The current year's depreciation for the home office portion of your house.

IRS Form 8829, *Expenses for Business Use of Your Home*, walks you through the calculation of your home office deduction, including how to compute the amounts that are disallowed for the current year and how to carry them over to the next year.

How to Claim a Home Office Deduction

Complete Form 8829 to calculate the amount of your deduction for the current year and the amount, if any, you must carry over to a future year. You claim the deduction itself on Schedule C, *Profit or Loss From Business*. Attach both Form 8829 and Schedule C to your income tax return.

Net Operating Loss

If you have a net loss from your business, you may claim it on your tax return and use it to offset other income, such as interest and dividends. If, after subtracting your business loss, you have negative taxable income, you might have a net operating loss (NOL). An NOL is a business loss that you are permitted to claim in a prior year (so you can obtain a tax refund for the earlier year) or in one or more future years (to reduce your tax liability in those years).

Determining whether you have an NOL is not simply a matter of figuring out whether you have negative taxable income. It could be that you have other losses—unrelated to your business—that have pushed your taxable income into negative territory. Also, you might have an NOL and not realize it. For example, your rental property might contribute to a net operating loss. Unfortunately, if you have negative taxable income, you won't be able to avoid the complex NOL calculation. For information and examples, see IRS Publication 536, *Net Operating Losses (NOLs) for Individuals, Estates, and Trusts*, and the instructions to Form 1045, *Application for Tentative Refund*.

When You Can Use a Net Operating Loss

If you have a net operating loss, you generally have two choices: You may carry the loss back two years and then forward for up to 20 years until it is used up, or you may forgo the two-year carry back and simply start carrying it forward.

> **CAUTION**
>
> **You might have to use different time periods.** Although the two-year carry back and 20-year carry forward periods are most common, there are special situations in which you might be permitted or required to use different time periods. See IRS Publication 536 for more information.

When you carry back your NOL, you claim the loss on the tax return for the second preceding tax year and claim a refund of your tax liability from that year. If you are not able to use the entire NOL in that year, you carry the remaining amount to your prior year tax return. If you still don't manage to use up the NOL, you may claim it on future year returns for up to 20 years, beginning with the tax year after you incurred the loss.

How to Claim a Refund for a Net Operating Loss

You may claim your NOL and request a refund for an earlier year's tax liability by filing Form 1045. You must file the form no later than one year after the end of the year in which you had the net operating loss. Alternatively, you may claim the NOL and tax refund on an amended tax return (Form 1040X). You generally have three years from the filing due date (including extensions, if you requested and received one) of the return for which you are requesting a refund. If you choose not to claim the NOL in an earlier year, you simply wait until next year and claim the loss as a negative number on the first page of Form 1040, on the "Other Income" line. You must also submit a statement showing how you calculated the net operating loss.

Self-Employment Tax

When you are self-employed, you must pay your own Social Security and Medicare taxes, in addition to regular income tax. You must pay those taxes even if you are already receiving Social Security and Medicare benefits. The good news is that you may deduct half of your self-employment tax as an above-the-line deduction.

Calculating Self-Employment Tax

When you work as an employee, your employer withholds money from your paycheck to fund Social Security and Medicare. However, you don't have to foot the whole bill: You pay half of your total contribution through payroll deductions (which tends to make it less painful than paying it out of your pocket at tax time), and your employer pays the other half.

When you're self-employed, the combination of Social Security and Medicare taxes is called self-employment tax. You must pay the entire amount yourself. And, if your net income is $400 or more, you must pay self-employment tax on all of your net income from your business, no matter what the rest of your income looks like.

If you aren't prepared for it, self-employment tax can be quite a shock, especially if you expect to owe little or no income tax. For example, suppose you have net business income of $2,500 and a capital loss of $3,000. Your taxable income is negative, but you will still owe self-employment tax on the business income.

To calculate the precise amount of your self-employment tax, see the form and instructions for Schedule SE, *Self-Employment Tax*. If you are subject to self-employment tax, you must file Schedule SE along with your tax return.

How to Claim the Self-Employment Tax Deduction

Use Schedule SE to compute your self-employment tax liability. You can deduct half of that amount on the first page of Form 1040, in the "Adjusted Gross Income" section.

Self-Employed Health Insurance

One of the more substantial tax benefits of self-employment is that your health insurance premiums might be deductible above the line (see "Restrictions" below). When expenses are deductible above the line, you may deduct them whether or not you itemize your deductions on Schedule A. And, unlike other medical expenses, which you may deduct only to the extent they exceed 7.5% of your adjusted gross income, you might be able to deduct your entire premium above the line. (See Chapter 4 for more information about medical expense deductions.)

This above-the-line deduction is limited to health insurance premiums. If you have other medical expenses, you must claim them on Schedule A, as usual. Self-employed health insurance premiums are those for policies purchased in the name of your business, or in your own name if you are a sole proprietor.

Included Premiums

You may deduct medical and dental premiums you pay to cover yourself, your spouse, and your dependents. You may also deduct the out-of-pocket premiums you pay for your own Medicare coverage (but not for your spouse's coverage). And, you may include the deductible portion of long-term care insurance you pay for yourself, your spouse, and your dependents. The deductible portion of long-term care insurance premiums is determined by the age of the person who is covered. (For more information about determining the deductible portion of such premiums, see Chapter 4.)

Restrictions

As good as this deduction is, there are a couple of restrictions. First, you may not claim your premiums for any months during which you were eligible to participate in a health plan subsidized by another employer or by your spouse's employer. You may still claim those expenses on Schedule A (if you itemize your deductions), but they will be deductible only to the extent that they, along with your other medical expenses, exceed 7.5% of your adjusted gross income.

> **TIP**
>
> **You can still deduct long-term care premiums.** Even if you are unable to claim an above-the-line deduction for medical insurance premiums because you were eligible to participate in another plan, you may still claim the deductible portion of long-term care insurance premiums as an above-the-line deduction, as long as that insurance is not subsidized by another employer.

Second, you may claim the self-employed health insurance deduction only to the extent you have net income from your business. If your business produces a loss, you may not claim the deduction. For purposes of determining whether or not you have net income from your business, you must reduce your net profit (revenue less expenses) by the self-employment tax deduction (described above) and by any retirement plan contribution you made, not including traditional or Roth IRA contributions.

Retirement Plans for Your Business

If your business makes a profit, you may establish and contribute to a retirement plan in the name of your business. Not only will doing so help you save money and bulk up your retirement nest egg, but you generally will be able to claim a deduction for the contribution and, in all likelihood, reduce your income tax liability. (Contributions to a retirement plan don't reduce your self-employment tax liability, however.)

Tax Strategy: Should You Contribute to a Retirement Plan Even If You Have Begun Taking Required Distributions?

Once you turn 70½, you are generally required to begin taking distributions from your retirement plans and traditional IRAs. Consequently, it might seem as though you shouldn't be permitted to make contributions to those accounts after age 70½. But in fact, the rules are not quite as simple as that.

If you are self-employed and past the age of 70½, you are not permitted to make a contribution to a traditional IRA. However, if you have net income from your business, you are permitted to contribute to a retirement plan that you have established for your business, no matter how old you are. So you might be in a situation where you are permitted to make a contribution to your retirement plan and required to take a distribution in the same year.

Does it make sense to contribute in that case? Generally, yes. Typically, the more net income you earn from your business, the more advantageous it is to make such a contribution because it reduces your tax liability.

Also, even though you may no longer contribute to a traditional IRA after turning 70½, you may still contribute to a Roth IRA. As long as you or your spouse has income from employment, you are permitted to make a contribution to a Roth IRA, no matter how old you are, if you otherwise qualify.

The following employer plans are those most commonly used by self-employed people running a small operation without employees.

Simplified Employee Pension (SEP)

A SEP is technically a type of IRA, but unlike a traditional IRA, it must be established by an employer—a business. If you establish a SEP, you may contribute up to 25% of your compensation. There is a ceiling, however: Your total contribution to your SEP cannot exceed $46,000 (for tax year 2008).

Calculating Compensation When You're Self-Employed

For purposes of retirement plan contributions, compensation is defined differently for self-employed people than it is for employees. Compensation for a self-employed person is "net earnings from self-employment," which is not quite the same as net income from your business. To compute your allowable retirement plan contribution, you must multiply your net profit—reduced by the self-employment tax deduction *and* the retirement plan contribution itself—by 25%. That sounds impossible, because you are trying to compute your retirement plan contribution and yet you need to use the amount of the contribution in the calculation. Fortunately, the math comes out the same if you reduce your net profit by the self-employment tax deduction and then multiply by 20% (instead of 25%). For more information about each of the retirement plans discussed in this section, including help figuring out how much you can contribute to each, see IRS Publication 560, *Retirement Plans for Small Business*.

A SEP is attractive because there are no reporting requirements. You simply set up the account, make the contribution, and claim a deduction on your tax return.

You are not permitted to make a contribution to a SEP for years in which you don't make a profit from your business. But you are also not required to make a contribution in the years you do make a profit.

Another advantage of a SEP is that it is the only employer plan that can be established after the end of the tax year. The only requirement is that you establish the plan and make your contribution by the due date of your income tax return, including any extensions you have received.

Savings Incentive Match Plan for Employees (SIMPLE) IRA

Like a SEP, a SIMPLE IRA must be established by a business. This plan works well for businesses that are not making money hand over fist. If the net income from your business is in the $15,000 range (or less), a SIMPLE IRA might be the best plan for you.

Contributions to a SIMPLE IRA comprise a salary deferral component and an employer contribution—typically, a matching contribution. Because you are both employer and employee, you may make both types of contributions to your account.

For 2008, the maximum salary deferral contribution to a SIMPLE IRA is $13,000 for those who are at least 50 years old (it's $10,500 for younger employees). The maximum employer contribution is a dollar for dollar match of your salary deferral contribution, but no more than 3% of your compensation. Bear in mind, however, that the total contribution to your SIMPLE IRA can never exceed your income from the business.

Like a SEP, a SIMPLE IRA typically has no tax reporting requirements. However, the plan generally must be established by October 1 of the year for which you want to make a contribution. If you miss that deadline, you will have to consider another type of plan.

401(k) Plan

You may establish a 401(k) plan for your business even if you are a sole proprietor with no employees. If your business nets more than approximately $15,000 or $20,000, this type of plan will allow you to contribute more than either a SEP or a SIMPLE IRA.

Like a SIMPLE IRA, a 401(k) plan has a salary deferral component and an employer contribution component. For 2008, the maximum salary deferral contribution is $20,500, if you are at least 50 years old ($15,500 for younger employees). In addition, you may make a maximum employer contribution of 25% of compensation. (See "Calculating Compensation When You're Self-Employed," above, for more information.) For 2008, the total of your salary deferral and employer contribution cannot exceed the smaller of your net income from your business or $51,000 for tax year 2008 ($46,000, if you have not yet turned 50).

Unlike SEPs and SIMPLE IRAs, 401(k) plans are required to file a Form 5500, *Annual Return/Report on Employee Benefit Plan*, once the assets in the plan exceed $250,000. If you have employees, you are required to file a Form 5500 regardless of the value of the assets in the 401(k) plan account.

TIP

Consider a Roth 401(k). If you establish a 401(k) plan, you have the option of making the salary deferral portion of that plan a Roth 401(k). If you do, then the salary deferral contribution is a nondeductible, after-tax contribution. The employer portion of the contribution is still deductible, but it must be held in a separate account. The advantage of establishing a Roth 401(k) is that the salary deferral portion and all of the earnings on that portion are potentially tax-free when distributed. For more information about distributions from Roth 401(k) plans and other types of retirement plans, see *IRAs, 401(k)s & Other Retirement Plans: Taking Your Money Out*, by Twila Slesnick and John Suttle (Nolo).

Defined Benefit Plan

A defined benefit plan is completely different from the IRAs and 401(k) plans discussed above. A defined benefit plan will serve you best if you are making significant amounts of money in your business (more than $150,000, for example) and you expect to continue doing so.

Once you establish a defined benefit plan, you are required to make contributions to your plan every year, even if your business is not making money. The only way out from under this requirement is to terminate the plan.

The advantage of a defined benefit plan is that it generally allows you to contribute far more than any other type of plan, because the contribution is not based on a percentage of compensation. Instead, the plan promises to pay you a life annuity at retirement. The payment amount is usually based on a combination of factors, such as the average of the highest three consecutive years of compensation, number of years of employment, and years until retirement.

The contribution you make each year is determined by an actuarial calculation that estimates how large the contribution must be to achieve the promised annuity payout. The annual contribution must be recalculated every year to make sure the plan will have enough assets to meet the benefit goal. Because of this complexity, establishing and maintaining such a plan can be expensive. The payoff is a large contribution and large deduction.

If you are making substantial amounts of money, a defined benefit plan generally allows you to build up your retirement account in a short time, which makes these plans especially good for those who are near retirement and need to fund a retirement plan quickly.

As with 401(k) plans, you must file an information return for a defined benefit plan once the assets in the plan exceed $250,000.

How to Claim a Deduction for Your Retirement Plan Contribution

Your retirement plan contribution is an above-the-line deduction. Claim the deduction on the first page of Form 1040, in the "Adjusted Gross Income" section, on the line "Self-Employed SEP, SIMPLE, and Qualified Plans."

Individual Retirement Accounts

The retirement plans discussed above are all for businesses. But how do individual retirement accounts (IRAs) fit into the picture? Both traditional IRAs and Roth IRAs are easy to establish and require little ongoing administration, other than managing the investments in the account. If you have income from employment (including self-employment), you generally will be able to make a contribution to some type of IRA, even if you also contribute to a retirement plan for your business. There are some restrictions, however. For example, you might not be able to claim a deduction for your contribution, or income limits might force you to contribute to a traditional IRA when you would prefer to contribute to a Roth IRA.

Traditional IRA

As long as you or your spouse has earnings from employment and you have not yet reached age 70½, you will be able to make a contribution to a traditional IRA. However, you might not be able to deduct your contribution if your income is higher than a threshold amount.

Contribution Limits

Your maximum contribution to an IRA is the smaller of your earnings from employment (or the combined earnings of you and your spouse, if you are married and filing a joint return), or $6,000 ($5,000 if you have not yet turned 50). Your spouse may also make a contribution to his or her own IRA of $6,000 ($5,000 if your spouse is not yet 50), as long as your IRA contributions do not exceed your combined earned income.

Deduction Limit

Once you determine your maximum contribution, you must calculate how much of the contribution, if any, is deductible. If you are not covered by an employer plan, then your contribution is fully deductible. Remember, however, that you are covered by an employer plan if you have established a retirement plan for your business. In that situation, the rules are a bit complicated.

If you are covered by an employer plan, your deduction begins to phase out when your modified adjusted gross income (AGI) exceeds a threshold amount. (For most people, modified AGI is the same as AGI. The most significant modification requires that you add back all earnings from overseas employment, if any, that you were permitted to exclude from U.S. taxation.) The phase-out ranges for 2008 are as follows:

Filing Status	Phase-Out Begins	Deduction Completely Phased Out
Single	$53,000	$63,000
Married filing jointly	$85,000	$95,000

IRS Publication 590, *Individual Retirement Arrangements*, contains a worksheet to help you compute your reduced deduction.

A nonworking spouse might also have the opportunity to make a retirement plan contribution. Here's how it works: If you are covered by an employer plan (for example, if you have started a business and established a retirement plan for that business) but your spouse is not covered by an employer plan, then your IRA deduction will be limited as described above. Your spouse's phase-out range is more generous, however. The phase-out doesn't begin until AGI reaches $159,000 and is complete when AGI reaches $169,000.

How to Claim a Traditional IRA Deduction

If your IRA contribution is deductible, you claim the deduction on the first page of Form 1040, in the "Adjusted Gross Income" section, on the "IRA deduction" line. If your contribution is not deductible or is only partially deductible, you must also complete Form 8606, *Nondeductible IRAs*, and attach it to your tax return.

Roth IRA

Roth IRAs differ from traditional IRAs in that no contribution to a Roth IRA is ever deductible. The advantage of a Roth IRA is that distributions are entirely tax-free as long as you satisfy certain criteria. Generally, if you are older than 59½ and you've had a Roth IRA for at least five years, your distributions (including investment earnings) are tax-free.

RESOURCE

Want more information about Roth IRAs? To learn about distributions from Roth IRAs and other types of retirement plans, see *IRAs, 401(k)s & Other Retirement Plans: Taking Your Money Out,* by Twila Slesnick and John Suttle (Nolo).

Contribution Limits

The contribution limits for a Roth IRA are exactly the same as they are for a traditional IRA. The hitch is that the contribution limit applies to all of your IRA contributions, traditional and Roth, combined. So, for example, if your maximum IRA contribution for the current year is $6,000, you may contribute that amount to a traditional IRA or to a Roth IRA but not to both. Alternatively, you may split the maximum contribution between your Roth and your traditional IRA, as long as the total contribution does not exceed $6,000.

Contributions to a Roth IRA are subject to an additional limitation: You are prohibited from making a contribution if your income exceeds a certain threshold. For 2008, the phase-out ranges are:

Filing Status	Phase-Out Begins	Deduction Completely Phased Out
Single	$101,000	$116,000
Married filing jointly	$159,000	$169,000

> ### Tax Strategy: Should You Split Your Contribution Between a Roth and a Traditional IRA?
>
> Generally, if you qualify to contribute to a Roth IRA, you should. Over the long term, it is likely to provide a larger benefit than a traditional IRA.
>
> If your Roth IRA contribution is limited because of your income, you might want to contribute as much as you can to a Roth IRA and put the remainder in a traditional IRA. In other words, if your maximum IRA contribution for the year is $6,000, but because of your high income, your Roth IRA contribution is limited to $2,000, you might want to contribute $2,000 to your Roth IRA and $4,000 to your traditional IRA.

Saver's Credit

If you make a contribution to an IRA, whether a traditional or a Roth IRA, or to a salary deferral retirement plan, such as a 401(k) plan or a SIMPLE IRA, then you might be able to claim a credit just for making the contribution. Furthermore, this credit is in addition to any deduction you are entitled to claim for your retirement plan contribution. As you might expect from such a generous tax benefit, however, the restrictions make it difficult to qualify for the credit.

Credit Amount

The amount you may claim is a percentage of your retirement plan or IRA contribution, up to a maximum credit of $1,000 per person, per year. The $1,000 maximum is reduced as your AGI increases. (See "Income Restrictions," below.)

Eligibility

To claim the Saver's Credit, you must satisfy all of the following requirements:
- You are at least 18 years old.
- You are not the dependent of another taxpayer.

- You are not a full-time student.
- You satisfy the income restrictions described below.

Income Restrictions

The Saver's Credit was conceived as a benefit for low-income tax payers, so the income restrictions make the credit unavailable to many people.

Married filing jointly. If you are married and filing a joint return with your spouse, you calculate your credit for the 2008 tax year as follows:

- If your AGI is $32,000 or less, your credit is 50% of all of your qualified retirement plan contributions (for example IRAs, 401(k) plans, and SIMPLE IRAs), but no more than $1,000.
- If your AGI is more than $32,000 but no more than $34,500, your credit amount is 20% of your retirement plan contributions, but no more than $400.
- If your AGI is more than $34,500 but no more than $53,000, your credit amount is 10% of your retirement plan contributions, but no more than $200.
- If your AGI exceeds $53,000, you may not claim a Saver's Credit.

TIP

Your spouse may also claim a credit. If your spouse also contributes to a retirement plan or IRA and qualifies for the Saver's Credit, you may each claim the credit. If your AGI is less than $32,000 then your maximum combined credit amount—if you both qualify—is $2,000.

Single. If you are single, you calculate your credit for the 2008 tax year as follows:

- If your AGI is $16,000 or less, your credit amount is 50% of all of your qualified retirement plan contributions, but no more than $1,000.

- If your AGI is more than $16,000 but no more than $17,250, your credit amount is 20% of your retirement plan contributions, but no more than $400.
- If your AGI is more than $17,250 but no more than $26,500, your credit amount is 10% of your retirement plan contributions, but no more than $200.
- If your AGI exceeds $26,500, you may not claim a Saver's Credit.

The above income thresholds for both married and single filers will increase for inflation from time to time.

Earned Income Credit

The earned income credit is another tax benefit crafted to provide tax relief to low-income taxpayers. To qualify for this credit, you must have earned income, which is income from employment (including self-employment).

Eligibility

If you do have earned income, you might qualify for the earned income credit in one of two ways:

1. You have a qualifying child and your income is below a threshold amount, as described below. A qualifying child is one who can be claimed as a dependent on your tax return. (See Chapter 10 for more information about the definition of a qualifying child.)

2. You do not have a qualifying child, but all of the following are true:
   - Your principal residence is in the United States.
   - You do not qualify to be claimed as a dependent on another individual's income tax return.
   - You (or your spouse) are at least 25 years old by the end of the year but not yet age 65.
   - Your AGI is under a threshold amount, as described below.

Credit Amount

If you qualify, you may claim a percentage of your earned income, up to a maximum credit amount. For 2008, the maximum credit is:

Qualifying Children	Percent of Earned Income	Maximum Credit
None	7.65%	$ 438
One	34%	$ 2,917
Two or more	40%	$ 4,824

However, the credit is also subject to an income phase-out. For 2008, the credit is reduced to zero once your AGI reaches the following amounts:

Qualifying Children	Maximum AGI (married)	Maximum AGI (single)
None	$ 15,880	$ 12,880
One	$ 36,995	$ 33,995
Two or more	$ 41,646	$ 38,646

In the instructions for Form 1040, the IRS provides tables for you to look up the precise amount of your earned income credit. You begin by completing the EIC Worksheet, which will serve as a guide when you turn to the tables. The worksheet is also included in the instructions for Form 1040.

The earned income credit is a refundable credit, which means you receive the credit amount even if your tax liability is less than the credit amount.

How to Claim the Earned Income Credit

Claim the earned income credit under "Payments" on the second page of Form 1040. If you qualify for the earned income credit because you have a qualifying child, you must also complete Schedule EIC and attach it to your income tax return.

Your Health

Tax Benefits in This Chapter

☐ **Are you at least 65 years old?**
- You may increase your standard deduction.
- You might qualify for a tax credit.

☐ **Are you blind?**
- You may increase your standard deduction.

☐ **Are you disabled?**
- You might qualify for a tax credit.

☐ **Do you have a high-deductible health plan?**
- You might be able to deduct your contributions to a health savings account (HSA).

☐ **Do you have significant medical expenses?**
- You might be able to deduct a portion of your out-of-pocket costs.

☐ **Have you remodeled your home to make it more accessible?**
- You might be able to deduct a portion of the cost.

☐ **Are you paying premiums for health insurance or long-term care insurance?**
- You might be able to deduct a portion of the cost.

☐ **Are you receiving ongoing care—in your home, a treatment center, nursing home, or hospital—for a medical condition?**
- You might be able to deduct a portion of the cost.

☐ **Did you pay an entrance fee for a continuing care facility?**
- You might be able to deduct part of the fee that goes toward paying your future medical expenses, as well as a portion of your monthly payments once you enter the facility.

☐ **Have you paid someone else's medical expenses?**
- You might be able to deduct a portion of those expenses as if they were your own.

M edical expenses tend to go up after retirement, and aging is only part of the reason. Once you leave your corporate employer behind, you bid farewell not only to your regular salary but probably to your health insurance coverage as well. From this point forward, you'll likely be paying your own way, at least until you reach age 65 when Medicare kicks in and picks up a portion of the tab.

Fortunately, Congress has seen fit to provide additional relief in the form of tax benefits to offset the increased costs of health care for seniors. Some of these benefits are available only to seniors or only to those with particular conditions (such as blindness or disability). Others are available to everyone but are especially helpful to seniors facing rising medical expenses. The benefits take many forms, from an increased standard deduction to special credits against tax.

Age and Blindness Deduction

If you are at least 65 years old and you don't itemize your deductions, you are entitled to an increased standard deduction. You may also increase your standard deduction if you are blind, regardless of your age. However, these increased deductions are available only if you claim the standard deduction on your tax return; if you itemize your deductions on Schedule A, you may not claim these additional amounts.

Deduction for Those 65 and Older

If you are single and you will be 65 years old by the end of the tax year, you may claim a larger standard deduction. The standard deduction and the additional amount increase each year for inflation. For 2008, the basic standard deduction is $5,450 if you are single. If you will turn 65 before the end of the year, you may claim an additional $1,350 for a total standard deduction of $6,800.

If you are married filing a joint return, you may also claim this increased standard deduction. For tax year 2008, you may add

$1,050 to the standard deduction ($10,900) if only one of you is 65 or older by the end of the year, and $2,100 if both of you are at least 65 years old.

> **TIP**
>
> **If you were born on New Year's Day.** If your birthday happens to fall on January 1, the IRS will let you open one of your presents early: You are allowed to claim the larger standard deduction based on age for the tax year before your 65th birthday.

Deduction for Blindness

If you are blind, regardless of your age, you may also take a larger standard deduction. Blindness is determined as of December 31 of the tax year. For 2008, you may add $1,350 to the standard deduction if you are filing single or $1,050 if married filing jointly. If you are blind and at least 65 years old, you may combine the additional amounts, for a total added amount of $2,700 (or $2,100 if married filing jointly) for tax year 2008. If you are married, your spouse is also entitled to these additional amounts. If both you and your spouse are blind and at least 65 years old, the additional standard deduction you may claim on your jointly filed tax return is $4,200.

> **EXAMPLE 1:** Sadie was single and age 68 in 2008. On her 2008 tax return, she could claim a standard deduction of $5,450 plus an additional $1,350 for being at least 65 years old. Sadie's total standard deduction for 2008 would be $6,800. To make sure she didn't pay more tax than necessary, Sadie also totaled up all of her itemized deductions, including deductible medical expenses, real estate taxes, state income taxes, mortgage interest, investment expenses, and charitable contributions. Her itemized deductions added up to $7,756. Because that total was more than her standard deduction, even with the additional amount based on age, Sadie elected to itemize her deductions on Schedule A. Because Sadie

elected to itemize her deductions, she could not claim any standard deduction at all. She didn't receive any benefit from the additional standard deduction.

EXAMPLE 2: Loretta was also single and age 68 in 2008. She was entitled to a standard deduction of $6,800 (the basic $5,450 plus $1,350 because she is at least 65). When Loretta added up her itemized deductions, she came up with a total of only $4,576. Because the standard deduction is higher, Loretta claimed the standard deduction instead of itemizing and did not file Schedule A with her tax return.

How to Claim the Age and Blindness Deduction

You may claim the higher standard deduction for age, blindness, or both on the second page of Form 1040. Check the appropriate box(es) in the "Tax and Credits" section, then you may use the worksheet in the Form 1040 instruction booklet to compute your standard deduction. Enter that amount on Form 1040. Remember, you may claim this additional amount only if you don't itemize your deductions on Schedule A.

Credit for the Elderly or Disabled

You might also reap a tax benefit simply by reaching your 65th birthday. This credit is also available to those who are disabled, regardless of age. If you qualify in both categories—in other words, you are at least 65 years old and disabled—you are not entitled to double the credit; you may claim it only once. (By the way, if you are reeling at the thought that the IRS considers you elderly once you reach your mid-60s, remember the adage, "Don't look a gift horse in the mouth.")

This credit won't benefit everyone, however. Even if you are over 65 or disabled, the amount of the credit you may claim is reduced or eliminated if you have any nontaxable income or if your adjusted gross income exceeds a threshold amount (see below). Also, the credit is nonrefundable, which means you may use it only to offset taxes you owe on your return. If you don't owe any taxes, you may not claim the credit.

Eligibility

To qualify for the credit, one of the following must be true:

- You must be age 65 by the end of the year (or January 1 of the following year).
- If you have not yet turned 65, all of the following must be true in the tax year for which you are claiming the credit:
  - You retired before the end of the year because of permanent and total disability.
  - You received taxable disability income from a former employer's disability plan.
  - You had not yet reached the company's mandatory retirement age (if it has one).

Permanent and Total Disability

The IRS considers you to be permanently and totally disabled if both of the following are true:

- You are unable to engage in any substantial gainful activity because of a physical or mental impairment.
- Your disability has lasted or is expected to last for at least a year, or is expected to result in your death.

In the instructions to IRS Schedule R, *Credit for the Elderly or the Disabled*, you will find a blank "Physician's Statement" that your physician must complete and sign, certifying the above. You are not required to file the statement with the IRS, but you must keep a copy in your files and produce it if and when the IRS requests it. You may not claim a credit based on disability unless you have a signed physician's statement.

Calculating the Amount of the Credit

If you meet one of the two eligibility criteria discussed above, you qualify for the credit. The exact amount you may claim (if any) depends on your income.

Your credit is 15% of a base amount determined by your age, income, filing status, and, if you are married filing jointly, the age and income of your spouse. (The base amount is sometimes called the "Section 22" amount, for the section of the tax code that allows the credit). As your income increases, your base amount decreases until it eventually reaches zero, which means you are no longer entitled to any credit.

To calculate the credit, follow these six steps.

Step 1: Determine the Initial Base Amount

Credit based on age: If neither you nor your spouse (if you are married) is disabled, your base amount is:

- $5,000 if you are single and at least 65 years old
- $5,000 if you file a joint return and either you or your spouse (but not both) is at least 65 years old, or
- $7,500 if you file a joint return and both you and your spouse are 65 or older.

If you are married and filing a separate return from your spouse, your own base amount is $3,750, but only if you lived apart from your spouse for the entire tax year. If you and your spouse lived together for any part of the year, you may not claim the credit if you file separate returns.

Credit based on disability: If you or your spouse (if you are married) is disabled, your base amount is determined according to the following rules:

- If you are single, younger than age 65, and permanently and totally disabled, then your base amount is either $5,000 or the amount of your taxable disability income for the year, whichever is less. (If you are at least 65 years old, you already qualify for the credit based on your age.)

EXAMPLE: You are single and 55 years old. You retired last year on permanent disability. This year, you received taxable disability payments of $3,500. Therefore your base amount is $3,500—the amount of your disability payments—because it is less than the standard base amount ($5,000).

If you are married and you and your spouse are both under the age of 65 but only you are disabled, then your base amount is either $5,000 or the amount of your taxable disability income, whichever is less.

If you and your spouse are both disabled and both under the age of 65, then the base amount is either $7,500 or your combined disability income, whichever is less.

- If you and your spouse are both disabled but only one of you is younger than 65, then the base amount is the lesser of:
  - $7,500 or
  - $5,000 plus the disability income of the younger spouse.

Step 2: Subtract Certain Government Benefits

Reduce the amount from Step 1 by the nontaxable portion of any Social Security or railroad retirement benefits you receive. Your income (both taxable and nontaxable) determines how much of your Social Security benefits are taxable. The taxable portion could be as low as zero or as high as 85%. The instructions to Form 1040 contain a worksheet that will help you figure out how much of your Social Security benefits are subject to income tax.

Step 3: Subtract Tax-Free Pension or Annuity Income

If you receive income from a pension or annuity, subtract any tax-free portion of that income from the total you reached in Step 2. If you made after-tax contributions to your pension plan, you do not need to subtract the portion of your distribution that is attributable to those contributions.

Step 4: Subtract Tax-Free Pension or Disability Income From the Veterans Administration

If you receive disability income or pension payments from the Veterans Administration, subtract the amount of any tax-free portion from the total you reached in Step 3. You do not need to subtract any tax-free disability income you receive as a result of your active service in the Armed Forces.

You do not need to subtract any workers' compensation you receive, unless the workers' compensation benefits are treated as Social Security benefits. If your Social Security benefits are reduced by the workers' compensation benefits you receive, you must subtract the workers' compensation benefits.

Step 5: Subtract a Portion of Your Adjusted Gross Income

If your adjusted gross income exceeds a certain amount (determined by your filing status), you must reduce the result you reached in Step 4 by 50% of the amount by which your adjusted gross income exceeds:

- $7,500, if you are single
- $10,000, if you are married filing a joint return, or
- $5,000, if you are married filing separately, but only if you've lived apart from your spouse for the entire year.

Step 6: Multiply by 15%

Take the result you reached in Step 5 and multiply it by 15% (0.15). This is the total amount you can claim as a credit.

Putting It All Together

Here's how a fictional couple, Mandy and Mark, calculated their credit using the six steps above. Mandy is 63 years old; Mark is 66 years old. On June 15, Mandy suffered a stroke and was no longer able to work. She retired July 1 on permanent disability. Between her retirement date and the end of the year, Mandy received $4,500 of taxable disability benefits.

At tax time, Mandy and Mark calculated their adjusted gross income (AGI) to be $18,000. They computed their Credit for the Elderly or Disabled as follows:

Step 1: Because Mark is over age 65 and Mandy is under age 65 but disabled, the initial base amount is the smaller of:

- $7,500, or
- $5,000 plus Mandy's disability income ($4,500), for a total of $9,500

Because the first amount is less, Mandy and Mark's initial base amount is $7,500.

Step 2: Neither Mark nor Mandy received any Social Security or railroad retirement benefits during the year, so the base amount is still $7,500.

Step 3: Although Mark is receiving a pension, it is fully taxable, so there is nothing to subtract here. The base amount for the credit remains at $7,500.

Step 4: Neither Mark nor Mandy received any benefits from the Veterans Administration. The base amount remains at $7,500.

Step 5: Because Mark and Mandy are married and filing jointly, they must reduce the result from Step 4 by 50% of the amount by which their AGI exceeds $10,000.

AGI	$ 18,000	
Reduction	− 10,000	
	$ 8,000	
×	0.5	(50%)
	$ 4,000	

They reduce their original base amount of $7,500 by $4,000. Their new base amount is $3,500.

Step 6: Mark and Mandy multiply $3,500 by 15%, for a total credit of $525. If Mark and Mandy owe less than $525 in taxes, they may claim a credit for only the amount they owe.

How to Claim the Credit for the Elderly or Disabled

Claim the Credit for the Elderly or Disabled in the "Tax and Credits" section of Form 1040. You must also complete Schedule R of Form 1040 or Schedule 3 of Form 1040A.

Health Savings Accounts

If you are covered under a high-deductible health plan, you might be able to contribute to a Health Savings Account (HSA) and deduct your contribution. An HSA is an account set up with an institution approved by the IRS (such as a bank, credit union, or insurance company), into which you deposit money to be spent on health costs. You may name a beneficiary to receive any funds left in the account when you die.

HSAs offer significant tax advantages during your lifetime. As explained below, you may contribute up to a certain amount each year and deduct that contribution from your taxable income. The money grows in the account, tax-free, and isn't taxed on withdrawal as long as you spend it on qualified medical expenses.

Eligibility

Many deductions found in the tax code are reduced or denied to you once your income exceeds a certain level, but those limits do not apply to HSAs. To contribute to an HSA, you must satisfy all of the following conditions:

- You may not be claimed as a dependent on another person's tax return.
- You may not be enrolled in Medicare. Once you turn 65 and are covered by Medicare, you may no longer contribute to an HSA.

Tax Strategy: Should You Have an HSA?

HSAs are most valuable if they can be left to grow tax-free for a long period of time. If your spouse is your beneficiary, your HSA automatically becomes your spouse's HSA when you die, as though it had belonged to your spouse from the start. This rule can give your HSA a long life during which the funds in the account continue to grow tax-free.

If you name someone other than your spouse as beneficiary, the funds in the HSA must be distributed upon your death and will be subject to income tax. However, if you are able to leave the funds untouched during your lifetime, you might still be able to leave a sizable account to your children or others you choose.

If you expect to be tapping into the HSA right away, you or your beneficiaries won't enjoy the benefits of long-term, tax-free growth. Although you will be able to claim a deduction, you must weigh the value of that deduction against the costs of a high-deductible plan. If you or your family members need frequent medical care, the high-deductible amount you must pay might eliminate the benefits of establishing and maintaining the HSA.

TIP

You may continue to use your HSA after age 65. Although you may no longer contribute to an HSA once you are covered by Medicare, you are still entitled to use the money in your account. The distributions you take to pay qualified medical expenses will be tax-free.

- You must be covered under a qualified high-deductible health plan (defined below).
- If you are also covered by a plan that does not qualify as a high-deductible plan, that plan may not provide coverage that overlaps with the high-deductible plan coverage.

What's a High-Deductible Plan?

A high-deductible plan is just what it sounds like: an insurance policy with a high deductible (the amount you have to pay out of pocket each year before the insurance company starts chipping in). The IRS sets the minimum deductible for a high-deductible plan, and the amount increases each year for inflation. For 2008, the deductible must be at least $1,100 for self-only coverage, or $2,200 for a plan that covers you and other members of your family. A qualified high-deductible insurance policy must contain other provisions as well. For example, the cost of prescription drugs must be applied to the annual deductible under the terms of the plan. Many health insurance providers offer (and, of course, advertise) high-deductible plans that conform to those requirements. See IRS Publication 969, *Health Savings Accounts and Other Tax-Favored Health Plans*, for more information about high-deductible plans.

Contributions

There are limits on how much you may contribute to an HSA each year. For 2008, the maximum amount you may contribute is $2,900 if you have self-only coverage or $5,800 if your plan covers you and other family members. The contribution limit increases each year for inflation.

If you are or will be 55 years old by the end of the year, you may make an additional contribution, called a catch-up contribution. These are the catch-up contribution amounts:

Year	Catch-Up Contribution
2008	$ 900
2009 and beyond	$ 1,050

For example, if you are age 58 and have self-only coverage, you may contribute $3,800 ($2,900 + 900) to your HSA for tax year 2008. If you have family coverage, you may contribute $6,700 ($5,800 + $900).

Only the owner of the HSA is entitled to make catch-up contributions. For example, if you have family coverage, and you and your spouse are both over the age of 55, the maximum you may contribute to your HSA for 2008 is $6,700—the family coverage limit plus a catch-up contribution for you.

On the other hand, if you and your spouse each establish a separate HSA in your own name, you could each make a catch-up contribution to your respective account. However, you may not contribute the basic family coverage amount of $5,800 to both accounts. You may contribute all of it to one account or you may divide it any way you like between the two accounts, as long as the total (not including catch-up contributions) does not exceed $5,800. For example, you could each contribute $3,800 (half of the $5,800 basic family contribution—which is $2,900—plus the $900 catch-up contribution). It's even permissible for one of you to contribute $6,700 (the entire $5,800 plus a $900 catch-up contribution) and the other to simply deposit his or her catch-up contribution of $900 in a separate account.

If you obtain coverage in the middle of the year, you may still contribute the maximum annual amount and claim a full deduction; you don't have to reduce it in proportion to the number of months you were covered during the year. However, you must be covered under the high-deductible plan in the last month of the year, and your coverage must continue for at least another 12 months (through the end of the following year) in order to qualify for the full deduction. If you discontinue your coverage before the end of the following year, you must amend your return and claim a reduced deduction (in proportion to the number of months you were covered during the tax year). You will also be subject to a 10% penalty on the addition amount you claimed as a deduction before amending your return.

EXAMPLE: Cassie, who is 57 and single, decides to establish an HSA and make a contribution for the current tax year. She obtains coverage under a high-deductible plan, which begins July 1, 2008. She contributes $3,800 to the plan and claims a deduction for that amount on the tax return she files the following April 15. In May 2009, she cancels the plan effective June 1.

Because she wasn't covered for all of 2009, Cassie is not entitled to deduct the full $3,800 on her tax return. Instead, she may deduct only $1,900 (half of $3,800) for the six months she was covered in tax year 2008. Cassie must amend her 2008 tax return to include the additional $1,900 in income. In addition, she will be subject to a 10% penalty ($190) on that amount. If Cassie had maintained her coverage until the end of 2009, she would have been able to claim the maximum $3,800 for the 2008 tax year even though she was covered under the high-deductible plan for only half of that year.

You must contribute to your HSA by the original due date of your tax return. No extensions are permitted.

Using the Money in Your HSA

All the money you withdraw from your HSA, including investment returns and your contributions, will be tax-free as long as you use the funds for "qualified" medical expenses. You may pay qualified expenses for yourself, your spouse, and any of your dependents. There is no waiting period before you may take money out of the account. You may even withdraw funds during the year you establish your HSA and make your first contribution.

TIP

You may reimburse yourself. You are permitted to withdraw funds from your HSA to pay qualified medical expenses directly or to reimburse yourself for expenses you have already paid. You may even reimburse yourself for expenses you incurred in an earlier year, as long as the expense was incurred after you established your HSA.

Qualified Expenses

You can use money from your HSA, tax-free, to pay most of the same medical expenses that qualify for a medical expense deduction on Schedule A of your tax return. (See "Medical Expense Deduction," below.) One notable exception applies to nonprescription drugs. Nonprescription drugs are not deductible on Schedule A, even if prescribed, but they qualify for tax-free treatment under HSA rules if they are prescribed by a physician.

Nonqualified Expenses

If you pay nonqualified expenses with your HSA funds, you'll have to pay income taxes on that amount—and perhaps penalties as well—so be sure you know that an expense is qualified before you withdraw the funds from the HSA. The following expenses are not qualified expenses:

- nonmedical expenses
- medical expenses for which you have claimed a medical expense deduction on Schedule A
- life insurance premiums, and
- all other insurance premiums, except for:
  - COBRA premiums (premiums you pay to continue health insurance through a former employer after you leave the job or become ineligible for coverage)
  - premiums paid while receiving unemployment insurance
  - premiums paid when you are age 65 or older
  - premiums for Medicare Parts A and B
  - your share of employer-based coverage, and
  - qualified long-term care insurance premiums up to the deduction limit, described below.

If you use HSA funds for anything other than qualified medical expenses, you must pay income tax, plus a 10% penalty, on the amount you withdraw. But once again, there are exceptions:

- If you take the money out after you have enrolled in Medicare, you will still owe income tax but no penalty.
- If you are disabled, you must pay income tax but no penalty.

> **CAUTION**
>
> **You might have to pay state taxes.** Although you won't owe federal income tax on money you take out of an HSA to pay qualified medical expenses, your state may impose a tax. Some states tax HSA distributions regardless of how the money is used.

How to Deduct Contributions to an HSA

You claim the deduction for your contribution to an HSA on the first page of Form 1040, in the "Adjusted Gross Income" section. You must also attach Form 8889, *Health Savings Accounts (HSAs)*, to your tax return.

Medical Expense Deduction

Many, if not most, people go through their entire working lives unable to claim a medical expense deduction on Schedule A. That's because medical expenses are deductible only to the extent they exceed 7.5% of your adjusted gross income (AGI). Your AGI is the total of your taxable income, less your "above-the-line" deductions. (See Chapter 1 for more on AGI and above-the-line deductions.)

> **EXAMPLE:** Woodrow's adjusted gross income last year was $25,000. He had medical expenses of $2,000. He itemized deductions on Schedule A and calculated his medical expense deduction as follows:
>
> | | |
> |---|---|
> | Total medical expense | $ 2,000 |
> | 7.5% of AGI (0.075 x $25,000) – | 1,875 |
> | Deductible medical expense | $ 125 |

> **CAUTION**
>
> **If you have to pay alternative minimum tax (AMT).** If you are subject to the AMT, the medical expense deduction threshold is 10% of your AGI instead of 7.5%. For more information about the AMT, see Chapter 1.

Unless you suffer a catastrophic illness or injury, your out-of-pocket medical expenses rarely, if ever, approach the 7.5% threshold while you are in the pink-cheeked vigor of youth. But after retirement, when medical expenses tend to go up and income tends to go down, you are more likely to cross the deduction threshold. And because you, rather than a former employer, will likely be the one footing the medical bills, it's a good idea to keep track of those expenses during the year, just in case you accumulate enough to deduct at tax time.

You may deduct medical expenses in the year you pay them, which is not always the year the medical service or treatment is provided. If you pay your medical bill with a check, the date you mail or deliver the check—not the date the check is cashed—determines the tax year for which you may claim the deduction. If you pay by credit card, the date you charge the expense is the date that determines the deduction year, not the date you pay your credit card bill. If you do your banking or bill-paying online, the payment date that appears on the financial institution's statement is the one you should use for tax purposes.

Tax Strategy: Will Filing Separate Returns Increase Your Deduction?

If you are married and you don't live in a community property state, you and your spouse might benefit from filing separate returns if one of you had large medical expenses during the year. When you file a separate return, you report only your own income and the medical expenses you paid. The combination of lower income and large medical expenses might result in a medical expense deduction that you wouldn't have if you filed a joint tax return.

This might not help if you paid your expenses from a joint account, however. You may claim on your return only expenses that you paid from your own separate account. If the expenses were paid from a joint account, they are generally considered paid equally by each spouse, and you would each claim half of the expense on your respective returns.

The separate account strategy usually doesn't work if you and your spouse live in a community property state: Alaska, Arizona, California, Idaho, Louisiana, Nevada, New Mexico, Texas, Washington, or Wisconsin. In these states, your funds are generally considered community funds, and expenses are deemed paid equally by each of you. You might be able to treat your funds as exclusively yours (and not community property) if you and your spouse have a property agreement (for example, a prenuptial or postnuptial agreement) to that effect or if you inherited assets that you have kept separate (for example, you kept inherited cash and investments in a separate account in your name only).

The potential downside of filing separate returns is that you each move more quickly into higher tax brackets than you would if you filed a joint return. So even if you live in a non-community-property state, make sure you are not trading ham for spam by filing separate returns. You might gain a medical expense deduction but lose something more significant. For example, certain education credits, like the lifetime learning credit, are not available to either of you if you file separate returns. The wisest strategy is to prepare your return both ways (filing jointly and filing separately) to see which is more beneficial overall.

Treatment and Medications

It would be a Herculean task to attempt to list every drug, treatment, or piece of equipment that the IRS might allow as a medical expense deduction. Even the IRS has not attempted a comprehensive list. But some guidelines have evolved through laws, regulations, and cases.

Drugs

Drugs and other medicines that require a prescription from a physician are deductible. The operative word here is "require." Although your neighborhood self-anointed tax expert might tell you that you may deduct those vitamin D tablets your doctor prescribed, the law says differently.

If a drug is available without a prescription, then the cost is not deductible, even if you have a prescription for it. In other words, the drug must be obtainable solely through a prescription. So, although your physician might have given you a prescription for those vitamin D tabs, you may not deduct the cost because vitamin D is also available without a prescription.

Who Is a Physician?
A physician, for prescription purposes, is defined to be a doctor of medicine (including psychiatrists) or osteopathy, a dentist, a chiropractor, or an optometrist.

As with most tax laws, there are some exceptions to the prescription drug rule:

- Even though some forms of insulin are available without a prescription, the cost of insulin in all its forms is deductible, whether or not the insulin is obtained through a prescription.

- The cost of a drug that is illegal under federal law, such as marijuana, is not deductible, even if the use of that drug is allowed in your state and you have a prescription.
- The cost of drugs that are imported illegally from other countries is not deductible. You may deduct only what you pay for drugs that have been approved by the FDA for importation by individuals.

Supplies, Equipment, and Home Remodels

Once you move into the realm of supplies, equipment, and building reconfigurations, distinguishing deductible from nondeductible medical expenses becomes a little trickier. If an expense is medically necessary, it is deductible. However, the tax code and regulations might not tell you whether a particular cost or item will qualify. In this situation, you must make your own good faith determination and hope that the IRS is of like mind.

If you avoid overreaching and apply a little common sense, you should be able to stay on the right path. Here are some examples of costs that the IRS has considered and found to be—or not to be—deductible.

Supplies and Equipment

Not surprisingly, you can patch yourself up after an accident and deduct the cost of bandages, crutches, and artificial limbs. You may also deduct the cost of a wheelchair and its maintenance, if it's medically necessary. However, if you are able-bodied and you have acquired a wheelchair simply as a convenient (and eco-friendly) mode of transportation, forget the deduction.

If you are diabetic and need to use a blood sugar monitor, the cost of the monitor is deductible.

You may deduct the cost of wigs if you have lost your hair because of a disease or treatment of a disease (such as chemotherapy), and your doctor recommends a wig for your continued mental health.

If your hearing is impaired, you may deduct the cost of hearing aids, batteries, and maintenance costs. If you need special equipment to use the phone or adapt your television to your hearing loss, those costs are also deductible.

Eyeglasses are deductible, as long as they are prescription glasses. If you choose contact lenses, the cost of the lenses, as well as the cost of cleaning (saline solution, for example) and maintenance is deductible. If you are blind and read Braille books and magazines, you may deduct the cost of those publications to the extent it exceeds the cost of the equivalent non-Braille publications. If you rely on a guide dog, the cost of the dog, including training and care, is deductible.

Home Remodeling

Some home remodel costs are clearly deductible. For example, the costs of making a home wheelchair-accessible are deductible. Such expenses might include constructing ramps, widening doors and hallways, installing railings, modifying bathrooms, and lowering kitchen counters. The cost of a lift designed to carry a disabled person up a flight of steps is also deductible.

There is a catch, however: Remodels or modifications are deductible only to the extent they do not increase the value of your house. For example, installing an elevator might well make your home more valuable, in addition to making it more accessible. In such cases, the cost of the improvement is deductible only to the extent it exceeds the home's increased value. For example, if you pay $20,000 to install an elevator, and a realtor appraises the house for $15,000 more than it was worth before the installation, your deductible expense is $5,000.

TIP

Certain remodeling costs are always deductible. Some remodeling projects to accommodate a disability are not improvements in the eyes of the IRS and are always deductible. These include things like widening doorways for wheelchair access or widening hallways and lowering counters. The entire cost of these projects is deductible as a medical expense.

Even if equipment you added to your home is not deductible, the ongoing maintenance might be. For example, the costs of operating and maintaining an elevator would be deductible as long as there is a medical need for the elevator, even if the cost of the installation was not deductible.

Treatment by Doctors, Dentists, and Therapists

During your retirement years, many of your doctor bills and most of your hospital care and prescription drug costs are paid or subsidized by Medicare. But your out-of-pocket expenses that are not reimbursed, such as co-payments or lab fees, are deductible. To make sure you don't miss any deductible expenses, keep good records of all of your medical costs.

Out-of-pocket dental expenses are deductible too, even those pesky full-mouth X-rays that your dentist seems to need every time you visit. Other deductible doctor bills include those from your orthodontist (never too late to correct that overbite!), psychiatrist or psychologist, optometrist, osteopath, physiotherapist, and even your oh-my-aching-back chiropractor.

Hospital Costs

Virtually all of the costs you incur after you are admitted to a hospital are deductible, including your room, meals, X-rays, and laboratory work.

Specialized Services and Nontraditional Treatments

You might be surprised to discover what seems to be a show of generosity on the part of Congress when it comes to deducting medical expenses for certain types of treatments. The IRS has allowed treatments that some people consider experimental or downright loopy, so don't assume (without doing some research) that your offbeat procedure would be disallowed. As far as the IRS is concerned, deductibility is determined by the purpose of the treatment or service, not by the title or qualifications of the person who provides it. As long as you are being treated for a disease or an injury, most forms of treatment will qualify, even holistic healing and naturopathy.

Acupuncture, for example, once considered a New Age experimental treatment, is now nearly mainstream. The fees you pay to your acupuncturist are deductible. However, if you purchase nonprescription vitamins or herbs recommended by your acupuncturist, those costs are not deductible.

The rules on allowable treatments are not cut and dried, of course. The IRS wouldn't be the IRS if it didn't create some gray areas by allowing a treatment expense under certain circumstances but not others. Here are some examples:

Cosmetic surgery. Although the section of the tax code that deals with medical expenses is quite short, two full paragraphs are devoted to cosmetic surgery. This suggests not only that cosmetic surgery is popular, but also that many people have tried to deduct it.

The IRS does not allow you to deduct the cost of cosmetic surgery, which it defines as a procedure that is meant to improve appearance but does not "meaningfully promote the proper function of the body ..." nor "...treat illness or disease." Under this rule, cosmetic procedures that are deemed by the IRS to have no medical purpose, such as teeth whitening, face-lifts, hair transplants, and liposuction, are not deductible.

Some procedures that we might consider to be a form of cosmetic surgery are allowed, however, if they have a medical purpose. Surgeries that are necessary to correct a congenital abnormality or a disfigurement from injury or illness—such as breast reconstruction surgery after a mastectomy—are deductible.

CAUTION

Surgeries to provide a more youthful appearance are not covered. The wide variety of surgeries intended to rejuvenate our bodies— such as face-lifts—are not deductible medical expenses. Although you might not agree, the aging process alone is not considered by the IRS to be a disfiguring illness.

We can all probably think of procedures that don't fall easily into the above categories and must be reviewed on a case by case basis. For example, the IRS and the courts have thus far disallowed deductions for gender reassignment surgery. But, lest you think the courts are universally prim, an exotic dancer was permitted to deduct the cost of implants.

Vision correction surgery. Although there is little doubt that many people elect to have vision correction surgery for no reason other than vanity, the IRS nonetheless routinely allows a deduction for the cost of such surgeries, including radial keratotomy and LASIK surgery.

Massage and exercise therapies. Here, the IRS follows a simple rule: The cost of treatments that are recommended by a doctor to treat injury or disease is deductible. For example, massages, whirlpools, and similar treatments are not allowed as deductible expenses if you use them simply to make you feel good or relieve the stresses of the day. If, however, they are recommended by a doctor to relieve "a physical or mental defect or illness," you may deduct their cost. The IRS doesn't completely trust your ability to make the determination, so the treatment recommendation must be substantiated by a physician's statement.

Even the cost of a health club program recommended by a doctor to treat a particular condition, such as hypertension or arteriosclerosis, has been allowed. Similarly, the cost of a swim club membership for a person with rheumatoid arthritis was allowed, because swimming therapy was prescribed by a doctor.

Treatment Programs

The cost of programs to treat addictions and obesity also are generally deductible. Here are the rules.

Weight loss. If a doctor has diagnosed you with a disease for which the prescribed treatment is weight loss, then you may deduct the cost of weight-loss treatment. For example, diabetes is a disease that requires the regulation of your weight, so diabetics may deduct the cost of a program that helps them lose weight.

Obesity is also considered a disease. If your doctor has diagnosed obesity and recommended a weight-loss program, the cost of the program is deductible. However, you may not deduct the cost of a general membership at a gym or spa, unless it is a designated part of a weight-loss program recommended by your doctor.

Deductible costs also include membership fees in a program like Weight Watchers, as well as travel costs to attend meetings. Diet food is a different story, however. The IRS figures you have to eat anyway, so why should you be able to deduct all of your food? Here's the compromise: If a doctor substantiates your claim that special food (such as food that is branded by the weight-loss program you have enrolled in) is required to treat your illness, you may deduct the cost, but only to the extent it exceeds what you would have paid for comparable normal (nonspecialty) food.

Drug addiction. The cost of drug addiction treatment programs is also deductible. If you receive inpatient treatment, the entire cost of that treatment is deductible, including transportation to the center and meals and lodging while you are there. If your spouse or dependent is in a treatment program and the doctor prescribes visits by you as part of the patient's treatment, you can deduct the cost of your travel to visit the patient. However, you may not include your meals and lodging in those travel costs.

Smoking. Treatment programs to help you stop smoking are deductible medical expenses. Fees that you pay to participate in the program, as well as prescription antismoking drugs you take, are deductible. However, over-the-counter drugs (such as nicotine gum or nicotine patches) are not deductible.

Alcoholism. The cost of treatment for alcoholism is also deductible. Such treatment includes all costs of any inpatient treatment you receive, including meals and lodging. You may also deduct the cost of your travel to and from Alcoholics Anonymous meetings, as long as your attendance at AA meetings is a recommended part of your treatment.

Deductible and Nondeductible Medical Expenses

IRS Publication 502, *Medical and Dental Expenses*, includes a long list of deductible and nondeductible medical expenses. This list is only a guideline, however. Although an expense might be listed in the "nondeductible" category, your particular situation might call for an exception.

Deductible Expenses

acupuncture	guide dog or other animal
alcoholism	health institute
ambulance	health maintenance organization (HMO)
artificial limb	hearing aids
artificial teeth	home care
bandages	home improvements
breast reconstruction surgery	hospital services
Braille books and magazines	insurance premiums
car	laboratory fees
chiropractor	lead-based paint removal
Christian Science practitioner	learning disability
COBRA (continuation health coverage)	legal fees
contact lenses	lifetime care—advance payments
crutches	lodging
dental treatment	long-term care
diagnostic devices	meals
disabled dependent care expenses	medical conferences
drug addiction	medical information plan
drugs	medical services
eyeglasses	medicines
eye surgery	nursing home

Deductible and Nondeductible Medical Expenses (continued)

Deductible Expenses (continued)

nursing services	telephone
operations	therapy
optometrist	transplants
osteopath	transportation
oxygen	trips
prosthesis	tuition
psychiatric care	vasectomy
psychoanalysis	vision correction surgery
psychologist	weight-loss program
special education	wheelchair
sterilization	wig
stop-smoking programs	X-ray
surgery	

Nondeductible Expenses

controlled substances	insurance premiums
cosmetic surgery	Medical Savings Account (MSA)
dancing lessons	medicines and drugs from other countries
electrolysis or hair removal	nonprescription drugs and medicines
funeral expenses	nutritional supplements
future medical care	personal use items
hair transplant	swimming lessons
health club dues	teeth whitening
household help	veterinary fees
illegal operations and treatments	

Travel

Among the grayest of areas in the category of deductible medical expenses is travel. The IRS is usually generous when it comes to allowing deductions for the cost of transportation (airfare, mileage, and so on), but a bit stingier about other travel-related costs, such as meals and lodging. Occasionally, some or all of the travel expenses of a companion are also deductible.

Transportation Expenses for the Patient

Generally, you may deduct expenses you incur when you travel to receive medical treatment, whether you go by car, bus, taxi, or airplane. If you use your own car, you may claim actual expenses, such as the cost of gasoline (but not depreciation, insurance, or general maintenance and repair). Alternatively, you may claim 19 cents per mile driven in the first half of 2008 and 27 cents per mile driven in the second half of 2008, and forgo your actual expenses. You may deduct parking and tolls regardless of which method (mileage or actual expenses) you choose.

If you must travel to another city for treatment, the cost of travel is deductible if the trip is "primarily for and essential to" your medical treatment. Sadly, a trip for your general well-being is not deductible, even if it is a doctor-advised vacation.

This doesn't mean that therapeutic travel is never deductible, however. If, on the advice of your doctor, you travel to another location to alleviate a specific medical condition, the cost is generally deductible. For example, your doctor might recommend that because of your heart condition you leave the high plains of Colorado and move closer to sea level. If your relocation is permanent, you may deduct your own transportation costs, but not the cost of moving your personal belongings.

Transportation Expenses of a Companion

If you travel with someone else on a medical-related excursion, the cost of your companion's travel is deductible only if your companion's presence is necessary. For example, a parent might need to accompany a sick child, or a family member might need to travel with someone who is too weak to travel alone safely. Perhaps you must hire a nurse to travel with you to give you injections, administer medication, or provide other medical assistance that you are unable to handle yourself. If so, the transportation expenses of both patient and companion are deductible.

Transportation expenses of a companion might be deductible in less critical circumstances as well. For example, a family member might need to travel with a patient in order to accompany the patient back home after a medical procedure. Or, your visits to the patient might be recommended as part of the patient's treatment.

Meals and Lodging

Meals and lodging generally are not considered medical expenses, because you must house and feed yourself whether or not you are ill. Consequently, situations in which meals and lodging are deductible are the exception rather than the rule. Here are some of those exceptions.

Lodging is deductible only if you are away from home and all of the following are true:

- The lodging is primarily for and essential to your medical care.
- The medical care is provided by a doctor in a licensed hospital or a medical facility affiliated with such a hospital. (You could be receiving treatment on either an inpatient or outpatient basis.)
- There is no significant element of pleasure (such as vacation-like activities) associated with the trip. For example, if you travel to Florida to see a specialist and stay an extra day or two to visit Disney World, you might have difficulty convincing the IRS that the lodging expense qualifies as a medical deduction.
- The accommodations are not extravagant.

You may deduct no more than $50 per night. This limit is per person: You may include lodging for the patient and another individual (one person only) who is traveling with the patient, for a total deductible limit for lodging expenses of $100 per night.

Meals are generally deductible only by a patient and only while he or she is receiving inpatient care (whether at a hospital or another treatment facility). However, there are two significant exceptions:

- You may deduct meals (and lodging) for a companion who is providing nursing-type services to you while you are away from home, unless that companion is your spouse.
- You may deduct meals and lodging while you are en route to another location for medical treatment—sometimes. Unfortunately, the IRS has allowed this deduction in some cases and not others, and court rulings on the subject are inconsistent. For example:

A patient who traveled from Kentucky to Minnesota for treatment at the Mayo Clinic was allowed to deduct meals and lodging on both legs of the round trip.

In another case, a court allowed a deduction for meals and lodging expenses for travel to a treatment facility, but not for the trip back home.

In yet another case, a court denied a deduction for meal expenses while traveling to a treatment facility. The IRS, in its wisdom, decided the trip should take only three hours, which meant the patient could have eaten at home before leaving and did not require a meal during the trip.

Let these rulings serve as a warning: If you decide to deduct the cost of meals and lodging en route to medical treatment, be prepared to defend your need to stop for that hot fudge sundae, salad bar, or whatever it was you had for lunch.

Conferences and Education

You may deduct the cost of attending a conference related to your own chronic illness, if your attendance is recommended by your doctor. You may also deduct your own costs of attending such a conference if the chronically ill person is your spouse or your dependent. Deductible costs may include conference fees and transportation, but not meals and lodging.

Insurance

Thankfully, the rules on deducting insurance premiums are clear. You may deduct insurance premiums you pay for policies that cover medical care and prescription drugs for you, your spouse, and your dependents.

Health Insurance Premiums

Your regular health insurance premiums are deductible, as are premiums for supplemental health insurance to fill in the gaps in your main policy. COBRA payments—the premiums you pay to maintain health coverage under a former employer's group health plan after you leave the job or otherwise become ineligible for coverage—are also deductible.

If Unused Sick Leave Pays for Your Coverage

Some employers give you the option of applying your unused sick leave to the cost of your continued participation in the company health plan when you retire. In this situation, you may claim that expense as a medical expense deduction. However, you must also report the sick pay as income. It's as though you received the sick pay (which is taxable compensation) and then used it to purchase insurance.

However, if your employer automatically applies your sick leave pay to your continuing health plan coverage, instead of giving you the option to receive the sick pay in cash, the rules are different. You don't need to report the income, but you may not claim a deduction, either.

If you are eligible for Medicare, the premiums you pay for Medicare Parts B and D are deductible. (Medicare Part B covers doctor care, while Medicare Part D covers prescription drugs). Medicare Part A covers hospital care, but those who are eligible for Social Security benefits are not required to pay Part A premiums. Those premiums are paid by the government. However, if you are not eligible for Social Security benefits and you are paying Medicare Part A premiums out of your own pocket, you may deduct those premiums, as well.

Prepayments of insurance premiums typically are not deductible. However, if you have entered into an agreement with an insurance provider to prepay insurance premiums that cover medical care for yourself, your spouse, or a dependent for the period after you reach age 65, you may claim a deduction for those prepayments if all of the following are true:

- You are not yet 65 years old.
- The premiums are payable in equal yearly (or more frequent) installments.
- The premiums are payable for at least ten years or until you are age 65, whichever comes first. However, you may not deduct your prepayments if the payment period is less than five years. So, if your payments begin when you are age 62, they must continue for at least five years, even though you will pass age 65 along the way.

Long-Term Care Insurance Premiums

Many people purchase long-term care insurance policies to cover expenses that are not covered by Medicare (nursing home care, for example). If you need to stay in a nursing home, Medicare will cover you only for a limited—and fairly short—period of time. So if you (or your spouse or dependent) become chronically or terminally ill and require care for a long period, you must pay for the care yourself or rely on a long-term care insurance policy that you have purchased.

Long-term care policies might also include coverage for home health care, respite care, and hospice care. The policy might cover an extended stay in an assisted living facility or adult day care for someone with Alzheimer's.

You may deduct premiums only for a qualified long-term care contract, and only up to a limit. To be qualified, a contract must meet all of the following requirements:

- The policy must provide insurance coverage only for qualified long-term care services (treatment or care for the chronically ill, prescribed by a licensed health care practitioner; see "Long-Term Care," below, for more information).
- It must be guaranteed renewable, which means that the insurer is required to renew the policy if you pay your premiums on time.
- It must not have a cash surrender value.
- Refunds and dividends from the policy must be used only to reduce future premiums or increase future benefits.
- The policy must not pay expenses covered by Medicare (unless Medicare is the secondary payer). However, the policy may allow benefits to be paid in the form of per diem payments: fixed amounts that you receive on a periodic basis (usually monthly), without regard to your actual medical expenses. (See "Long-Term Care," below, for more information about the taxability of benefits paid in this way.)

Once you confirm that the premiums on your long-term care policy are deductible, you must determine whether your deduction is limited. The deciding factor is your age. For 2008, you may deduct your annual premiums up to the following limits (these amounts are increased for inflation from time to time).

Age	Premium Limit (Per Person)
Age 40 or under	$ 310
Age 41 to 50	$ 580
Age 51 to 60	$ 1,150
Age 61 to 70	$ 3,080
Age 71 or over	$ 3,850

If more than one person is covered under the policy, the limit applies to each person separately. For example, if you are married filing jointly, you and your spouse are both under the age of 40, and both of you are covered under a long-term care policy, your maximum deductible amount is $620 ($310 each).

Taxability of Long-Term Care Benefits and Viatical Settlements

If you are receiving benefits from a long-term care insurance contract, the payments are generally excludable from income (that is, they are not taxable). However, if you are paid a fixed amount per day (a "per diem") instead of being reimbursed for your actual expenses, you may exclude only $270 per day from your income (for the 2008 tax year). If your contract allows you to receive a per diem amount that is more than $270 per day (or $98,550 per year), you may exclude only up to your actual unreimbursed expenses. (The $270 limit is for each individual covered under the policy.)

Accelerated death benefits paid to a terminally ill patient under a life insurance policy—known as viatical settlement proceeds—are handled differently. These settlements are not taxed at all, regardless of the amount. To receive a viatical settlement, the patient sells his or her life insurance policy to a third party to generate cash, often for medical expenses. The buyer pays the seller an agreed sum immediately and also takes over the premium payments on the policy. In exchange, the buyer receives the proceeds of the policy when the insured dies.

If a patient is chronically, but not terminally, ill, viatical settlements may be excluded from income only up to $270 per day (or the amount of the patient's actual long-term care costs, if greater). The excess, if any, is taxable and must be reported on Form 8853, *Archer MSAs and Long-Term Care Insurance Contracts.*

Other Premiums

The premiums for other types of insurance are not deductible. You may not deduct premiums you pay for:

- life insurance
- loss of earnings insurance
- insurance against loss of limbs (and other disabilities)
- insurance that provides guaranteed pay if you are hospitalized
- car insurance that covers medical care for anyone injured by your car, or
- Medicare payroll taxes (these are not technically insurance premiums).

Care

Most people will eventually need some assistance in handling the daily activities of life as they age or become ill or infirm, but the level of care necessary will vary dramatically from one person to the next. Some might simply need a caretaker to come to their homes once or twice a week. Others might require an extended stay in a skilled nursing facility. An increasingly popular strategy for aging seniors is to move into a retirement community where doctors and nurses—not to mention companionship— are readily available. Many of the costs associated with these different levels of care are deductible.

Nursing Homes

If you must stay in a nursing home for medical reasons, the costs of meals, lodging, medical treatment, and other medical or care-related expenses are all deductible. If, on the other hand, your stay in a nursing home is not medically necessary (perhaps your roommate is out of town and you don't want to stay alone in your home), then the cost of your stay is not deductible unless you actually receive medical care. If you do, then the expense of the medical care are deductible, but other expenses, such as meals and lodging, are not.

In-Home Care

In-home care is deductible if it is medically necessary. Typically, expenses for caring for a chronically ill patient are deductible. (See

"Long-Term Care," below, for more information.) But, if a person is not ill and care is provided only for convenience, the cost is not deductible. For example, if you hire a companion to stay with you just in case you need emergency help and you are not currently ill, the expenses of having that companion nearby are not deductible. Similarly, if you hire a housekeeper to clean your house, the service is considered a personal expense and is not deductible, unless you are chronically ill and unable to clean the house yourself.

Long-Term Care

If you are chronically ill, you may deduct the cost of your care, whether you're paying for a full-time caretaker in your home or for inpatient care at a long-term care facility.

To qualify for this deduction, you must have been certified "physically or cognitively chronically ill" by a doctor, social worker, or licensed health care worker within the last 12 months. The statement must certify that for at least 90 days, you have been unable to perform at least two of the following "activities of daily living":

- eating—the ability to feed yourself
- toileting—the ability to get to and from the toilet, and on and off the toilet
- dressing—the ability to put on and take off clothes and other items you wear, such as braces and artificial limbs
- bathing—the ability to get in and out of a tub or shower
- continence—the ability to control your bowel and bladder or to maintain hygiene if you are physically incontinent, or
- transferring—the ability to move from a sitting position to a standing position, to move from a chair to a bed, and similar changes of position and location.

Once you are certified as chronically ill, you may deduct the expenses of your care. Care is broadly defined and can include the cost of maintenance and personal care services (such as housekeeping), if prescribed by a licensed health care practitioner. If you are cared for by a relative, the relative must be a licensed health care provider. You may, of course, deduct the salary you pay the caretaker, as well as any payroll taxes, such as Social Security, Medicare, or FUTA (unemployment) taxes.

If your caretaker lives with you, you may deduct the additional board and lodging expenses, but only to the extent the costs with the caretaker exceed your costs without the caretaker. For example, if you must move to a larger apartment to accommodate your live-in caretaker, you may deduct the amount by which your new rent exceeds what you were paying for your previous home.

Continuing Care Facility—Prepaid Medical Care

Generally, you are not permitted to deduct what you pay for future medical services. Instead, you pay for services after they are rendered and then deduct the expenses in the year you paid them. If you pay in advance, the IRS will allow the deduction only if the services are rendered within a time period that is not "substantially beyond" the close of the year.

However, the IRS carved out a significant exception to this advance payment rule in 1975, when it decided that entrance fees paid to a life care facility may be deducted when they are paid. Many seniors decide to move to a facility that provides them with not only their own apartment, but also the services of a doctor or nurse on call, and perhaps even a skilled nursing wing in the building. Such an arrangement provides the security of knowing that you will have skilled care if it becomes necessary. But that security comes at a price—often a steep one. To move into a facility like this, you will almost certainly be required to pay an entrance fee. Often, a significant part of that fee is to cover the cost of your future medical care, should you ever need it.

To the extent the advance payment is specifically for medical care, even though it is for future medical care, you may deduct it. And, if you pay a monthly fee after you move in, and a portion of that fee is allocable to your future medical care, you may deduct that portion of your fee each year. The administrator of the facility generally will provide you with a letter at tax time, informing you of the portion of your entrance fee and monthly rent that can be treated as a deductible medical expense for the year.

The IRS granted another exception to the advance payment rule in 1986. In that case, a taxpayer made a nonrefundable payment in advance to a private institution for lifetime care of his disabled child. The prepayment was to cover continuing care of the child after the taxpayer's death. The IRS determined that this type of payment may be deducted only if it is a condition of the institution's future acceptance of the child. This decision was issued in a private letter ruling, which applies only to the taxpayer who requested the ruling; however, it provides some insight into how the IRS is likely to rule in similar situations.

Paying Medical Expenses of Others

You may, of course, deduct your own medical expenses. However, you are also permitted to deduct your spouse's expenses or your dependents' (even if they aren't related to you), if you are the one paying the bills. You may also deduct:

- **Medical expenses you pay for someone who would be your dependent if he or she were not claimed as a dependent by your former spouse under the terms of a divorce decree.** For example, if your divorce agreement allows your former spouse to claim your daughter as a dependent, you may claim, as a medical expense deduction on your own tax return, any qualified medical expenses you pay for your daughter, even though you do not claim her as your dependent.

- **Medical expenses you pay for someone you could claim as a dependent, except that this person files a joint return or earns too much money to be claimed as your dependent.** For example, you might pay the medical expenses of your married son just to help out. Because he and his wife file a joint tax return, you are not permitted to claim him as a dependent on your tax return. But if he would otherwise qualify as your dependent, you may claim medical expenses you pay on his behalf.

- **Medical expenses you pay for someone you could claim as a dependent on your return if you could not be claimed as a dependent by someone else.** You may not claim any dependency exemptions on your tax return if someone else can claim you as a dependent, whether or not that person actually does so. In this situation, too, you may deduct the medical expenses you pay for the person who would otherwise be your dependent.

Claiming a Decedent's Medical Expenses

If someone dies before paying all of his or her medical expenses, and those bills are paid out of the estate of the deceased person (that is, with cash that belonged to him or her at the time of death), the expenses may be claimed on the decedent's estate tax return.

Alternatively, the medical expenses may be claimed on the decedent's final income tax return. This might make sense if no estate tax return is required or if the income tax deduction is more valuable.

If the expenses are paid within one year of the date of death—even if they are paid after the decedent's death and after the close of the tax year—the expenses are considered paid at the time the medical services were rendered. Therefore, expenses for services provided in the year of death may be claimed on the final return of the decedent. If the services were provided before the year of death, the executor or administrator may file an amended tax return to claim the expenses in that prior year.

If the executor claims the expenses on the decedent's income tax return, the executor or administrator must include a statement (in duplicate) declaring that the expenses were not claimed on an estate tax return. In that statement, the executor should also waive the right to claim the deduction on any estate tax return at any time in the future. (For more information, see IRS Publication 559, *Survivors, Executors, and Administrators*.)

Reimbursements

One of the cardinal rules of the tax code is that there shall be no double dipping. (Although there are exceptions even to that rule, none of them apply here.) As applied to medical expenses, this means that you can't deduct money you get back. For example, if your medical expenses are reimbursed by an insurance company or by Medicare, then you must reduce your deduction by the amount of the reimbursement. A personal injury settlement payment is not treated as a reimbursement unless the settlement is earmarked for medical expenses.

If you claim a medical expense deduction in one year and receive reimbursement in a later year, you must report the reimbursement as income in the year you receive it. (You report it as "Other Income" on the first page of your Form 1040.) The reimbursement is taxable only to the extent it reduced your tax bill in the previous year.

> **EXAMPLE 1:** McGee's adjusted gross income last year was $25,000. He had enough deductions to itemize (instead of claiming the standard deduction). He also had medical expenses of $3,000. He calculated his medical expense deduction as follows:
>
> | | |
> |---|---|
> | Total medical expense | $ 3,000 |
> | 7.5% of AGI (0.075 x $25,000) | − $ 1,875 |
> | Deductible medical expense | $ 1,125 |
>
> This year, McGee received a medical expense reimbursement of $100. McGee must include the $100 in his income this year because he received a tax benefit from deducting the expense last year.

> **EXAMPLE 2:** Last year, Molly did not itemize deductions. Instead, she claimed the standard deduction. This year, she received a $500 reimbursement for a medical expense she paid last year. Molly does not have to include the reimbursement

in her income because she did not claim a deduction for the medical expense last year. Therefore, she received no tax benefit.

On occasion, you might receive a reimbursement that exceeds the expense for which you requested reimbursement. If so, you must first apply the reimbursement against the expense for which you are being reimbursed, and then apply the remainder against other deductible medical expenses. If there is still some left over, you must report the remaining amount as income if the total reimbursement exceeds $98,550 (for 2008).

This rule applies if you have been paying your own insurance premiums. If your insurance premiums were paid by an employer or a former employer and the cost was tax-free to you, then you must report your entire excess reimbursement as income on your tax return, regardless of the amount.

How to Claim a Medical Expense Deduction

Claim your medical expense deduction in the first section of Schedule A. You attach Schedule A to your Form 1040 when you file your tax return.

Charitable Contributions and Volunteer Work

Tax Benefits in This Chapter

☐ **Did you donate cash to a charitable organization?**
  • You may be able to claim a deduction for your donation.
  • If you receive any property or services in exchange for your donation, you might have to reduce your deduction by the value of the property or services.

☐ **Did you donate used clothing or household goods to charity?**
  • You may deduct the fair market value of your property, as long as it's in good condition.

☐ **Did you donate a car to charity?**
  • If the charity sells your car, your deduction will generally be limited to the sales proceeds.
  • If the charity keeps your car, gives it away, or sells it for less than market value to a needy person, you may generally deduct the car's fair market value.

☐ **Did you donate stock or real estate to a charitable organization?**
  • You may be able to deduct its fair market value, if you owned it for more than one year. But there are some exceptions and limitations.

☐ **Did you donate artwork to charity?**
  • If the charity plans to display the artwork, you may generally deduct its fair market value.
  • If the charity sells the artwork, your deduction is probably limited to your basis.
  • If you created the artwork, you may deduct only the cost of your supplies.

☐ **Did you do volunteer work for a charitable organization?**
  • You may deduct your out-of-pocket costs, but not the value of your time or services.

☐ **Do all of your donations for the year add up to more than 20% of your adjusted gross income?**
  • The amount you may deduct this year may be limited, although you may carry over any amounts you can't deduct to future years.

For many, the retirement years offer the first opportunity to indulge—through volunteer work—passions and interests acquired over the years. Whether you decide to continue using the expertise you developed during your paid career or throw yourself into something new, volunteer work can be a highly rewarding way to spend some of your newly acquired free time.

Charitable giving often takes on more importance after retirement as well, particularly for those who are fortunate enough to have large estates, with cash or valuable property to donate to favorite causes. Charitable donations offer an opportunity to fund worthwhile endeavors—and the attendant tax breaks are nothing to sneeze at, either.

This chapter covers the following three main categories of charitable contributions:

- **Cash.** This is the simplest category. There are no questions about what cash is worth, no issues of shared ownership, and no disputes over whether it should be hung on the wall or sold. However, the amount you can deduct might be limited by your income or by goods or services you receive in exchange for your contribution.

- **Property.** You may donate almost any type of property, whether used or new (although certain types of property must be in good condition, so you can skip the running shoes with holes in the soles). Property contributions run the gamut from used clothing and cars to investment securities, real estate, artwork, and other collectibles.

- **Volunteer work.** Unfortunately, neither your time nor the value of the services you provide to a charitable organization is deductible. However, you may deduct many of the expenses you incur for volunteer work, such as the cost of gasoline, supplies and phone calls.

Contributions You May Not Deduct

Although it's usually easy to figure out whether a donation qualifies for a charitable deduction on your return, there are certain types of donations that are never deductible, even though it might seem that they should be. These include:

- **Gifts to individuals.** You might give someone money just to help out or because you want to support the work he or she is doing. However, gifts to specific people are not deductible.

- **Political contributions.** A donation to the political campaign of your favorite candidate is not deductible, nor are contributions to groups whose primary function is lobbying.

- **Contributions to foreign charities.** Donations to foreign charities generally are not deductible. There are exceptions for donations to Canadian, Mexican, or Israeli organizations, but only if you have income from that country. Even if you qualify, your donation will be subject to certain limitations spelled out in tax treaties between the United States and the three countries. IRS Publication 526, *Charitable Contributions*, summarizes the rules for deducting donations to charities in these countries. If you need to dive into the tax treaties, you can find them on the IRS website.

- **Free use of vacation home or other property.** Many charities raise money by holding auctions and allowing participants to bid on items that have been donated, from baked goods to professional services to weekend getaways. If you offer free use of your vacation home to a charitable organization— whether for the charity's own use or for the charity to auction off—you may not deduct the rental value of the property for that period of time.

- **Your services.** As valuable as your time is, or perhaps as expensive as your services would be if you charged for them (if you are donating professional services as an accountant or architect, for example), you may not deduct the value of your time or service. Only your out-of-pocket volunteer expenses are deductible. The tax courts have also disallowed home office deductions if the office is used for charity work.

- **Bingo, raffles, and lottery tickets.** You may not deduct the cost of raffle and lottery tickets sold on behalf of charities, nor the cost of bingo games sponsored by charities.

Partly because taxpayers are eclectic in their interests and creative when fashioning their charitable pursuits, the laws governing contributions have become more and more complex. Just for starters, the deductibility of both your charitable volunteer work and your contributions of cash and property depend on a variety of factors, including:

- the type of organization receiving your contribution
- what you give (whether services, property, or cash)
- the conditions or restrictions, if any, you place on your gift, and
- how much you give.

For example, you might be able to deduct the full fair market value of a contribution to one organization, but not to another. Your income level might curtail how much you may deduct in the current year. And certain gifts of property are automatically restricted, simply because of the nature of the property. On top of all that, contributions of different types and amounts of property have vastly different reporting requirements.

This chapter covers the basic rules for charitable contributions and provides some detail about the most common areas of charitable volunteer work and charitable giving. It explains the tax benefits available—and the restrictions that apply—when you donate money, property, or services. And it touches on the ramifications of making gifts to or from an entity such as a trust.

RESOURCE

Want more information on the tax benefits of charitable giving? For more arcane donation strategies and less traditional contributions, you might take a look at IRS Publication 526, *Charitable Contributions*. Particularly if you are making large gifts, you will almost certainly also want to confer with a tax professional to ensure that the tax benefits of your contribution meet your expectations.

Charitable Organizations

No matter what or how much you decide to donate, your gift will be deductible only if you make it to a qualified organization. You can't simply start giving cash or property away and claiming deductions: The group to which you give must meet certain requirements.

A charitable organization must qualify as such under one of several different sections of the tax code. If the organization qualifies, then it is tax-exempt, which generally means that it qualifies to receive your tax-deductible contribution and that it doesn't have to pay tax on donations. Your donations to most public charities are deductible, as are your donations to many nonprofit private foundations. If you are uncertain whether an organization qualifies to receive deductible donations, you should ask the organization for a copy of the IRS letter approving the organization's tax-exempt status.

Using the IRS List of Qualified Charities

Many of the organizations that are eligible to receive tax-deductible contributions are listed in IRS Publication 78, *Cumulative List of Organizations described in Section 170(c) of the Internal Revenue Code of 1986*. However, because the list is based on applications for tax-exempt status received by the IRS, several large categories of eligible organization are not included. For example, churches are automatically tax-exempt and are not required to file an application. Also, public charities that have annual gross receipts of less than $5,000 are not required to complete an application and therefore will not appear in Publication 78. Federal, state, and local governments, as well as Indian tribal governments, also are not required to submit an application for exempt status.

If you do not find an organization listed in Publication 78 and are not able to verify tax-exempt status with the organization itself, the IRS recommends that you call its Tax Exempt Customer Account Services line at 877-829-5500.

Typically, your contributions to the following types of organizations will be deductible, as long as they are operating on a nonprofit basis:

- churches
- educational institutions
- hospitals and other medical facilities
- organizations that operate exclusively for charitable purposes, such as the American Red Cross, Salvation Army, and United Way
- government or government supported organizations (if the donation is for public purposes), and
- private nonprofit foundations that meet certain requirements.

Many other types of organizations satisfy the qualification requirements; you might need to do some research to determine whether the charity you want to support is one of them.

Cash Donations

As long as you give to a qualified organization, donating cash is usually fairly straightforward, taxwise. If, however, you receive something in exchange for your cash donation, calculating your deduction can be a bit trickier.

Cash

If you donate cash to a qualified organization and receive nothing in exchange, your donation will be fully deductible (as long as your contribution isn't too large relative to your income; see "Contribution Limits," below). However, you may not deduct a cash donation unless you have a tangible record of the donation, no matter how small the amount. You might know that you put $5 in the church basket every week, but without a receipt, that donation is not deductible. To claim a cash donation, you will need one of the following:

- a canceled check
- a bank statement showing the name of the charity and the date and amount of the check, or
- a written receipt from the charity that includes the name of the charity and the date and amount of your contribution.

If you donate $250 or more, you must obtain a written acknowledgement from the charity. The acknowledgment must state the amount of your donation and whether or not you received goods or services in exchange for the donation. If you did receive a benefit, the acknowledgment must contain an estimate of the value of the goods or services you received.

You won't need to send in these records with your tax return, but you will be required to produce them if the IRS asks for them.

Cash With Benefits

If you receive something in return for your cash donation, such as services, items of property, or even benefits (if they are financial in nature), then you must reduce your deduction by the value of the items or benefits you received.

For example, if you pay $200 for tickets to a charity dinner, but the dinner itself was worth $50, you may deduct only $150 as a charitable contribution. Or, if you donate $300 to a charity and the charity sends you a coffee table book of photographs worth $65, your deductible contribution is $235.

> **TIP**
>
> **Give back those unused event tickets.** Have you ever bought tickets to a charity event, then been unable—or just haven't wanted—to go when the date rolls around? You might think that you could deduct the full price of the tickets, with no reduction, because you didn't attend the event and therefore received no benefit. According to the IRS, however, you still must subtract the value of the benefit because you had the right to attend. For example, if you paid $200 for tickets to a charity dinner you didn't attend, you may deduct only $150, if the meal is worth $50. The

better option, if you can plan ahead, is to return the tickets to the charity for resale. That way, you can deduct the full purchase price of your tickets.

If you donate more than $75, the charity generally must provide you with an estimate of the value of benefits you received in exchange for your donation. The IRS has said that you may rely on the charity's written estimate of the value of those benefits.

The Benefits of Membership

Often, an organization asks you to become a member by paying a certain amount each year. If you make a contribution to a qualified organization and receive a membership in return, you may still deduct the full amount of your contribution as long as the membership costs $75 or less and the benefits you receive in exchange are limited to:

- Privileges like these that you may exercise frequently as a member:
    - discounted or free admission to the organization's events, facilities, goods, and services that are also available to the public
    - preferred access to goods or services, or
    - discounted or free parking.
- Admission to member-only events, but only if the cost to the organization (per person) does not exceed $9.10.

If your membership perks fall into the above categories, the charitable organization will generally indicate in its acknowledgment of your gift that you received no benefits in exchange for your contribution.

Cash With Token Benefits

At this point, you are probably wondering about the mug you received for donating to your local public radio station or the SPCA. You are not always required to reduce your deduction by benefits received if those benefits are deemed by the IRS to be of "insubstantial value." Happily, the IRS has given us a definition to work with in this situation. For tax year 2008, a benefit is of insubstantial value if it falls into one of the following categories:

- The value of the benefits you receive is no more than $91 or 2% of your donation, whichever is less.
- Your contribution amount is at least $45.50 and the only benefits you receive are token items with the organization's logo on them, which cost the charity no more than $9.10 total.
- The item or benefit you receive comes to you unsolicited with a request for a contribution and with the statement that you may keep the gift or benefit whether or not you make a contribution. In this case, too, the total cost to the charity of the items you receive may not exceed $9.10.

When Is a Cash Donation Made?

As is the case with most deductions, you claim a charitable contribution deduction for the tax year in which you actually made the contribution. But if you are like many people, you write one or more of your checks to charity at the end of the year. What if you don't get around to writing that check until December 31? Is the contribution date the same as the date on the check? Is it the postmark that counts? Or is it the date the charity cashes the check? If you make your contribution by credit card, is the contribution made when you charge the card or when you pay the credit card bill?

Rulings in a variety of tax court cases provide the following guidelines:

- If you deliver your check before the end of the current year, it is deductible in the current year even if the charity doesn't cash it until the following year.
- If you mail the check instead of delivering it to the charity, the same rule applies. If you date and mail it before the end of the current year, you may deduct it in the current year.

- If you postdate your check for next year but deliver it to the charity before the end of the current year, it will be deductible next year, not in the current year.
- If you charge your contribution to your credit card, you claim the deduction for the year in which the card is charged, not the year in which you actually pay your credit card bill.
- If you make the contribution directly from your bank account to the charity, the date of the debit that appears on your bank statement determines the year of the deduction.

Although these guidelines should serve you well, bear in mind that the default rule is that contributions are deductible in the year they are paid. For example, in one case that went to court, a check written on December 12 did not clear (according to the bank statement) until January 17. Strict adherence to the above guidelines would suggest that the payment should be deducted in the year the check was written. However, the court determined that the payment should be deducted in the year the check cleared. The fact that it took so long for the check to clear suggested that the check was not delivered until after the end of the year. On the other hand, if the taxpayer had been able to provide evidence that he actually did deliver the check before the end of the year, he might have prevailed.

How to Deduct Charitable Contributions of Cash

You may claim your deduction on Schedule A, in the "Gifts to Charity" section. Before you claim your deduction, see "Contribution Limits," below, to find out whether it is subject to a reduction based on your adjusted gross income.

Property Donations

Donating property is not as straightforward as donating cash, because of the following complications:

- When you donate property, your deduction is sometimes limited to your basis in the property rather than its fair market value when you donate it. (For help figuring out your basis, see Chapter 1.)

- With some exceptions, if you donate property valued at more than $500, you are required to complete and attach IRS Form 8283, *Noncash Charitable Contributions*, to your income tax return.
- If you donate property worth more than $5,000, you might need to have it appraised.
- Contributions of certain types of property (such as vehicles), or partial interests in property, have additional reporting requirements.

Used Clothing and Household Goods

Your deduction for used clothing and household goods is limited to the fair market value of those items, which typically is far less than you paid for them. It is up to you, not the charity, to estimate the fair market value. Try to be as accurate as possible. Thrift store prices are often a good indicator of what your goods are worth.

You may not claim a deduction at all for household items that are not in "good" condition, with one exception: If an item is worth more than $500, as verified by an appraisal, you may deduct the fair market value of the item regardless of its condition. (You must also complete Form 8283 and attach the appraisal to your tax return; see "Rules for Appraisals," below.)

If the total value of all of your property donations (to one or more charities) exceeds $500, you must also complete Form 8283 and attach it to your tax return. That form requires you to provide detailed information about the charitable organization and the items you donated.

Acknowledgments and Appraisals

If the value of a single contribution is more than $250, you must obtain a written acknowledgment from the charity. The acknowledgment must contain a description of the property donated and indicate whether or not you received goods or services in exchange. If you did receive a benefit, the acknowledgment must contain an estimate of the value of those goods or services. You are not required to include the acknowledgement with your tax return, but you should keep it with your other records in case the IRS asks to see it.

If you donate a single item, or a group of similar items, valued at more than $5,000, not only must you complete Form 8283, but you must also obtain an appraisal of the item(s). You need not submit the appraisal with your tax return, except in certain circumstances (see "Rules for Appraisals," below).

Rules for Appraisals

Although you might have to have an item appraised before you may claim a deduction for donating it to a charity you don't have to attach the appraisal to your tax return unless one of the following is true:

- You claim a deduction of more than $500 for an item that is not in good condition.
- You claim a deduction of $20,000 or more for donated artwork.
- You claim a conservation contribution for certain types of easements (that is, you give an interest in real property to be used for conservation purposes).
- You claim a deduction of more than $500,000 for a single item (or group of similar items).

If you are required to obtain an appraisal (whether or not you have to attach it to your tax return), the appraisal must meet all of these requirements:

- It must be made by a qualified appraiser. (To see how the IRS defines "qualified appraiser" see the instructions to Form 8283.)
- It must be made no more than 60 days before you donate the item.
- You must receive it before the due date (or extended due date) of your income tax return.
- You must obtain a separate appraisal for each item or group of similar items requiring an appraisal.

How to Deduct Charitable Contributions of Clothing and Household Goods

If the total value of property donated is $500 or less, you may simply claim the amount on Schedule A, in the "Gifts to Charity" section. If the total value of property donations exceeds $500, you must complete and attach Form 8283 as well. If an appraisal is required, it need only be attached to your return in certain circumstances. (See "Rules for Appraisals," above.)

Cars and Other Vehicles

The rules for donating cars are very similar to those for donating clothing and household goods, with a couple of additional twists. There are two typical scenarios for vehicle donations, each with its own rules: (1) you give a car to an organization that keeps it or gives it away to someone in need, or (2) you give a car to an organization that sells it at market value to raise funds.

Car Will Be Used or Given Away

If the organization plans to keep the vehicle or give it (or sell it for less than fair market value) to a needy person "in furtherance of the organization's charitable purpose," then you must meet certain substantiation requirements intended to offer proof of the car's value. The requirements depend on what the car is worth:

- If you plan to claim a deduction of more than $250 but no more than $500, you will need a written acknowledgement from the charity. You don't have to attach the acknowledgement to your return.
- If you plan to claim a deduction of more than $500 but no more than $5,000, you must obtain a written acknowledgement from the organization. The preferred form of acknowledgement is a completed Form 1098-C, *Contributions of Motor Vehicles, Boats, and Airplanes*, which you must attach to your tax return. However, a written statement from the organization containing the same information is also acceptable.

- If you plan to claim a deduction of more than $5,000, you will need to have the vehicle appraised. In addition, the charity must provide you with a copy of Form 1098-C or an equivalent written acknowledgement of your donation.

Car Will Be Sold to Raise Funds

If the organization plans to sell the car and use the proceeds for its own charitable purposes, the following substantiation requirements apply:

- If the vehicle sells for more than $500, the charity must report the sale on Form 1098-C and send you a copy of the form (or an equivalent substitute) within 30 days. Your deduction is limited to the gross sales proceeds reported on Form 1098-C.
- If the vehicle sells for more than $250 but no more than $500, the charity must send you a written acknowledgement but is not required to send you a Form 1098-C. Because Form 1098-C also satisfies the written acknowledgement requirement, some charities will send you a 1098-C anyway. If so, you should see a checkmark in box 7, which alerts you that you are not permitted to deduct more than $500. Generally, you may deduct the amount of the sales proceeds. However, if you can prove that the car's fair market value was more than the proceeds, you may claim the fair market value, as long as it does not exceed $500.

If the charity gives your vehicle to a needy person as part of its charitable work or sells the vehicle to a needy person at below fair market value, these rules don't apply. This is considered giving the car away, not selling it to raise funds. In this situation, you may deduct the fair market value of the vehicle; your deduction is not limited to the gross proceeds from the sale.

How to Claim a Deduction for Donating a Vehicle

If the value of your donation is less than $250, simply report the amount of the deduction on Schedule A, in the "Gifts to Charity" section.

If the claimed value of the vehicle is more than $250 but no more than $500, you must also obtain an acknowledgment from the charity to keep in your files. You are not required to submit the acknowledgement with your return.

If the claimed value of the vehicle is more than $500, you must complete and attach Form 8283 and you must also attach a copy of Form 1098-C (or an equivalent statement from the charity) to your tax return.

If you are claiming a deduction of more than $5,000, you must obtain an appraisal. In addition, the charity must send you a Form 1098-C, which you must attach it to your tax return along with Form 8283.

> **CAUTION**
>
> **Form 8283 is required for property donations of more than $500.** If the total value of all of your property donations for the year (regardless of the type of property) exceeds $500, you must always complete and attach Form 8283 to your tax return.

Capital Gain Property

The donation rules are even trickier if you donate property that would produce a long-term capital gain if sold. Capital gain property is typically property that you have held for more than a year and that has increased in value since you acquired it. (If you have not held the property for more than a year, your deduction is generally limited to your basis, rather than the fair market value of the property when you donate it. There are some exceptions—for property you received as a gift or inheritance, for example.)

The rules for calculating the amount of your deduction depend on the type of property, the type of organization you plan to give it to, and how that organization plans to use it. This section takes a closer look at some of those rules for specific types of capital gain property.

Stock

If you donate publicly traded stock, you may deduct its fair market value as long as you have held the stock long term (that is, for more than one year) and you give the stock to a "50% limit organization." A 50% limit organization is a public charity or qualified private foundation to which you may make the largest deductible contribution. As explained in "Contribution Limits," below, you generally may deduct no more than a certain percentage of your adjusted gross income. That percentage might be 20%, 30%, or 50%, depending on the organization to which you donate and the property you give.

In the case of stock, your deduction generally will be limited to 30% of your adjusted gross income. This might be somewhat confusing: After all, if you donate to a 50% limit organization, shouldn't you be entitled to a deduction of up to 50% of your adjusted gross income? It might seem so, but the answer is no. If you choose to calculate your deduction based on the stock's fair market value (rather than its basis), you are subject to the 30% limit. See "Contribution Limits," below, for more information.

 TIP

Give appreciated stock. When you donate stock that has increased in value, you may deduct the full fair market value, even though you might have paid quite a bit less for it. This gives you the benefit of the stock's current value without having to pay tax on the gain. If you have stock that has not appreciated, your donation is still the fair market value of the stock (not your basis). In this situation, it would be better for you to sell the stock, claim the loss on your tax return, and then donate the proceeds to charity.

Real Estate

The rules for donating real estate are similar to those for donating stock: You may deduct the fair market value of the property if you have held it for more than a year and you donate it to a 50% limit organization. (If you have not held the property for more than a year, your deduction is generally limited to your basis.) Your deduction will be limited to 30% of your adjusted gross income (again, assuming you donate to a 50% limit organization).

But donations of real estate differ from donations of stock in the following ways:

- If you donate real estate to a private foundation that is not a 50% limit organization, your deduction is limited to 20% of your adjusted gross income. What's more, you may deduct only your basis in the property, not its fair market value.
- If the property you plan to donate is mortgaged, you should probably confer with a tax professional before making the donation. In general, your deduction will be limited to your equity (the difference between the fair market value of the property and the amount of the mortgage). However, when you give away mortgaged property, the amount of the mortgage is usually treated as cash you received, so the transaction is likely to result in a tax liability. A tax professional should review the transaction before it's a done deal to help you determine the potential tax consequences.

If you donate property that has been subject to depreciation (such as rental real estate), then to the extent you would have to report the gain as ordinary income if the property were sold, you must limit a prorata portion of your deduction to your basis in the property. This can be a complicated calculation. See the "Depreciation Recapture" section of IRS Publication 544, *Sales and Other Dispositions of Assets*, for more information. You might also want to confer with a tax professional before donating property that has been depreciated.

Artwork

The amount you may deduct for a donation of art depends on how long you have owned the artwork, the type of organization to which you plan to donate it, and how the organization plans to use the art. And, there are severe restrictions on your deduction if you donate art of your own creation, even if you happen to be a famous artist.

Donations of Art Created by Someone Else

If the artwork you donate was created by someone else and has appreciated in value since you purchased or acquired it, the general rules for donating appreciated property, described above, will apply. As long as you have owned it for more than a year and you donate it to a 50% limit organization, you may claim a deduction for its fair market value rather than limiting the deduction to your basis in the artwork.

However, there is another variable in the mix. If the charity plans to use the art for its exempt purpose (if, for example, an art museum plans to display the art you donate), then you may deduct its fair market value. If the charity plans to sell the art and use the proceeds, however, your deduction must be reduced by the amount the art has appreciated while in your possession. Generally, this means your deduction is limited to your basis.

> **CAUTION**
>
> **If the charity eventually sells the artwork you donated, you may have to pay back part of your deduction.** If you claimed a deduction for the full fair market value of art you donated, and that value was more than $5,000, you might have to return some of the tax benefit if the charity later sells the art. If the organization sells the art either in the year you donate it or in any of the following three years, your deduction is limited to your basis. Because you've already taken a larger deduction, you must report the excess as ordinary income for the year in which the organization sells the art.

Art Created by You

If you create art and donate it to a charitable organization, your deduction is limited to the lower of its fair market value or your out-of-pocket costs to produce it (canvas, paints, and so on, but not your time).

Selling Appreciated Property for Less Than It's Worth

Instead of donating appreciated property, you could sell it to the organization for less than its fair market value. In this situation, the transaction is treated as part gift—for which you may claim a charitable contribution—and part sale—on which you might owe tax. The amount of your gift is the difference between the fair market value of the property and the amount you received from the sale. If your deduction is limited to your basis, your basis is allocated between the gift portion and the sale portion in the same ratio as the sales proceeds are allocated between gift and sale.

EXAMPLE: You sell some art valued at $20,000 to an art museum (a qualified 50% limit organization) that plans to hang the art in one of its galleries. Your basis in the art is $15,000 and you sell it to the organization for that amount ($15,000). Your charitable contribution is $5,000, the difference between what it is worth and what you actually received for it.

Because you sold appreciated property, you must also determine whether you have a taxable gain on the sale part of the transaction. To compute your gain on the sale, you must allocate a portion of your basis to each part of the transaction. Your charitable contribution of $5,000 (as computed above) represents 25% of the proceeds ($20,000) from the sale of the artwork. Consequently, 25% of your $15,000 basis in the art ($3,750) should be allocated to the charitable contribution. The remaining 75% of the basis ($11,250) is allocated to the sale portion of the transaction. Therefore, your gain from the sale portion of the transaction is:

Share of sales proceeds	$ 15,000
Less basis allocated to sale portion	(11,250)
Gain reportable on tax return	$ 3,750

Partial Interest Contributions

As a rule, to claim a deduction for a charitable contribution, you must give away your entire interest in the donated property. But the exceptions to this rule—which allow partial-interest gifts—are what make the world of charitable giving go around. These exceptions make it possible for donors to make gifts of property even if they still need—or want—some benefit from it.

> **SEE AN EXPERT**
>
> **Contributing a partial interest in property can be a tricky undertaking.** You will want to make sure that your donation is structured in such a way that you may claim a charitable deduction on your tax return. That will usually require some legal assistance. Often the charitable organization itself will provide the legal documents you need, but you might want to confer with your own attorney, as well. This section provides an overview of the basic issues involved in donating a partial interest in property; if this sounds like something you might want to explore, talk to a tax professional.

You may claim a deduction for the following partial-interest gifts to charity:

- **A remainder interest in your personal residence (or farm), whether it is your principal residence or a vacation home.** A remainder interest is one that is left when another interest terminates. For example, your gift to charity might provide that you may live in your house until you die, after which your house will go to charity. In that case, the charity has a remainder interest in your home.
- **An undivided portion of your entire interest in a property.** An undivided interest in property exists when more than one person or entity shares ownership of property that cannot be separated into autonomous pieces. For example, a tennis court might be owned by the residents of a community, but the residents may not divide up the court into separate pieces for

each owner. Instead, they all have an undivided interest in the tennis court.

- **One of two or more contributions in which you give your entire interest to one or more qualified charitable organizations.** In this type of partial-interest donation, you make two or more donations in the process of giving away your entire interest. For example, you might donate half of your interest in a piece of land to a charity in one year and donate the remainder in the following year.

- **A partial interest in property where the portion you donate represents your entire interest.** For example, suppose your grandmother owned her own home. She left the house to you when she died, but gave your mother the right to occupy the home for as long as she lived. Your mother has an interest in the property during her lifetime (a life estate), and you have a remainder interest. You may donate your remainder interest to charity and claim a deduction for that portion.

- **A qualified conservation contribution.** A qualified conservation contribution is a contribution of an interest in real estate, either your entire interest or a partial interest (such as an easement), which is to be used exclusively for conservation purposes.

You may also deduct your contribution of a partial interest that is made in trust and meets one of the following conditions:

- **It is a remainder interest in a charitable remainder annuity trust.** A charitable remainder annuity trust is one that requires a fixed annual payment (no less than 5% of the initial fair market value of the trust) to a noncharitable beneficiary—such as you—for the life of the beneficiary or a set number of years. Once the beneficiary dies or the set term ends, the remainder goes to charity.

- **It is a remainder interest in a charitable remainder unitrust.** This type of trust requires payments to a noncharitable beneficiary based on the current fair market value of the trust, determined annually. The payment must be at least 5% of the fair market value of the trust. Again, the payments must continue for a fixed term or until the beneficiary dies. Once the term ends or the beneficiary dies, the remainder goes to the charity.

- **It is an income interest in a charitable lead trust.** In a charitable lead trust, the trust's income is paid to charity, either for a set period or until the death of one or more specific individuals. Once the term ends or the specified individuals die, the remainder of the trust is paid to a named noncharitable beneficiary.

- **It is a remainder interest in a pooled income fund.** This is a fund, set up by a charity, to which a number of different people contribute. Income from the trust goes to the contributors during their lifetimes in proportion to the size of their donations. When a contributor dies, a remainder portion goes to the charity.

Complicated though they are, these rules are just the tip of the iceberg. Special rules might apply if you want to contribute a fractional interest in personal property (such as art), you want to contribute an additional partial interest in the same property, or you fail to contribute 100% of the property within ten years of your initial donation. Because the partial contribution rules are so complex, it is important that you seek the counsel of a tax professional before completing such a transaction.

Charitable Donations From an IRA

What if you want to give funds from your IRA rather than from your regular bank account? To spur charitable giving, Congress enacted a measure that allows certain taxpayers to do just that through tax year 2009.

Eligibility

To be eligible to make a donation from your IRA, you must meet all of these requirements:

- You must be age 70½ or older on the day you make the donation.
- The donation must come from a traditional IRA or a Roth IRA. No other plan qualifies, not even other types of IRAs (like SEPs and SIMPLEs; see Chapter 3 for more information about these retirement plans). Other employer plans, such as a 401(k) plan, do not qualify either.
- The donation must be a direct transfer from the IRA to the charity. You may not take the money out of the IRA and deliver it to the charity yourself. The custodian of your IRA must arrange to transfer the funds directly to the charity.
- Your total charitable donations from one or more of your qualified IRAs may not exceed $100,000 for the year. However, if you are married and filing a joint return, you and your spouse may each donate up to $100,000 from your respective IRAs.
- You may not make a donation to a donor-advised trust (see "Gifts to a Donor-Advised Trust," below, for more information on this option).
- You may not make a split-interest gift. A split-interest gift is one in which less than 100% of the gift goes to the charity. For example, you may not make a gift to a charitable remainder trust, which provides income to you for life and gives the remainder to charity.

Tax Benefits

If you qualify to make charitable donations from your IRA, there are significant tax benefits that might sway you to take the plunge. Although you can't deduct the amount you donate in the usual way, you may exclude it from your income *and* count it as your required distribution for the year.

Because you don't have to report the charitable distribution as income, you will derive a tax benefit even if you don't itemize your deductions on Schedule A. Also, a number of tax benefits are reduced or eliminated as your adjusted gross income increases. For example, the portion of your Social Security benefits that is subject to income tax increases as your adjusted gross income increases. If you use part of your required distribution from your IRA to make a charitable contribution, you can reduce your adjusted gross income and perhaps enjoy additional tax benefits.

And, because the contribution that goes from your IRA to charity is considered a distribution from the IRA, it satisfies the required distribution rules. As you probably know, you are required to start taking money out of your IRA(s) once you reach the age of 70½. You must take at least a minimum amount each year, determined by a statutory formula. When you make a charitable contribution from your IRA, you may count it as your required distribution under these rules.

How to Claim a Charitable Donation From an IRA

You don't claim a charitable donation from an IRA as a deduction, either on Schedule A or above-the-line. Instead, you exclude the amount from your income.

Gifts to a Donor-Advised Trust

In recent years, donor-advised trusts have become popular vehicles for charitable giving. When you use a donor-advised trust, you typically donate a lump sum to a trust that is sponsored (and controlled) by a public charity. You claim a deduction on your tax return for the year in which you contribute the funds. Your donation is held in trust and contributions are made to a variety of charities, but not necessarily in the year of your donation. Because you have relinquished control of the funds to the sponsoring organization, you may deduct the full amount of your gift in the year you make the donation.

Tax Strategy: When Should You Establish a Donor-Advised Trust?

If you are in the habit of making sizable annual contributions to charity, you might benefit from contributing to a donor-advised trust in a year when your income is unusually high. Sometimes, that will be the year you retire. After retirement, you might find that your income is substantially lower. By contributing what you might have donated in future years to a donor-advised trust, you might be able to maximize the tax benefit by claiming a large deduction in your highest-income year.

The sponsoring charity has legal ownership and control of the trust. However, one of the characteristics of such a trust is that the donor (you, presumably) is permitted to offer advice regarding how the funds are invested, which charities will receive the funds, and in what amounts.

Those privileges suggest that you, the donor, actually retain some control over the funds you have donated. The IRS was troubled by those features of this charitable vehicle. Consequently, it tightened the rules somewhat. Beginning in 2007, you may not deduct your contribution unless you have a written acknowledgement from the sponsoring organization indicating that the organization itself has exclusive legal control over the funds you contributed.

Volunteer Work

People who volunteer their time and expertise believe they have something valuable to offer. So, you may find it distressing that your services, expert though they may be, are worth a tax deduction of precisely zero. If it makes you feel any better, this rule is not unique to volunteer work. In fact, it is quite consistent with other tax laws. With only rare exceptions, the general rule is that you must spend cold, hard cash before you may claim a deduction.

In spite of this rule, you might have more deductible volunteer expenses than you realize. Whenever you spend money to do volunteer work, you might be eligible for a deduction.

Miscellaneous Volunteer Expenses

You may claim a deduction for expenses you incur while providing services to a charitable organization as long as you are not reimbursed for them. Be sure to obtain an acknowledgement of your volunteer work from the organization if you deduct more than $250.

These are some of the expense you may deduct:
- the cost of hosting a party or fundraiser for the organization
- advertising you buy on behalf of the organization
- supplies you purchase to be used in volunteer work, such as stamps and stationery
- the cost of a required uniform (and the cost of keeping it clean), and
- telephone expenses.

Travel

Travel is often the most significant out-of-pocket expense volunteers incur, whether they are traveling locally or out of town to provide services.

Local Travel

Your deductible local travel expenses might include bus, train, or taxi fares or the cost of similar travel. You may also deduct the cost of parking fees and tolls.

If you use your own car, you may deduct the cost of your gas and oil for those miles you travel for the charity. But that is the extent of your deductible car expenses. You may not deduct the cost of insurance, maintenance, registration fees, or depreciation, as you could if you were using your car for business.

As an alternative to keeping track of your actual car expense (gas and oil), you may simply keep a log of the miles you travel for your volunteer work and deduct 14 cents per mile (for tax year 2008).

You may not deduct the cost of meals. Meals and lodging are deductible only if you are traveling away from home and must be gone overnight.

Travel Away From Home Overnight

If you must be gone overnight, either while performing services on behalf of the charitable organization or while serving as a delegate for the organization at a convention, you may deduct your travel costs, including meals and lodging. However, your deduction will be denied if the trip has "any significant element of personal pleasure." So, if you combine your charity work with a vacation or you spend significant amounts of time sightseeing, you will lose the charitable deduction for the cost of the trip.

If you attend a convention as a member—but not a delegate—of the charitable organization or church, you may not deduct your travel costs.

Contribution Limits

Rest assured, there are no restrictions on the amount you may donate to charity: If you wish to give away all of your worldly possessions, you are free to do so. The law restricts only the amount you may claim as a deduction on your tax return. Your deduction might be limited in one of two ways:

- **Value of donated property.** As explained in "Property Donations," above, your deduction for property you give to charity might be limited to your basis rather than the fair market value of the property (or the portion of the property you are donating).

- **Income restrictions.** The total amount you may deduct in any year for charitable contributions is limited to a percentage of your adjusted gross income (AGI). The percentage limit might be 50%, 30%, or 20%, depending on the type of property you are donating and the type of organization that receives it. As long as your charitable contributions aren't more than 20% of your AGI, you don't have to worry about these limits.

 CAUTION

You might also face an overall limit on your itemized deductions. As explained in Chapter 1, certain high-income taxpayers might be unable to claim all of their itemized deductions. Although this limit doesn't apply specifically to charitable deductions, it could reduce your total itemized deductions, including donations to charity.

 TIP

Some qualified conservation contributions have higher limits. If you are a rancher or a farmer and you donate an interest in real property to an organization for conservation purposes, your deduction limit might be as much as 100% of your AGI (instead of 50%, 30%, or 20%). See IRS Publication 526 for more information about this type of donation.

Adjusted Gross Income Limits

In the world of charitable giving, organizations are divided into two large categories. The first category is "50% limit organizations." You may contribute up to 50% of your AGI to such organizations and claim a current year deduction for that amount, as long the property you give also qualifies. (See "50% AGI Limit," below.) See IRS Publication 526 for a detailed description of qualifying 50% limit organizations.

All other organizations—those that qualify to receive deductible contributions but are not 50% limit organizations—fall into the catch-all category of non-50% limit organizations. Your deduction for donations to those organizations is limited to 30% or 20% of your AGI, depending on the type of property you give.

If you are not sure whether an organization is a 50% limit organization, you can ask the organization or you can check IRS Publication 78. Generally, the following organizations, if operated on a not-for-profit basis, fall into the 50% limit category:

- churches
- educational organizations
- hospitals
- U.S., state, or local governments (including tribal governments)
- publicly supported charitable, religious, educational, or scientific foundations, and
- other private foundations that meet certain requirements.

50% AGI Limit

Your deduction for all of your charitable contributions for the year can never exceed 50% of your AGI (except for certain conservation contributions, described above). However, some of your contributions might be limited to a smaller percentage of your AGI.

To qualify for the higher 50% limit, your contribution must be made directly to a 50% limit organization (as explained in "Adjusted Gross Income Limits," above) and it must be either:

- a cash donation, or
- a contribution of capital gain property for which you have made an election to limit your deduction to the basis of the property. You make this election by attaching a statement to your income tax return, or simply by reporting the correct amount of the deduction on Schedule A and also on Form 8283, if you are required to file it.

CAUTION

Your election applies to all capital gain property for the year. If you elect to limit your deduction to the basis of property, that limit applies to all other capital gain property you donate in the current year.

30% AGI Limit

Your deduction for contributions to qualified charitable organizations are limited to 30% of your AGI if any of the following is true:

- You contribute cash or property (except capital gain property) to a qualified organization that is a non-50% limit organization.
- You contribute capital gain property to a 50% limit organization and you do not make an election to limit your deduction to your basis in the property.
- You contribute cash or property "for the use of" any qualified organization (whether a 50% limit or a non-50% limit organization), rather than giving it directly to the organization. Such a contribution might be in the form of an interest in a charitable unitrust or annuity, or certain types of charitable remainder trusts. If you are making a donation through a trust or you are donating an interest in a trust, you should confer with a tax professional to make sure your gift is deductible and help you determine the limit of your deduction, if any.

20% AGI Limit

Your charitable deduction is limited to 20% of your AGI if you make a contribution of capital gain property to a non-50% limit organization.

Computing Your Deduction Limit

If your total charitable contributions exceed 20% of your AGI, then you must check to see whether your deduction will be limited. When calculating your deduction limit (if any), you are required to claim the deduction for your various contributions in the following order:

1. First, claim contributions that are subject to the 50% limit as described above. You may not claim a deduction for more than 50% of your AGI.
2. Next, claim all contributions you made to a non-50% limit organization, except for contributions of capital gain property. This portion of your deduction is limited to the smaller of:

- 30% of your AGI, or
- 50% of your AGI reduced by all contributions of any type to 50% limit organizations.

3. Next, claim your contributions of capital gain property to 50% limit organizations, except for contributions of capital gain property for which you made an election to limit your deduction to the basis of the property. This portion of your deduction is limited the smaller of:
   - 30% of your AGI, or
   - 50% of your AGI reduced by all other contributions to 50% limit organizations.

4. Finally, claim contributions that are subject to the 20% of AGI limit—that is, contributions of capital gain property to non-50% limit organizations. This portion of your deduction is limited to the smaller of:
   - 20% of your AGI, or
   - 50% of your AGI remaining after taking into account deductions described in Steps 1 through 3, above.

If you make contributions of various types that are subject to different AGI limits, the calculation of the deductible amount of each donation (and the carryover, if any—see below) can be complicated. IRS Publication 526 (in the section "How to Figure Your Deduction When Limits Apply") includes a detailed example followed by a completed worksheet. That worksheet is duplicated below. The example is for a taxpayer who:

- has an AGI of $50,000
- gave $2,000 in cash to a church
- gave land to the church (the fair market value was $28,000 and the taxpayer's basis in the land was $22,000, but the taxpayer did not choose to limit his or her deduction to the basis), and
- gave $5,000 in cash to a private foundation (a 30% limit organization).

The completed worksheet (including amounts that may be carried over and deducted in a future year) looks like this:

Filled-in Worksheet 2.　**Applying the Deduction Limits**
If the result on any line is less than zero, enter zero. For other instructions, see page 17.　　　　*Keep for your records*

Step 1. Enter any qualified conservation contributions (QCCs).

			Carryover
1.	If you are a qualified farmer or rancher, enter any QCCs eligible for the 100% limit **1**	-0-	
2.	Enter any QCCs not entered on line 1. Do not include this amount on line 3, 4, 5, 6, or 8 . . . . . . **2**	-0-	

Step 2. List your other charitable contributions made during the year.

3.	Enter your contributions to 50% limit organizations. (Include contributions of capital gain property if you reduced the property's fair market value. Do not include contributions of capital gain property deducted at fair market value.) **Do not** include any contributions you entered on line 1 or 2 . . . . **3**	2,000	
4.	Enter your contributions to 50% limit organizations of capital gain property deducted at fair market value **4**	28,000	
5.	Enter your contributions (other than of capital gain property) to qualified organizations that are not 50% limit organizations **5**	5,000	
6.	Enter your contributions "for the use of" any qualified organization. (But do not enter here any amount that must be entered on line 8.) **6**	-0-	
7.	Add lines 5 and 6 . . . . **7**	5,000	
8.	Enter your contributions of capital gain property to or for the use of any qualified organization. (But do not enter here any amount entered on line 3 or 4) **8**	-0-	

Step 3. Figure your deduction for the year and your carryover to the next year.

9.	Enter your adjusted gross income **9**	50,000	
10.	Multiply line 9 by 0.5. This is your 50% limit. **10**	25,000	

			Carryover
	Contributions to 50% limit organizations		
11.	Enter the smaller of line 3 or line 10 . . . . **11**	2,000	
12.	Subtract line 11 from line 3 . . . . **12**		-0-
13.	Subtract line 11 from line 10 . . . . **13**	23,000	
	Contributions not to 50% limit organizations		
14.	Add lines 3 and 4 . . . . **14**	30,000	
15.	Multiply line 9 by 0.3. This is your 30% limit. **15**	15,000	
16.	Subtract line 14 from line 10 . . . . **16**	-0-	
17.	Enter the smallest of line 7, 15, or 16 . . . . **17**	-0-	
18.	Subtract line 17 from line 7 . . . . **18**		5,000
19.	Subtract line 17 from line 15 . . . . **19**	15,000	
	Contributions of capital gain property to 50% limit organizations		
20.	Enter the smallest of line 4, 13, or 15 . . . . **20**	15,000	
21.	Subtract line 20 from line 4 . . . . **21**		13,000
22.	Subtract line 17 from line 16 . . . . **22**	-0-	
23.	Subtract line 20 from line 15 . . . . **23**	-0-	
	Other contributions of capital gain property		
24.	Multiply line 9 by 0.2. This is your 20% limit **24**	10,000	
25.	Enter the smallest of line 8, 19, 22, 23, or 24 . . . . **25**	-0-	
26.	Subtract line 25 from line 8 . . . . **26**		-0-
27.	Add lines 11, 17, 20, and 25 . . . . **27**	17,000	
28.	Subtract line 27 from line 10 . . . . **28**	8,000	
29.	Enter the smaller of line 2 or line 28 . . . . **29**	-0-	
30.	Subtract line 29 from line 2 . . . . **30**		-0-
31.	Subtract line 27 from line 9 . . . . **31**	33,000	
32.	Enter the smaller of line 1 or line 31 . . . . **32**	-0-	
33.	Add lines 27, 29, and 32. Enter the total here and on Schedule A (Form 1040), line 16 or line 17, whichever is appropriate **33**	17,000	
34.	Subtract line 32 from line 1 . . . . **34**		-0-
35.	Add lines 12, 18, 21, 26, 30, and 34. Carry this amount forward to Schedule A (Form 1040) next year **35**		18,000

Carryover

If your contributions in any category exceed your deduction limit for that category, then you may carry over your excess deduction for up to five years.

The carryover amount will be subject to the same deduction limit in the carryover year as it was in the current year. In other words, if you have excess contributions to a 30% limit organization, the excess will be subject to the 30% of AGI limit in later years, as well.

In future years, all contributions for the current year are deducted first, including current year contributions subject to the 50%, 30%, and 20% of AGI limits. After deducting current year contributions, if the various deduction limits have not been exceeded, you may deduct carryover amounts in the order described above (in the section "Computing Your Deduction Limit").

Education

Tax Benefits in This Chapter

☐ **Are you going back to school?**
  - You may be eligible for a Lifetime Learning Credit or a higher education expense deduction.

☐ **Will you be enrolling as a freshman or sophomore in college?**
  - You may be eligible for a Hope Credit.

☐ **Are you paying interest on a student loan?**
  - You may be able to deduct up to $2,500 per year in interest payments.

☐ **Are you saving money for your own education?**
  - If you put funds in a Section 529 plan account, you won't have to pay tax on withdrawals you use for certain education expenses.

When you turned eighteen, did you tell everyone within earshot that you would never set foot in a classroom again? Was your education something you were eager to finish and get behind you? Or are you one of those people who could never quite get enough of school, taking classes and learning new skills throughout your adult life?

Whether or not you've seen the inside of a classroom since your teen years, you have certainly continued your education in some fashion or another through school, work training, or hobbies. And now, if you are like many retirees, your plans for this phase of your life probably include spending some time learning subjects or skills you bypassed earlier. Maybe you would like to take up a new trade, like carpentry, and you need some training. Or you might be headed off to college for the first time, or back to college for a second degree.

If you are ready to spend some of your hard-earned free time hitting the books, you are probably highly motivated. And Congress would like to offer you its support and encouragement as well, through tax incentives. Whether you are taking a course or two or enrolling in a degree or certificate program, you'll likely find a tax benefit that fits your circumstances.

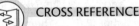 CROSS REFERENCE

Tax benefits for funding someone else's education. The focus of this chapter is on tax benefits that are available to you for your own educational endeavors. But if you are providing financial assistance for the education of your children, grandchildren, or other relatives or friends, you will want to read Chapter 10, which contains information about tax benefits that are available to you when you pay the education expenses of others.

Tax Strategy: Should You Use Retirement Account Funds to Pay Education Expenses?

Have your "financial advisors"—your know-it-all neighbor, for example—told you that there's a great tax benefit available to you if you use IRA funds to pay education expenses? And has your imagination turned that benefit into "tax-free withdrawals to pay for education?" Beware your active imagination. There is no such benefit.

Here are the facts: Whenever you take money out of your retirement account, you must pay tax on it (unless you are withdrawing after-tax money, or nondeductible contributions, you deposited earlier). With a few exceptions, your retirement funds should be the last resource you turn to when you need cash. Generally, you will want to leave the funds in your IRA to grow tax-deferred for as long as possible.

The common misconception about using IRA funds for education probably comes from the rules on paying penalties—which you don't have to worry about any more, as long as you are at least 59½ years old. If you are younger and are subject to early distribution penalties when you withdraw money from your IRA or other retirement plan, a special exception allows you to avoid the penalty if you use the funds to pay education expenses. However, you still have to pay income tax on the money you withdraw; it's only the early distribution penalty that is waived. If you are retired and older than 59½, the penalty doesn't apply to you no matter what you use the money for, so this benefit doesn't help you.

Tuition and Fees

Whether you enroll in a degree or certificate program or simply take a few courses, you might have at least two tax benefits from which to choose: a Lifetime Learning Credit or a higher education expense deduction. And, if you are enrolled in a college degree program as a freshman or sophomore, you might also be eligible for a third type of benefit, the Hope Credit. But here's the catch: You may claim only one of these three benefits in any given year, even if you qualify for more than one. In subsequent years, you may again use the credit or deduction for which you qualify. However, you may claim the Hope Credit only twice for the same student.

Lifetime Learning Credit

The Lifetime Learning Credit allows you to claim a credit—a dollar-for-dollar offset of your income tax liability—for a portion of the tuition and fees that you pay for postsecondary coursework, up to a credit limit of $2,000 per year. The course or courses you take must satisfy both of the following requirements:

- The course must be offered by an "eligible educational institution," which generally means an accredited public, nonprofit, or proprietary (private for-profit) postsecondary institution.
- You must be enrolled in an undergraduate degree program, a graduate degree program, or a nondegree program directed toward improving job skills or acquiring new ones. However, you are not required to be a full-time or half-time student. You may take a single course if you like. (Sports or hobby-related courses do not qualify.)

Calculating Your Credit

You may claim 20% of your eligible expenses (tuition and required fees) up to a maximum credit of $2,000. Eligible expenses must be reduced by any tax-free scholarships and grants you receive. When computing your credit, you may also include qualified expenses incurred by your spouse and your dependents, but the total credit may not exceed $2,000 for the year.

 TIP

Choose the optimum tax benefit for each eligible student.
If you and your spouse both paid tuition and fees, you are not required to use the same tax benefit. For example, if your spouse qualifies for the Hope

Credit and you qualify for the Lifetime Learning Credit, you may claim the Hope Credit for your spouse's expenses and the Lifetime Learning Credit for your expenses. (See "Hope Credit," below, for information about how to qualify for the Hope Credit and the separate dollar limits that apply.)

The IRS generally doesn't permit you to claim a credit or deduction for payments you make in the current year for services you will receive in a future year. However, there is an exception for tuition payments. You may claim a tax benefit in the current year if your payment is for a term that begins no later than the end of the third month of the next calendar year—that is, by the end of March of the following year.

Credit Phase-Out for Higher-Income Filers

If your income exceeds a certain level, you won't be allowed to claim the full credit. Instead, the portion you can claim decreases as your income increases. In 2008, if you are single, the phase-out begins when your modified adjusted gross income reaches $48,000 and the credit is completely wiped out when your income reaches $58,000. If you are married filing a joint return, the phase-out range is $96,000 to $116,000. (For most people, "modified adjusted gross income" is the same as adjusted gross income. The most significant modification requires that you add back earnings from overseas employment that you were permitted to exclude from U.S. taxation, if any.)

If your income falls within the phase-out range, you must complete Part III of IRS Form 8863, *Education Credits (Hope and Lifetime Learning Credits)*, to compute your reduced credit. That section of the form looks like this:

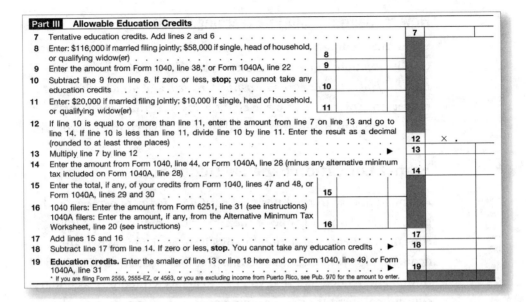

	Part III	**Allowable Education Credits**				
7	Tentative education credits. Add lines 2 and 6			**7**		
8	Enter: $116,000 if married filing jointly; $58,000 if single, head of household, or qualifying widow(er)	**8**				
9	Enter the amount from Form 1040, line 38,* or Form 1040A, line 22 .	**9**				
10	Subtract line 9 from line 8. If zero or less, **stop;** you cannot take any education credits	**10**				
11	Enter: $20,000 if married filing jointly; $10,000 if single, head of household, or qualifying widow(er)	**11**				
12	If line 10 is equal to or more than line 11, enter the amount from line 7 on line 13 and go to line 14. If line 10 is less than line 11, divide line 10 by line 11. Enter the result as a decimal (rounded to at least three places) . . . . ▶			**12**	× .	
13	Multiply line 7 by line 12			**13**		
14	Enter the amount from Form 1040, line 44, or Form 1040A, line 28 (minus any alternative minimum tax included on Form 1040A, line 28)			**14**		
15	Enter the total, if any, of your credits from Form 1040, lines 47 and 48, or Form 1040A, lines 29 and 30	**15**				
16	1040 filers: Enter the amount from Form 6251, line 31 (see instructions) 1040A filers: Enter the amount, if any, from the Alternative Minimum Tax Worksheet, line 20 (see instructions)	**16**				
17	Add lines 15 and 16			**17**		
18	Subtract line 17 from line 14. If zero or less, **stop.** You cannot take any education credits . ▶			**18**		
19	**Education credits.** Enter the smaller of line 13 or line 18 here and on Form 1040, line 49, or Form 1040A, line 31 . . . . ▶			**19**		

* If you are filing Form 2555, 2555-EZ, or 4563, or you are excluding income from Puerto Rico, see Pub. 970 for the amount to enter.

EXAMPLE: After retiring from a 35-year career in the insurance industry, you decide to begin your retirement by going to law school. During 2008, you racked up tuition and fees totaling $9,000. Your maximum Lifetime Learning Credit is the smaller of $2,000 or 20% of your expenses. Because 20% of $9,000 is only $1,800, that amount is your maximum credit. However, because you and your spouse have adjusted gross income for the year of $100,000, your maximum credit of $1,800 will be limited. To compute the reduced credit, you complete Part III of Form 8863 as follows to arrive at the reduced credit amount of $1,440.

	Part III	**Allowable Education Credits**				
7	Tentative education credits. Add lines 2 and 6			**7**	1,800	
8	Enter: $116,000 if married filing jointly; $58,000 if single, head of household, or qualifying widow(er)	**8**	116,000			
9	Enter the amount from Form 1040, line 38,* or Form 1040A, line 22 .	**9**	100,000			
10	Subtract line 9 from line 8. If zero or less, **stop;** you cannot take any education credits	**10**	16,000			
11	Enter: $20,000 if married filing jointly; $10,000 if single, head of household, or qualifying widow(er)	**11**	20,000			
12	If line 10 is equal to or more than line 11, enter the amount from line 7 on line 13 and go to line 14. If line 10 is less than line 11, divide line 10 by line 11. Enter the result as a decimal (rounded to at least three places) . . . . ▶			**12**	× .800	
13	Multiply line 7 by line 12 . . . . ▶			**13**	1,440	

How to Claim the Lifetime Learning Credit

Claim the credit on the second page of Form 1040, in the "Tax and Credits" section. You must also complete Form 8863, *Education Credits (Hope and Lifetime Learning Credits)*, and attach it to your tax return. You may claim the credit every year that you incur qualified expenses and are enrolled in an eligible course or program.

Higher Education Expense Deduction

As an alternative to the Lifetime Learning Credit (remember, each person may claim only one of the education credits or the higher education expense deduction in any given year), you may claim a deduction for your education costs. You may deduct the qualified tuition and related fees that you pay to an accredited postsecondary educational institution. Qualifying courses and expenses are the same as they are for the Lifetime Learning Credit.

A quick note on terminology: The section of the tax code that governs this deduction is titled "Qualified Tuition and Related Expenses." However, the deduction is often referred to as the "Higher Education Expense Deduction" to avoid confusing it with "Qualified Tuition Programs," also known as college savings plans or Section 529 plans. For clarity, we'll refer to it as the higher education expense deduction as well.

Although this benefit is a deduction, rather than a more valuable credit, it is an "above-the-line" deduction, which means that you subtract it when calculating your adjusted gross income (AGI). These deductions tend to be more valuable than "itemized deductions" (those you claim on Schedule A, after computing your AGI) for two important reasons. First, you may claim above-the-line deductions even if you do not itemize your deductions (and instead claim the standard deduction). Second, above-the-line deductions reduce your adjusted gross income, which is used to determine your eligibility for a number of other credits and deductions. With a lower AGI, you might qualify for tax benefits that are phased out for higher-income taxpayers.

Calculating Your Deduction

If you are married filing a joint return, and your modified AGI is $130,000 or less, you may claim a deduction for the tuition and fees you paid during the year up to a maximum of $4,000. You may also include any amounts you paid on behalf of your spouse and your dependents, but the total deduction—for everyone's expenses combined—still has an upper limit of $4,000. If your income exceeds $130,000 but is no more than $160,000, your deduction is capped at $2,000.

If you are single, the corresponding income levels are $65,000 (for a deduction of up to $4,000) and $80,000 (for a deduction of up to $2,000).

Your qualified expenses are the same as for the Lifetime Learning Credit, explained above. And, as you must for the Lifetime Learning Credit, you must subtract any tax-free scholarships and grants that you (or your spouse or dependents, if you are claiming their expenses as well) received during the year to come up with your qualified expenses.

> ## Tax Strategy: Should You Choose the Lifetime Learning Credit or the Higher Education Expense Deduction?
>
> As explained above, each eligible student must choose either the Lifetime Learning Credit or the higher education expense deduction (or the Hope credit, if you qualify)—you can't claim both. If you qualify for both, which is more advantageous?
>
> For many taxpayers, the Lifetime Learning Credit will provide greater benefits. Credits are generally more valuable than deductions, because they directly reduce your tax liability rather than reducing the income on which you must pay tax (like a deduction). If your marginal tax rate is 25%, for example, each dollar you deduct saves you 25 cents in taxes, while each dollar you claim as a credit saves you a dollar in taxes.
>
> However, you might find that you qualify for the higher education expense deduction when you don't qualify for the Lifetime Learning Credit. That's because the income level at which you become ineligible for the deduction is higher than it is for the credit. If you qualify for both, you should calculate your tax liability with each to see which provides the greater benefit.

How to Claim the Higher Education Expense Deduction

Claim the deduction on the first page of Form 1040, in the "Adjusted Gross Income" section.

Hope Credit

If you were just too busy to go to college when you were 18 and you decided to save that pleasure for your retirement years, you might be able to take advantage of yet another education tax credit. The Hope Credit is a third alternative to the Lifetime Learning Credit and the higher education expense deduction. (Again, you may claim only one of these three tax benefits.)

Qualified expenses and eligible institutions are the same for the Hope Credit as for the Lifetime Learning Credit and the higher education expense deduction. And, eligibility for the Hope Credit is subject to the same income phase-out that applies to the Lifetime Learning Credit. However, it's a bit more difficult to qualify for the Hope Credit than for either the Lifetime Learning Credit or the higher education expense deduction, because you must meet all of the following additional requirements for the Hope Credit:

- You must be enrolled in one of the first two years of college (freshman or sophomore year).
- You must be enrolled in a degree program.
- You must be attending school at least half-time.
- You may claim the credit in only two tax years.

EXAMPLE: You enroll as a college freshman in September 2008 and claim a Hope Credit on your tax return for that year. In January 2009, you decide to take a year off. You drop out of school before completing your freshman year. In January 2010, you enroll again and finish your freshman year, after which you decide to take another break. You claim a Hope Credit on your tax return for 2010. Because you have now claimed the Hope Credit on two separate tax returns, you may not claim it again, even if you enroll later as a sophomore. Of course, you might still qualify for either the Lifetime Learning Credit or the higher education expense deduction, either of which can be claimed for as many years as you qualify.

Calculating Your Credit

The Hope Credit differs from the Lifetime Learning Credit and the higher education expense deduction in that the maximum benefit is applied per person, not per family. For 2008, the maximum Hope Credit is $1,800 per qualified individual. So, for example, if you and your spouse both qualify, you may claim up to $3,600 in Hope Credits.

For each qualified individual, you may claim 100% of the first $1,200 of tuition and fees, and 50% of the remaining qualified expenses up to $1,200 of additional expenses, for a maximum credit of $1,800.

> **EXAMPLE:** You paid $1,800 worth of tuition and fees for the year and you qualify to claim the Hope Credit. Your maximum credit amount is $1,500: 100% of the first $1,200, plus 50% of the remaining $600.

Credit Phase-Out for Higher-Income Filers

Once you compute your maximum credit, you must determine whether you can claim the full amount. The phase-out ranges for the Hope Credit are identical to those for the Lifetime Learning Credit, explained above. If your income falls within the phase-out range, you must compute the reduced credit on IRS Form 8863, *Education Credits (Hope and Lifetime Learning Credits)*.

How to Claim the Hope Credit

Claim the credit on the second page of Form 1040, in the "Tax and Credits" section. You must also complete Form 8863 and attach it to your tax return.

Student Loan Interest

If you are really serious about getting your degree, you might decide to apply for a student loan to make it happen. Taking on new debt during retirement probably isn't a terribly appealing idea, but at least you might be able to deduct the interest. The maximum deduction is $2,500. And there's more good news: This deduction, like the higher education deduction, is claimed above the line.

Your student loan interest is deductible if you (and the loan) satisfy all of the following requirements:

- You must be enrolled at least half time.
- You must be enrolled in a degree or certificate program.

- The loan proceeds must be used to pay qualified higher education expenses. (You may include expenses you pay on behalf of your spouse or your dependents, as well, but the maximum deduction is still limited to $2,500.) Qualified expenses include tuition and fees, room and board, books, equipment, and even transportation. However, you must reduce your qualified expenses by any tax-free scholarships or other tax-free assistance you receive.
- The loan may not be from a relative.
- The loan may not be from a qualified retirement plan (such as a 401(k) plan).
- The interest must not be deductible under another provision of the tax code. For example, if you obtain a home equity loan and use the proceeds to pay for your education, you must deduct the interest as home mortgage interest rather than as student loan interest.
- The entire proceeds of the loan must be used for education. For example, you may not deduct any interest on the loan if you spend some of the funds on your education and the rest on a new car.
- You may not claim the deduction if another taxpayer claims you as a dependent.

Deduction Phase-Out for Higher-Income Taxpayers

The maximum deduction of $2,500 is gradually phased out when your modified adjusted gross income exceeds a certain level. For 2007, the phase-out range for single filers is between $55,000 and $70,000. If you're married and filing a joint return, the phase-out range is $110,000 to $140,000.

The IRS provides a worksheet (see below) to help you calculate how much interest you can deduct if your income falls within the phase-out range. This worksheet is part of the instruction booklet for Form 1040.

Student Loan Interest Deduction Worksheet—Line 33   *Keep for Your Records*

Before you begin: ✓   Figure any write-in adjustments to be entered on the dotted line next to line 36 (see the instructions for line 36 on page 31).
                        ✓   Be sure you have read the **Exception** above to see if you can use this worksheet instead of Pub. 970 to figure your deduction.

1. Enter the total interest you paid in 2007 on qualified student loans (see above). **Do not** enter more than $2,500 **1.** _____

2. Enter the amount from Form 1040, line 22 . . . . **2.** _____

3. Enter the total of the amounts from Form 1040, lines 23 through 32, plus any write-in adjustments you entered on the dotted line next to line 36 . . . . **3.** _____

4. Subtract line 3 from line 2 . . . . **4.** _____

5. Enter the amount shown below for your filing status.
   • Single, head of household, or qualifying widow(er)—$55,000   ⎫
   • Married filing jointly—$110,000   ⎬ . . . . **5.** _____
                                                                     ⎭

6. Is the amount on line 4 more than the amount on line 5?
   ☐ **No.**   Skip lines 6 and 7, enter -0- on line 8, and go to line 9.
   ☐ **Yes.** Subtract line 5 from line 4 . . . . **6.** _____

7. Divide line 6 by $15,000 ($30,000 if married filing jointly). Enter the result as a decimal (rounded to at least three places). If the result is 1.000 or more, enter 1.000 . . . . **7.** _____ . _____

8. Multiply line 1 by line 7 . . . . **8.** _____

9. **Student loan interest deduction.** Subtract line 8 from line 1. Enter the result here and on Form 1040, line 33. **Do not** include this amount in figuring any other deduction on your return (such as on Schedule A, C, E, etc.) . . . . **9.** _____

How to Claim the Student Loan Interest Deduction

Once you have used the IRS worksheet to calculate your deduction (if you are subject to a reduction), you claim the deduction on the first page of Form 1040, in the "Adjusted Gross Income" section.

Section 529 Plans

Section 529 plans (named after the section of the tax code that permits them) have become wildly popular, even though taxpayers can't deduct or claim a credit for contributions to these plans. The plans, also known as Qualified Tuition Programs, offer a variety of other benefits that appeal to middle-income and wealthy taxpayers alike, in part because of the estate planning and wealth transfer opportunities they provide.

The most common variety of 529 plan allows you to establish an account for any beneficiary you choose (including yourself) and make nondeductible contributions up to a maximum per beneficiary. The maximum varies by state; typically, the cap is several hundred thousand dollars. You may make the entire contribution in one year or contribute smaller amounts over a period of years.

> **CAUTION**
>
> **Unless you're the beneficiary, contributions are subject to the usual gift tax rules.** As you may know, you must file a gift tax return if you give more than $12,000 (for 2008) to any one person in a single year. This limit applies to contributions you make to a 529 plan for another person as well: If you contribute more than $12,000, you will need to file a gift tax return. For more information about paying for someone else's education, see Chapter 10; see Chapter 11 for information on gifts. Of course, if you're the beneficiary of the plan, you don't need to worry about gift tax.

The tax benefits surface when it comes time to pay for college. The beneficiary of the account—the student—doesn't have to pay tax on distributions that are used to pay qualified education expenses. In other words, a 529 account can grow completely tax-free; neither the contributor nor the beneficiary will have to pay tax on the interest your money earns, as long as the funds are used for qualified expenses. Of course, if you set up a 529 account for your own education, those benefits are yours to enjoy.

Types of 529 Plans

The tax code provides for two different types of 529 plans: prepaid tuition programs and savings programs. Prepaid tuition programs must be sponsored by either a state government or by a private institution. Savings programs may be sponsored only by a state government.

> **RESOURCE**
>
> **Your state might not sponsor both types of plans.** Although the tax code allows all states to offer both types of 529 plans, not every state does. To find out about the options available through your state, check your state's website: www.[your state's postal code, such as MN or CA].gov. You can also check the Saving For College website, www.savingforcollege.com.

Prepaid Tuition Program

If you choose a prepaid tuition program, you typically purchase "tuition credits" for future education, usually at a particular institution. For example, you may purchase one semester's tuition credit today to be used when you start attending the state university after you retire in a few years. That credit will be good for one semester's worth of education regardless of how much tuition costs have risen by the time you're ready to head back to school.

Savings Plan

If you choose a savings plan instead of a prepaid tuition plan, you may contribute any amount at any time, up to a maximum contribution. The funds in the account are invested and, when you go to college, the entire account will be available to you for educational expenses.

Tax Strategy: Which Type of 529 Plan Should You Choose?

One of the difficult decisions you must make is whether to select a prepaid tuition program or a savings plan. Unfortunately, there is no easy answer. Prepaid tuition programs purport to give you some protection against future tuition increases. But on the flip side, prepaid programs typically cover tuition only, not other fees. Furthermore, your prepayment typically can be used only at specified institutions—not just any school you (or the beneficiary) might choose when the time comes.

Savings plans permit funds to be used for a broad range of expenses. And because this type of plan is an investment account, you might be able to build up a sizable nest egg for yourself or your student beneficiary if the investments do well. On the other hand, if the returns are not as high as you hoped, the account's funds might not be adequate to pay for all of the beneficiary's college expenses.

Beneficiaries

Although you may set up 529 plan accounts for as many different beneficiaries as you like, each account must name only one beneficiary. The beneficiary, or prospective student, is the person who will be using the account to pay for his or her own postsecondary education.

The beneficiary must be a person (as opposed to an entity like a trust, for example), but anyone, including you, will qualify. There are no age or income restrictions.

At this point, you might be wondering what happens if you decide not to go back to school after all. Or, in a best-case scenario, what happens if you finish school without using up all of the money in the account? The answer is that you may change the beneficiary on the account at any time, as long as all of the following conditions are met:

- The new beneficiary must be a member of the former beneficiary's (your) family. For this purpose, a family member includes the beneficiary's:
  - spouse
  - child (or child's descendant)
  - stepsons and stepdaughters
  - siblings, half-siblings, and step-siblings
  - father, mother, and the ancestors of either
  - stepmother and stepfather
  - niece, nephew, uncle, aunt, or the spouse of any of them
  - son-in-law, daughter-in-law, mother-in-law, father-in-law, brother-in-law, sister-in-law, or the spouse of any of them, and
  - first cousin (but not the first cousin's spouse).
- If the funds are moved to a different 529 plan account, the funds must be deposited in the new account within 60 days of removing them from the old account.
- If the new beneficiary is at least one generation younger than you (the former beneficiary), the transfer is deemed to be a gift from you to the new beneficiary, and all the regular gift tax rules would apply. (See Chapter 11 for more about gifts.)

Contributors

Any adult person, regardless of income, may contribute to a 529 plan for any given beneficiary. Contributions from entities, such as a trust or an estate, are also permitted. Minors (unless they are emancipated) may not contribute to a 529 plan, although a guardian or custodian for the minor might be able to make contributions on a minor beneficiary's behalf.

Contributions

You may not deduct contributions you make to a Section 529 plan on your federal tax return. However, most states now offer an income tax deduction to residents who contribute to a plan sponsored by that state.

Each state-sponsored plan establishes its own contribution limit per beneficiary, and the rules for contributions can vary from state to state.

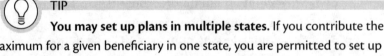

TIP
You may set up plans in multiple states. If you contribute the maximum for a given beneficiary in one state, you are permitted to set up another account in a different state for the same beneficiary and contribute up to the new state's maximum dollar amount for that beneficiary.

Here are some common restrictions imposed by state plans:
- Contributions must be in cash. This is true in every state.
- Although the maximum contribution varies by state, contribution limits are generally several hundred thousand dollars (per beneficiary).
- If a state plan permits multiple contributors to a single account (some states do not), the maximum contribution applies to the beneficiary, not the contributor. For example, if the state sets a maximum contribution of $200,000 for a given beneficiary,

any number of individuals may contribute to that beneficiary's account, but the total of all contributions may not exceed $200,000. If a beneficiary has multiple 529 plan accounts, the combined contributions to all accounts may not exceed $200,000.

- Account maximums are often based on a formula that takes into account the age of the beneficiary, the estimated cost of completing college, estimates of tuition increases, and estimates of investment returns.

Tax Strategy: Should You Use Your State's Plan or an Out-of-State Plan?

You are not required to contribute to a 529 plan that is sponsored by the state where you live (or where your student beneficiary lives, if you are setting up an account for someone else's education). However, it might be to your advantage to contribute to your own state's plan, particularly if it offers an income tax deduction for contributions by residents.

If the state income tax deduction is not a consideration, you might prefer an out-of-state plan simply because you like the investment opportunities offered by the plan or because the plan has unusually low expenses. Here are a couple of websites specifically designed to help you compare plans: www.savingforcollege.com and www.collegesavings.org.

Distributions

When it comes time to use 529 plan funds for your postsecondary education, each distribution of funds will be tax-free, as long as both of the following conditions are met:

- You must be attending a postsecondary institution that meets the all of following requirements:
  - The institution is accredited.

- It offers an AA degree, a bachelor's degree, a graduate degree, or a credential. (Certain vocational and proprietary (private, for-profit) institutions qualify as well.)
- The institution is eligible for the Department of Education's student aid programs.
- The distribution must be used to pay qualified education expenses, which include:
  - tuition and fees required for enrollment
  - books and supplies
  - equipment, and
  - room and board (but only if you are at least a half-time student).

CAUTION

You may not claim a Hope or Lifetime Learning Credit for expenses paid with 529 plan funds. You may claim a Hope or a Lifetime Learning Credit in the same year you use 529 plan funds to pay education expenses, as long as you don't claim a credit for expenses that you actually paid with 529 plan funds. Similarly, you may not claim a higher education expense deduction for expenses you paid with funds from your 529 plan.

If There's Money Left Over

If you decide to cancel a 529 plan account you have established, either because you have graduated or for some other reason, you may take a distribution of the remaining funds. There are some tax consequences, however.

If you distribute the remaining funds but do not use them to pay your education expenses, you must pay income tax plus a 10% penalty on the portion of the distribution that is attributable to investment earnings.

If you die, the remaining funds are included in your estate, and the estate (or your heirs) will be liable for the income tax on the distributed funds.

> **TIP**
>
> **Roll over funds to a new 529 plan with a new beneficiary.** If there's still money in the account when you finish college, you may name a new beneficiary, rather than canceling the account and paying taxes and penalties on the remaining funds. If you decide to change the beneficiary, you have only 60 days after taking a distribution of the funds to set up the new account and deposit the funds.

If Your Account Loses Money

You might be unlucky enough to have a poorly performing 529 plan: one for which the total distributions are less than your total contributions. If you're in this situation (and we hope you're not), you may claim a loss. However, you may not claim a loss until the year the funds in the account are completely distributed.

You must claim the loss as a miscellaneous itemized deduction on Schedule A. The loss will be deductible only if you itemize deductions, and only to the extent that this loss plus certain other miscellaneous itemized deductions exceeds 2% of your adjusted gross income.

> **EXAMPLE:** You have contributed $50,000 to your 529 plan. You paid a total of $45,000 out of the account for your qualified expenses. Now, you're finished with school, and you decide to cancel the account this year and take a distribution of the rest of the money. The remaining account balance is $2,800.
>
> You have a loss of $2,200. Although you started with $50,000, you took out only $45,000 plus $2,800 for a total of $47,800. ($50,000 − $47,800 = $2,200.) If you itemize your deductions, you may claim that loss on Schedule A of your current year's tax return.

How to Claim Deductions
Associated With 529 Plans

Because contributions to your 529 plan are not deductible, you are not required to report them on your federal income tax return. However, if your state permits a deduction for state income tax purposes, you must claim the deduction as prescribed by your state taxing authority. Check the instructions for your state income tax return.

If the total of all of your distributions from your 529 plan account exceeds all of your contributions, you may claim a loss on Schedule A, in the "Job Expenses and Certain Miscellaneous Deductions" section. Use the line labeled "Other Expenses" and note on your tax return that the expense is a 529 plan account loss.

Investments

Tax Benefits in This Chapter

☐ **Do you pay an accountant or tax preparer to prepare your tax return?**
   • You may claim the cost as a miscellaneous itemized deduction.

☐ **Do you have an advisor who manages your investment portfolio?**
   • The fee you pay is deductible as a miscellaneous itemized deduction.

☐ **Have you borrowed money to invest in stock, bonds, or other investments?**
   • The interest you pay on that loan might be fully deductible if you have enough investment income.

☐ **Have you purchased bonds this year?**
   • You may be able to subtract accrued interest you paid to the previous holder of the bond when you calculate your taxable interest on Schedule B.

☐ **Have you paid taxes in another state?**
   • You might be able to claim a credit for those taxes on your tax return.

☐ **Have you invested in any foreign securities on which foreign taxes were withheld?**
   • You generally will have a choice between claiming a deduction or a credit for the foreign taxes you paid.

Now that you're retired, you might be paying more attention to your investments. Many retirees make some changes to their portfolios, to reflect changes in their income and lifestyle. And, after spending most of their work lives saving for retirement, most retirees begin living off their investments. You might even be spending some of your newfound free time taking a more active interest in managing your portfolio.

Keeping your financial affairs in order can be an expensive proposition. It seems like there are fees for everything. You pay an annual fee for the privilege of having a brokerage account, and perhaps a fee to an investment advisor. You pay a lawyer to put together an estate plan for you. Perhaps you pay an accountant to prepare your tax return or to give you tax advice. If you prepare your own return, then it is likely you purchase software each year to prepare the return and pay a fee to file it electronically.

As the old saying goes, it takes money to make money. And, as luck would have it, you can deduct at least a portion of what you spend to invest and manage your finances. The tax code allows you to deduct expenses you incur "for the production of income." You may also deduct expenses for "managing, conserving or maintaining property held for the production of income," which includes managing your various investments. And finally, you may deduct expenses in connection with "the determination, collection or refund of any tax."

Those categories of expenses might sound vague enough to be generous. However, IRS rulings and court cases have long since determined which of the most common investment expenses you may deduct and which you may not. This chapter explains the rules on deducting the costs of managing your money, including investment costs, portfolio management fees, tax preparation fees, and attorney fees. It also describes benefits that are available to help you avoid paying a double tax (to another state or another country) on your investment income.

> (!) CAUTION
>
> **Investment expenses are deductible only if you incur them in the production of taxable income.** Expenses allocable to the production of tax-exempt income are not deductible. For example, suppose you hire a portfolio manager to manage your investments. If your portfolio contains securities that generate taxable income as well as securities that generate tax-exempt income, you may deduct only the portion of the portfolio manager's fee that is allocable to the taxable income produced by the portfolio.

Investment Expenses That Qualify as Miscellaneous Itemized Deductions

The expenses covered in this section are categorized by the IRS as "miscellaneous itemized deductions subject to the 2% floor," which means you can deduct them only in part. Although businesses are permitted to deduct virtually all of their operating expenses, the government has traditionally been less generous to individuals. To keep the peace and still bring in revenue, Congress has enacted laws that allow individuals to deduct certain nonbusiness expenses, including some they incur when managing their finances. However, these expenses are not fully deductible: Because they are categorized as miscellaneous itemized deductions subject to the 2% floor, you can deduct them only to the extent they exceed 2% of your adjusted gross income.

> **EXAMPLE:** Your adjusted gross income (AGI) is $100,000, and you've spent a total of $4,500 on miscellaneous itemized deductions. However, you may deduct only $2,500, the amount by which your expenses ($4,500) exceed 2% of your AGI ($2,000).

CAUTION
High-income taxpayers may face further limits on their itemized deductions. Until tax year 2010, if your income exceeds a certain threshold, all of your itemized deductions will be subject to additional limits. For more information about the itemized deduction phase-out for high income taxpayers, see Chapter 1.

Tax Accounting and Legal Fees

Although tax preparation and tax planning fees are generally deductible as miscellaneous itemized deductions, estate planning fees and other legal fees might or might not be deductible, depending on the nature of the service your attorney provides.

Tax Preparation and Audits

The expenses you incur to compute your tax liability, prepare your return, and file it with the IRS are all deductible. If you hire a tax preparer, you may deduct the fee as well as the cost of phone calls and travel to and from your tax preparer's office.

If you prepare your own return, you may deduct the cost of any software and books you purchase to help you complete the forms. If you mail your return the old fashioned way, you may deduct the cost of postage. If you pay someone to electronically file your return, you may deduct that fee, as well. However, you may not deduct the convenience fees you must cough up for the privilege of paying your taxes with a credit card.

You may deduct tax preparation costs for all types of tax, whether they are imposed by the federal government or by state or local taxing authorities. That means you may deduct the cost of preparing state and local income taxes, fiduciary income tax returns (to pay tax on income generated by estates and trusts, for example), and federal gift and estate tax returns.

If the tax audit you dread becomes a reality, you may also deduct expenses related to the audit, from the cost of copying your records to the fees you pay an accountant or lawyer to fight the assessment of additional tax.

TIP

Allocate some tax preparation costs to your rental or your business. If you have rental property and report rental income and expenses on your tax return, you may deduct your costs for preparing that portion of your tax return as a rental expense on Schedule E. Similarly, if you report business income and expenses on Schedule C, you may deduct your costs for that part of the tax return as a business expense. (If you hire an accountant to prepare your return, ask for a breakdown of costs so you know how much to allocate to each category.) The advantage of dividing your expenses this way is that tax preparation costs associated with a rental or business are fully deductible; they aren't subject to the 2% rule explained above.

Tax Planning and Estate Planning

If you pay an accountant to give you tax advice, that fee is generally deductible as long as the advice is specific to your situation. For example, if you meet to discuss the tax ramifications of selling your rental property, the fees are deductible. But if you meet with your accountant just to obtain general information about how the tax system works, the IRS is likely to deny the deduction. Remember, you are permitted to deduct expenses related to managing or conserving the assets you currently own and using them to produce taxable income.

When it comes to estate planning, the same principles apply. You may deduct the fees you pay an attorney for tax-related work and advice. For example, if you pay your attorney to prepare a trust that will help you (or your heirs) save estate taxes, the related fees are deductible. But if your attorney simply prepares a will for you, the fee for that service is considered a nondeductible personal expense.

It can be tough to figure out how much of an attorney's or accountant's fee is related to tax advice. And if it's murky to you, you can be sure it will be murky to the IRS. If the IRS cannot determine how much of a fee is for tax advice, it will either disallow the deduction entirely or come up with its own allocation of the fee—one that's probably less advantageous to you than you'd like.

To avoid this problem, ask your attorney or accountant to provide a breakdown of his or her bill, showing the cost of services provided. Although having a detailed billing record doesn't ensure that the IRS will accept your allocation, the IRS usually gives such backup information great weight.

Other Attorney Fees

Of course, there are many other issues for which you might seek an attorney's advice. Even though it might seem to you that the attorney's services are directly related to managing or conserving your income-producing property, the IRS might not see it that way. Deductible attorney fees are more the exception than the rule.

For example, if you pay an attorney to help you purchase real estate, the expense is not deductible but instead is added to the basis of the property, which you use to figure out your depreciation deduction (if you rent the property out, for example) or your capital gain (if you sell the property). Attorney fees that relate to title, whether acquiring title in the first place or mediating or litigating a title dispute, are treated the same way.

To be deductible, attorney fees must be tied directly to the production of taxable income. For example, if an attorney helps you obtain Social Security benefits, the attorney fees are deductible only to the extent the Social Security benefits are taxable. If your income is low enough that you are able to exclude (not pay tax on) all of your Social Security benefits, then none of the attorney fees are deductible, either.

Over the years, there have been many cases dealing with the deductibility of attorney fees in a divorce proceeding. Although it might seem like the fees you pay a divorce attorney should be deductible because the attorney is helping you preserve your assets (by keeping them out of the hands of your former spouse), the IRS generally treats those fees as capital expenditures, which means you add them to the basis of the assets, as explained above. However, if you pay an attorney to advise you on the tax ramifications of a divorce-related property settlement, those fees are deductible. Also, if you hire an attorney to help you obtain alimony, that fee is deductible because it relates to generating taxable income for you. In contrast, if you hire an attorney to help you avoid paying alimony, the fees are not deductible.

To make sure you can provide documentation if the IRS challenges your attorney fee deductions, you should ask your attorney to provide a detailed bill.

 TIP

Use different attorneys for different services. Because an attorney's breakdown of time spent on various services can be somewhat arbitrary, the IRS would much prefer that you obtain different advice from different attorneys. For example, you should see a divorce attorney for your divorce and a tax attorney for tax advice. This way, you can deduct your entire fee from the tax attorney (and probably can't deduct anything you pay to the divorce lawyer).

Investment Expenses and Portfolio Management Fees

Most expenses that are directly related to your investments are deductible, with some exceptions discussed below. Like the expenses discussed above, these are miscellaneous itemized deductions, deductible only to the extent they exceed 2% of your AGI (see above). Bear in mind, too, that any money you spend to earn tax-exempt interest is not deductible—you can only deduct what you spend to create taxable income.

Deductible Investment Expenses

Here are some of the most common investment expenses you can deduct.

Investment Advisor Fees

If you pay an investment advisor to manage your portfolio, those fees are generally deductible, whether you pay a flat dollar amount or a percentage of the value of your portfolio.

> **CAUTION**
>
> **Commissions aren't deductible.** If your investment advisor does not charge you a flat fee or a percentage of your assets, but instead earns commissions when you purchase or sell securities, you may not deduct those commissions. Instead, you add them to your basis, which you use to calculate your taxable gain (if any) when you sell the securities.

However, if your portfolio contains assets that generate tax-exempt income, you must allocate a portion of the fee to those tax-exempt assets. That portion of the fee is not deductible. Unless you can trace particular expenses to the production of either taxable or tax-free income, you must use a "reasonable" method of allocation. If there is no direct link between an expense and the income produced, a reasonable approach, which also generally will give you a favorable result, is to allocate the fee based on the relative value of the taxable and tax-exempt assets in the portfolio.

> **EXAMPLE:** The total value of your investment portfolio is $100,000. Your investment advisor charges you $1,000 per year to manage your portfolio. Your portfolio contains $25,000 of tax-exempt municipal bonds; the remaining $75,000 is invested in stocks and taxable corporate bonds. To determine how much of your advisor's fee you can deduct, you must determine how much of the fee is allocable to taxable securities. Three-quarters of the portfolio is invested in taxable securities, so you may deduct three-quarters of the fee: $750.

IRA Account Fees

If you pay a fee to establish an IRA or other retirement plan account, those fees are deductible as long as they are paid from funds outside the IRA or plan. The same is true of annual maintenance fees. If you pay those fees with assets from the IRA, they are not deductible.

TIP

Pay IRA fees from a taxable account, not from your IRA. Unless you arrange to pay it separately, your annual IRA maintenance fee will probably be deducted automatically from the assets in your IRA. As convenient as that may be, there are two reasons to avoid it. First, the fee will not be deductible. As explained above, you may deduct IRA (or other account) fees only if they are paid with after-tax dollars (from a taxable account). Second, you will deplete your IRA account. Generally, you want to leave assets in your IRA for as long as possible, drawing on them only when you are required to (at age 70½) or when you need money for living expenses. If you pay your IRA fee from a taxable account, you can leave that much more in your IRA to grow tax deferred.

Other Account Fees

If you have a brokerage account or a securities account with a bank, you might be charged an annual fee. Generally, the fee covers such services as collecting interest and dividends on your behalf. Those fees are deductible only to the extent your account generates taxable income. If you hold tax-free investments in your account, you will have to allocate a portion of the service fee to your tax-exempt income. That portion of the fee is nondeductible.

Publications

Subscriptions to investment services or publications that provide you with information and advice about your investments are all deductible, as are books related to taxes and investments. The IRS has allowed deductions for subscriptions to such publications as the *Wall Street Journal, Barrons, Financial World, Fortune*, and even the *New York Times*. On the other hand, the IRS has denied deductions for subscriptions to *National Geographic, Reader's Digest,* and *Newsweek*, for lack of evidence that the publications had any significant relationship to generating taxable income.

Office Expenses

You may deduct the administrative cost of maintaining your investments. Such expenses might include the cost of a bookkeeper to help you track your investments, phone calls to your broker, and even travel to and from your broker's office. If you rent office space strictly to manage your investments, the equipment and supplies you purchase, as well as the office rent, are all deductible.

If you set up an office in your home, you may deduct what you pay for supplies, equipment, and phone calls. However, you may not deduct the cost of a home office. Even if you have a room that you use exclusively to work on your investments, you may not deduct a portion of your house expenses—such as mortgage, real estate taxes, and depreciation—as an investment expense.

It might seem inconsistent that you can deduct the expenses of an office outside the home but not one inside the home. However, the home office deduction is permitted only if you are engaged in a trade or business. If you are simply managing your retirement nest egg, you are not considered (by the IRS) to be engaged in a trade or business. Those same constraints do not apply to expenses related to an outside office.

If you purchase a computer to track your investments, and you use the computer for other personal activities as well, you may deduct only the portion of the cost that is allocable to investment use of the computer. For example, if you use your computer 30% of the time to manage your investments and the remainder of the time (70%) to watch YouTube videos, you may deduct only 30% of the cost of the computer as an investment-related expense.

Depreciating a Computer Used for Investment Purposes

Computers fall into a category that the IRS calls "listed property." Listed property includes assets that can easily be used for personal purposes as well as business or investment purposes. Because of the potential blurring of the lines between uses, deductions for listed property are subject to some additional restrictions. Most important, if you use the property at least 50% of the time for personal purposes (which includes using the computer for your investments), you are required to claim the business and investment portion of the cost through straight-line depreciation, instead of through an accelerated method that might allow you to recover your cost more quickly. (See Chapter 3 for more information about depreciation of listed property.)

On the other hand, if you use the computer more than 50% for your business (remember, this doesn't include managing your investments), then you may use accelerated depreciation

> EXAMPLE: You paid $2,000 for a computer, which you use 70% of the time in the consulting business that you run out of your home. You spend an additional 20% of your computer time managing your investments and the remaining 10% for personal entertainment. Business and investment use of your computer are both deductible. Consequently, 90% of the cost of the computer, or $1,800, is eligible for depreciation partly as a business expense and partly as an investment expense. Because you use the computer more than 50% of the time for business, you may claim accelerated depreciation. Once you compute the depreciation amount, you claim a portion of it as a business expense and a portion as an investment expense.

Safe Deposit Box Rental

Many people routinely claim a deduction for the annual fee they pay to rent a safe deposit box. However, the fee is deductible only to the extent that you use the box to store taxable securities or other income-producing assets (such as gold coins) and related documents. If the box is used for personal effects such as jewelry, or to store tax-exempt securities, the fee must be apportioned between personal and investment use. You may deduct only the portion of the fee that is allocable to taxable investments.

Travel

You may deduct travel costs that are linked directly to investments that generate taxable income. For example, travel to manage a rental property is deductible. (See Chapter 8 for details about which travel expenses qualify as a rental expense deduction.) You may also deduct the cost of traveling to meet with your broker, attorney, or accountant if the purpose of the meeting is to manage or obtain advice about your own personal investments.

Nondeductible Investment Expenses

Most of the time you will find it easy to distinguish between non-deductible personal expenses and deductible investment expenses. But a handful of investment-related expenses that might seem like they should be deductible sit firmly on the IRS's verboten list.

Tax-Exempt Securities

As mentioned previously, you may not deduct investment expenses allocable to the production of tax-exempt income. If you incur investment fees (such as portfolio management fees) related to a portfolio that contains both taxable and tax-exempt securities, the safest course of action is to ask to be billed separately for the taxable and tax-free portfolios. Alternatively, you might ask for a clear allocation on the bill. If all else fails, you can allocate the fee according to the amount of income generated by taxable and tax-exempt securities.

Home Office

As mentioned in "Office Expenses," above, if you maintain an office in your home to manage your investments, you may deduct only your direct expenses (such as postage, telephone calls, and supplies). You may not deduct a portion of the expenses you pay to maintain your home (such as real estate taxes, mortgage interest, and depreciation), as you could if you used your home office for a business.

Investment Seminars

You may not deduct the cost of attending an investment seminar. None of these expenses—from tuition to travel and accommodations—are deductible as an investment expense. The IRS's rationale for excluding investment seminars is that the information is general, not specific to you and your investments. Rail against the rationale if you must, but the issue is settled as far as the IRS is concerned.

Stockholder Meetings

You may not deduct the cost of attending stockholder meetings, at least in most cases. However, if you can demonstrate that you attended a meeting in order to bring about a policy change that would directly affect the value of your own investments, you might be able to defend a deduction for travel expenses.

How to Claim Miscellaneous Itemized Deductions

Claim these deductions on Schedule A, in the "Job Expenses and Certain Miscellaneous Deductions" section. Remember, you may claim the above miscellaneous itemized deductions only if, and to the extent that, all of your miscellaneous deductions (those that are subject to the 2% floor) together add up to more than 2% of your adjusted gross income. If you claim the standard deduction instead of itemizing your deductions on Schedule A, you may not claim these expenses on your tax return.

Casualty and Theft Losses

By the time you reach retirement, your portfolio of diversified investments might include some fine art or perhaps a coin collection you have built up over the years. The collection might be valuable enough that you would be devastated if it were damaged or stolen. Once you recovered from the shock of the calamity, you might wonder if you can recover some of your loss through tax benefits.

A casualty loss is one that results from a sudden, unexpected, and unusual event, such as a car accident, a fire, an earthquake, a hurricane or tornado, a flood, or an act of vandalism. A theft loss is even easier to define. The item must actually have been stolen from you by another person, intentionally. If you simply lost the item, you do not have a theft loss.

Casualty and theft losses are treated differently for tax purposes, depending on the type of property that was lost and how the property was used. For purposes of identifying the appropriate tax treatment for the casualty, property is generally divided into two categories: (1) personal use property, and (2) business or income-producing property. Your investment assets fall into the category of income-producing property.

Total Amount of Loss

When you experience a casualty or theft loss of investment assets, you may claim a deduction for the loss on your tax return, but it might not be precisely the amount you expect. Your loss is either the amount by which the property declined in value (the value immediately before the casualty or theft reduced by the value immediately after) or your basis, whichever amount is smaller. (For information on calculating your basis, see Chapter 1.)

If you experienced a total loss of the property—for example, a valuable painting was destroyed in a fire—then your loss is deemed to be the basis of the property. This is true even if the fair market value of the property was less than your basis just before the loss.

Once you determine the amount of the loss, you might need to make some additional adjustments to arrive at the deductible amount.

Deductible Amount of Loss

Your investment casualty or theft loss must be reduced by any reimbursement you receive from insurance or from any other source. The result, after reductions for reimbursement, is the amount you may deduct on your tax return.

Although you claim casualty losses on Schedule A as itemized deductions, they are not subject to the 2% floor. As long as you itemize your deductions, you are permitted to deduct the full amount of your loss, less any reimbursement you receive.

In addition, if your income is high enough that your itemized deductions are subject to a phase-out, you may exclude your casualty loss when computing this additional reduction. (See Chapter 1 for more information about the itemized deduction phase-out.)

How to Report an Investment Casualty or Theft Loss

If you have an investment-related casualty or theft loss, you must complete IRS Form 4684, *Casualties and Thefts,* and attach it to your tax return for the year of the casualty or theft. If you expect to receive insurance reimbursement for the casualty or theft loss, then you claim the loss in the year you receive the insurance recovery. You claim the loss itself on Schedule A, on the line "Other Miscellaneous Deductions." In the space provided on that line, you must identify the deduction as a "casualty loss." If the loss is to rental real estate that you own, you must also complete IRS Form 4797, *Sales of Business Property,* and attach it to your tax return.

Casualty Loss of Personal-Use Property

If you suffered a loss not to investment or business property, but to personal-use property, such as jewelry, an iPod, or similar items, the loss is deductible on Schedule A (on the "Casualty and Theft Losses" line), but you may not deduct the full amount of your loss. In fact, your deduction is limited in several ways.

First, your loss is limited to the lower of your basis or the fair market value of the property just before your loss. And that's just your starting point: You must reduce the loss by any insurance recovery. Next, you reduce the loss by an additional $100, and finally, reduce the result by 10% of your adjusted gross income. If you still have a loss after all of those calculations, you may deduct that amount.

If you were reimbursed for your entire loss by an insurance company or any other source, you may not claim a deduction. And, if the insurance or other recovery you receive exceeds the loss you incurred, you might have to report the excess as taxable income.

Although the deduction for this type of loss is restricted by the above rules, there's also some good news: The deduction isn't subject to the 2% floor, nor to the phase-out of itemized deductions that applies to high-income taxpayers (covered in Chapter 1).

You claim a casualty loss of personal property on Schedule A, on the line "Casualty and Theft Losses" (this line is only for personal-use property, not real estate, business property, or investment property). You must also complete IRS Form 4684 and submit it with your tax return.

Investment Interest Expense Deduction

Your neighbor has given you a hot stock tip, and you're eager to invest. The only problem is, you don't have the cash. If you borrow money to purchase the stock, can you deduct the interest you pay on that loan?

In general, the interest you pay on a loan used to purchase or carry investments—or more specifically, to purchase "property held for investment"—is deductible as investment interest. There's even a separate line for it on Schedule A of your tax return. But, as usual, certain exceptions and restrictions might prevent you from deducting as much as you might expect; for one thing, you may not deduct more than your net income from your investments. This section explains how to calculate your investment income and expenses, and then use those amounts to calculate your investment interest expense deduction.

Investment Interest Expense

You incur investment interest expense whenever you borrow money to purchase securities or other investments. For example, if you have a margin account with your broker, you might borrow against the securities in your account to purchase additional securities. The interest you pay on such a loan is margin interest, which is generally deductible as investment interest. Even if you borrow money from a friend or family member, the interest on the loan is deductible as investment interest as long as you use the money to purchase investments.

However, you may not be able to deduct all of the interest you pay in a year. When you tally up your deductible investment interest expense, you may not include interest on any portion of a loan that is used to purchase or carry any of the following investments:

- **Tax-exempt securities.** You may deduct interest only on the portion of the loan used to purchase taxable securities.
- **Straddles.** A straddle is an investment strategy involving options. In a straddle, the investor purchases both a put—an option that pays off if the value of the underlying stock goes down—and a call—which pays off if the value of the stock goes up. An investor's profit is based on how much the price of the underlying stock changes, regardless of whether the price rises or falls. In general, interest expense on the purchase

of straddles is not deductible as interest expense. However, there are certain esoteric exceptions. If you are involved with straddles or you are planning to invest in them, you should confer with an expert to become familiar with the potential tax ramifications.

- **First or second home.** Qualified home mortgage interest (as described in Chapter 2) is not considered investment interest.
- **Passive activities.** If you use loan proceeds in a passive activity, and the interest on the loan is taken into account when calculating your income (or loss) from that activity, the interest is not deductible as investment interest. Passive activities include rental real estate, a limited partnership, or an S corporation in which you invest but don't materially participate. This rule simply prevents you from double dipping. For example, if you own rental property (which is considered a passive activity), the mortgage interest you pay is deductible as a rental expense on Schedule E (see Chapter 8), not investment interest on Schedule A.

Once you have determined how much of the interest you pay qualifies as investment interest, you need to determine how much of it is actually deductible. Your investment interest deduction is limited to your net investment income; in other words, you can't deduct more than you earn. Net investment income is your total taxable investment income, reduced by all of your investment expenses (except investment interest expense).

Investment Income

In today's complex financial world, an individual might receive income from a variety of sources, including stocks and bonds, limited partnerships, businesses, and a plethora of esoteric vehicles that most people know nothing about. Some of the income these money-generating enterprises produce qualifies as investment income for tax purposes, but some does not. To further complicate matters, you may elect to treat certain types of income as investment income, if doing so would give you a tax benefit.

What Qualifies as Investment Income

Here are the most common types of investment income:

- **Interest.** If your investments generate interest, it qualifies as investment income.

- **Nonqualified dividends.** Nonqualified dividends are those that are taxed at ordinary income tax rates (as opposed to "qualified" dividends, which are eligible for special capital gains tax rates). Dividends you receive from most domestic corporations are qualified dividends, as long as you satisfy holding period requirements. Your qualified dividends are reported to you on Form 1099-DIV, *Dividends and Distributions*, at tax time. (For more information about qualified dividends, see IRS Publication 17, *Your Federal Income Tax*.) In some situations, you may elect to include qualified dividends and long-term capital gains in investment income (generally, you have a long-term capital gain if you sell stock or other investment assets that you have held for more than one year); see "Income You May Elect to Include," below, for more information.

- **Annuity income.** Annuity income is investment income if the annuity is not connected with your employment. For example, if you are receiving annuity payments from an employer's retirement plan, those annuity payments are not considered investment income. However, if you purchased a commercial annuity from an insurance company—perhaps a single-premium tax-deferred annuity—as an investment independent of your prior or current employment, the income from that annuity qualifies as investment income.

- **Royalty income.** Similarly, royalty income counts as investment income only if the source of the royalties is not your business. For example, if you receive royalties from a book you wrote or a film you produced, the royalties are considered compensation for employment, not investment income. But if you invest in a limited partnership and receive a share of royalty payments for use of patents or copyrights, that is generally investment income.

- **Certain short-term capital gains.** If you have a net short-term capital gain, meaning your short-term capital gains are greater than your short-term capital losses, then the net short-term gain is treated as investment income, but only if you have a net gain when you tally all capital gains and losses—both short-term and long-term. For information on including long-term capital gains in investment income, see "Income You May Elect to Include," below.

EXAMPLE 1: For the current year, you have long-term capital gains of $10,000, short-term capital gains of $15,000 and short-term capital losses of $8,000. To include your net short-term capital gains in investment income, both of the following must be true:

- Your short-term capital gains must exceed your short-term losses.
- You must have a net gain when you combine all of your capital gains and losses (both long- and short-term).

You satisfy the first condition because you have a net short-term capital gain of $7,000 ($15,000 – $8,000). You satisfy the second condition because you have a total net gain of $17,000 ($10,000 + $15,000 – $8,000). Because you satisfy both conditions, your short-term capital gain of $7,000 is included in investment income for purposes of determining how much investment interest expense you may deduct.

EXAMPLE 2: For the current year, you have a long-term capital loss of $10,000 and a short-term capital gain of $7,000. Because you have a net loss when you combine short-term and long-term gains and losses, you may not include the short-term gain in investment income for purposes of determining how much investment interest expense you may deduct.

Income You May Elect to Include

Although long-term capital gains and qualified dividends are not considered investment income, you may choose to include some or all of that income in your investment income total for purposes of determining how much investment interest you may deduct. If you elect to treat long-term capital gains and qualified dividends as investment income, however, those gains and dividends will not be eligible for special tax rates. They will be taxed as ordinary income. You may have the favorable rates or the additional deduction, but not both.

If you elect to include only part of your long-term capital gains and qualified dividends in your investment income total, then only the amount you elect to include will be taxed at ordinary rates. The remainder will still be eligible for long-term capital gains tax rates.

To qualify to make any election with respect to your capital gains transactions, however, you must have a net gain when you combine all short- and long-term capital gains and losses. In Example 1, above, the short-term gain of $7,000 is automatically included in investment income. If you make the election to include all of your net capital gain, you may include the additional $10,000 of long-term capital gain.

Why would you make the election to include long-term capital gains and qualified dividends if you would lose the favorable rates? Because you might be able to deduct more investment interest, which in turn might result in lower overall tax liability for you than if you had used capital gains rates. You will almost certainly need to calculate your tax liability both ways to see which makes more sense for you.

What Doesn't Qualify as Investment Income

You may not treat any of the following items as investment income for purposes of calculating your investment interest expense deduction:

- tax-exempt income
- business income, or
- income from passive activities. The most common passive activities in investor portfolios are rental real estate, limited partnerships, and the occasional passive investment in an S corporation.

> **TIP**
>
> **If your passive activity generates investment income.** Many limited partnerships and other entities in which you are a passive investor might have portfolios of their own that generate interest and dividends. Some of that portfolio income might be passed through to you. (If so, it is reported on a Schedule K-1, which you receive at tax time.) That income also qualifies as investment income. However, if the limited partnership generates income from other sources, such as business income or passive income (for example, from rental real estate), that income is not treated as investment income for purposes of computing your investment interest expense deduction.

Once you have determined your total investment income, you must subtract your investment expenses to arrive at your net investment income.

Investment Expenses

Your investment expenses are those described in "Investment Expenses and Portfolio Management Fees," above. Because investment expenses on Schedule A are miscellaneous itemized deductions subject to the 2% of AGI floor, you might not be required to use the full amount of your investment expenses to arrive at net investment income. Instead, your investment expense (for purposes of determining net investment income) is the smaller of:

- the investment expenses included on the line "Other Expenses" in the "Job Expenses and Other Miscellaneous Deductions" section on Schedule A, or

- the total amount reported on the last line of the section "Job Expenses and Certain Miscellaneous Deductions" on Schedule A. (The amount on that line is all of your miscellaneous itemized deductions reduced by 2% of your AGI.)

EXAMPLE: You listed $4,000 of investment expenses on the line "Other Expenses" in the "Job Expenses and Other Miscellaneous Deductions" section of Schedule A. However, on the last line of the "Job Expenses and Certain Miscellaneous Deductions" section on Schedule A, you listed only $3,500. That number represents the total of all of your miscellaneous itemized deductions reduced by 2% of your AGI. Therefore, your investment expenses are deemed to be $3,500 for purposes of calculating your net investment income.

Net Investment Income

Net investment income is your total investment income less your investment expenses (as described above). Net investment income sets the limit on how much investment interest expense you may deduct. If your investment interest expense exceeds your net investment income, you may carry over the excess to the following year. You may continue to carry over any unused amounts until you have deducted the full amount.

EXAMPLE: Your wheeling and dealing in your brokerage account resulted in total margin interest of $5,500 for the year. You had no other investment interest expense. However, your net investment income for the year was only $4,500. You may deduct only $4,500 of your margin interest for the year. You may carry over the remaining $1,000 and deduct it in a future year when you have the investment income to cover it.

How to Claim a Deduction for Investment Interest

You claim the deductible amount of your investment interest on Schedule A, on the line "Investment Interest." You must also complete and file IRS Form 4952, *Investment Interest Expense Deduction*, unless *all* of the following are true:

- Your investment income from interest and nonqualified dividends alone exceeds your investment interest expense.
- You do not have any deductible investment expenses (other than investment interest expense).
- You do not have any investment interest expense from a previous year that you have carried over to the current year.

If you want to treat some or all of your long-term capital gains or qualified dividends as investment income (for the reasons explained in "Income You May Elect to Include," above), you must make the election on Form 4952 and attach it to your tax return. On the form, you indicate how much of your long-term gain or qualified dividends you would like to include. You are not required to include all of it.

If all of the conditions listed above apply and you are not electing to treat any long-term capital gains or qualified dividends as investment income, you are not required to complete Form 4952. You can simply enter your investment interest expense on the "Investment Interest" line of Schedule A.

Accrued Interest

If you invest in corporate bonds, don't overlook your deduction for any accrued interest you might have paid to the bond's previous owner. You can subtract that amount from the total interest on which you have to pay tax.

What Is Accrued Interest?

Accrued interest works like this: When you purchase a bond, you earn interest from the day you acquire it. However, bond interest is typically paid on a quarterly or semiannual basis, not daily. That payment includes interest for the entire period and is paid to the current owner of the bond.

Because of this payment schedule, some of the interest you receive might not belong to you. For example, let's say you purchase a bond on April 1 and that bond pays interest on January 1 and July 1 of each year. When you receive your July payment, a portion of the interest you receive rightfully belongs to the person who owned the bond between January 1 and April 1.

To solve this problem, you are required to purchase the interest from the previous owner when you buy the bond. That means you must pony up the cost of the bond plus the amount of interest that accrued between January 1 and April 1—the amount that was earned by but not paid to the previous owner. Come July, you will receive an interest payment that includes all interest earned from January 1. You may keep all of it because you already paid the previous owner his or her share.

At the end of the year, you will receive a tax statement reporting the amount of interest you earned on your new bond. However, that statement will include the interest you paid to the previous owner. Because you are required to report the full amount of the interest payment on Schedule B of your tax return, you can claim a deduction for the interest you paid to the previous owner, so you don't pay tax on money you never received.

How to Claim a Deduction for Accrued Interest

The tax forms do not include a separate line for an accrued interest deduction. Instead, on part 1, line 1 of Schedule B, *Interest and Ordinary Dividends*, you must list the full amount of interest income reported to you. Then, as your final entry on line 1, write "Accrued

Interest" and enter as a negative number the interest you paid to the previous owner of the bond. When you total your entries for line one, be sure to treat that final item as a subtraction.

Taxes Paid to Other States

Occasionally, you might need to file a nonresident tax return in another state. Once you are retired, this is most likely to happen if you hold rental property in another state. However, it might also happen if you receive income from an investment in a limited partnership or another entity that is doing business in another state.

If you do pay taxes to another state, those taxes are deductible on Schedule A as "State and Local Taxes."

Foreign Taxes

If you have a diversified portfolio, some of your funds are probably invested in foreign securities. You might invest in these securities directly or perhaps through a mutual fund that invests some or all of its assets globally.

Occasionally, taxes are withheld from your account and paid to foreign countries on your behalf. Those amounts are foreign income taxes you owe for investment income you received from your foreign investments. However, the United States also taxes that income. To ease the pain of a double tax, the tax code allows you to claim either a deduction or a credit for the foreign taxes you pay. You may choose the benefit that provides you with the greater tax reduction. But, as is the case with most tax benefits, your credit or deduction might be limited or even eliminated altogether under certain circumstances.

TIP
You may be entitled to a foreign tax credit or deduction for other types of income. Although this chapter covers investment income, there are other kinds of income on which you might owe tax to another

country. For example, if you are working or doing business in a foreign country, you might have wages or business income from which foreign taxes were withheld. The rules for claiming a foreign tax credit or deduction are much the same, regardless of the type of income.

Credit

In the best-case scenario, the foreign tax credit will directly offset your tax liability. For example, if you paid foreign taxes (on foreign-source dividends you received) in the amount of $150, you might be able to reduce your overall tax liability by $150. (You may take a credit only for amounts that were taxed in the United States; otherwise, you have no double taxation to offset with a credit.)

However, you might encounter some roadblocks. The first potential problem is the source of your foreign income. If your foreign income came from a country on the U.S. Government's list of "countries that engage in terrorist activities," you may not claim a credit for any taxes paid to that country. The list changes from time to time, but currently looks like this:

- Cuba
- Iran
- North Korea
- Sudan
- Syria
- Libya (but only for income taxes paid or accrued on or before December 9, 2004).

If your income didn't come from any of these countries, you must next check to see whether your credit is limited. The general rule is that your foreign tax credit should offset only the amount of your tax liability that is allocable to foreign-source income.

For example, suppose you have taxable income of $50,000, which includes $5,000 of dividends from a French stock in which you have invested. Your total federal income tax liability is $1,000. During the tax year, France withheld $500 (U.S.) to cover French tax. Because your foreign-source income represents only one-tenth of your taxable income, you would not be permitted to claim a credit of $500 because it would offset 50% of your tax liability—a disproportionate amount.

Figuring out precisely how much of a foreign tax credit you may claim is fairly complicated. The fine points of the calculation can be found in the voluminous instructions for IRS Form 1116, *Foreign Tax Credit (Individual, Estate, or Trust)*, on which you calculate your allowable credit.

Now for some good news: Relief from these complex calculations comes in the form of a *de minimus* rule. Under that rule, you may elect to *not* file Form 1116 and in effect be exempt from the credit limitations. To be eligible to make this election, all of the following must be true:

- All of your foreign-source income must be qualified passive income. Passive income for this purpose generally includes interest, dividends, royalties, rental income, annuities, and gain from the sale of investment property.
- All of your foreign income and foreign taxes must be reported on a Form 1099, Schedule K-1, or equivalent substitute statements.
- Your creditable foreign taxes must total $300 or less ($600 if you are married filing a joint return).

If you make the election, you are not required to file Form 1116. However, if you are unable to use all of your foreign tax credit (which is limited to your tax liability), you are not permitted to carry back or carry over the unused portion of the credit, as you would if you filed Form 1116.

Deduction

As an alternative to the foreign tax credit, you may claim a deduction for all of the foreign taxes you paid during the year. And, although taxes paid on income from countries that appear on the federal government's terror list (above) are not creditable, you may nonetheless claim a deduction for those taxes, provided you are not claiming a credit for any other foreign taxes paid. (You may claim either a foreign tax credit or a foreign tax deduction in any given year, but not both.)

Also, for deduction purposes, you can include foreign taxes you paid on interest income that is exempt from U.S. income tax.

Tax Strategy: Should You Claim a Credit or Deduction?

Assuming that your foreign-source income does not come from a country on the federal terror list, you must decide whether to claim the credit or the deduction. In general, a credit will provide the bigger benefit because:

- The credit provides a dollar for dollar offset of your tax liability, but a deduction simply reduces the amount of income subject to tax.
- You may claim the credit whether or not you itemize your deductions, but the deduction is not available to you if you claim the standard deduction.
- You may take advantage of unused credits by claiming them in the prior year or by carrying them forward for up to ten years until they are used up.

On the other hand, a deduction might provide a greater benefit if the foreign tax rate is high and the ratio of your foreign income to your U.S. income is low. In any case, you should compute your tax liability once with the credit and again with the deduction to determine which provides the greater benefit.

In any given year, you may claim either a credit or a deduction for foreign taxes, but not both. In other words, if you claim any foreign tax credit at all, even if you are unable to claim all of the foreign taxes you paid, you are barred from claiming a deduction in the same year for the remainder.

How to Claim a Foreign Tax Credit or Deduction

To claim a foreign tax credit, complete Form 1116 to calculate your allowable credit. You can then claim that amount on the second page of Form 1040, in the "Tax and Credits" section. There is a separate line for the Foreign Tax Credit. You must also attach Form 1116 to your tax return.

To make the election to claim *de minimis* foreign taxes without filing Form 1116, you simply claim the credit on the appropriate line of Form 1040 (in the "Tax and Credits" section on the line "Foreign Tax Credit").

To claim a foreign tax deduction, enter the amount of foreign taxes you paid during the year on Schedule A, in the "Taxes You Paid" section. Enter the deduction on the line "Other Taxes" and indicate that the source of your number is "foreign taxes paid." You may deduct foreign taxes only if you are itemizing your deductions instead of claiming the standard deduction.

Your Rental Property or Vacation Home

Tax Benefits in This Chapter

☐ **Do you own rental property?**
- You may deduct many expenses associated with the rental.
- You may claim a depreciation deduction based on the value of the building.
- If all of your deductions exceed your rental income, you might be able to claim the resulting loss (up to $25,000) against other income to reduce your tax bill.

☐ **Do you own a second home?**
- You may deduct mortgage interest and real estate taxes, as you do for your principal residence.
- If you pay points to obtain the loan, you may deduct a portion of them each year.

☐ **Do you own a vacation home that you use part of the year and rent out part of the year?**
- You may offset certain rental-related expenses against rental income.
- If you treat the property as a second home, you might be able to deduct all of the mortgage interest and real estate taxes.

As you enter your retirement years, you may be the proud owner of more than one home. Perhaps you've recently downsized to smaller digs, but have decided to rent out your previous home rather than sell it. Maybe you've purchased a second home in a location that's closer to your grandchildren. Or, you might have spent some of your nest egg on a vacation home in a tropical paradise where winters aren't so harsh.

No matter what type of real estate you own, your enjoyment of the property will certainly be enhanced if you know that you are taking advantage of all the tax benefits to which you are entitled. Chapter 2 explains the unique benefits available to you if you own your principal residence: the home you live in most of the time. The deductions available to you for other types of property—rental property, vacation homes, and second homes—are covered in this chapter.

Sorting out these tax benefits can be a bit complicated. The deductions available to you are not the same for every type of property you own. Instead, the deductions you may claim depend on how you use the property. The tax code distinguishes between rental property, property that is part rental and part residence (usually called a "vacation home"), and property that serves as your own alternative residence and is not rented out to others (usually called a "second home").

 **SKIP AHEAD**

If you don't own more than one piece of real estate. This chapter explains the deductions available for homes you own but don't live in most (or any) of the time. If you don't own a second home or any rental real estate, skip ahead to Chapter 9.

Rental Property

Some retirees own rental property: property that they don't live in for any part of the year, but instead rent out (or offer for rent) 100% of the time. You might have purchased the rental to add some real estate to your investment portfolio or to generate rental income to live on during your retirement years. Or, you might have become a landlord by happenstance. For example, you might have moved into a bigger and better home and decided to rent out your previous home rather than go to the trouble of selling it. And now, lo and behold, you are a landlord and your property is producing income for you.

Because your rental property produces taxable income in the form of rent, you will want to be sure to deduct all the applicable expenses of operating, repairing, and improving the rental. Claiming all of the deductions available to you will help you offset the taxable rental income—and, most likely, your tax liability, as well.

There are three basic ways that you can recover some of the costs associated with the purchase and maintenance of rental property. Some of the costs are deductible as current-year expenses, other costs must be recovered through depreciation, and still others through amortization. (Unfortunately, some costs cannot be recovered at all; see "Nondeductible Expenses," below, for more information.)

- **Deductible expenses.** Certain expenses are deductible in the year you pay them. You report those expenses on a rental schedule (Schedule E, *Supplemental Income and Losses*), which you submit with your tax return. Many of the day-to-day costs of maintaining your property are deductible; see "Deductible Rental Expenses," below, for more information.

- **Depreciable expenses.** The cost of the house itself (but not the land), as well as improvements you make later (such as renovating or upgrading the rental), are depreciable. Although you are permitted to claim a deduction for the cost of the house on your rental schedule, you may not deduct the entire cost in one year. Instead, you must recover the cost a little bit at a time, over a period of years. (See "Depreciation," below, for more information.)

- **Amortizable expenses.** Costs associated with obtaining or refinancing a loan are also recovered over a number of years—specifically, over the term of the loan. Such expenses might include loan points, underwriting fees, appraisal fees, mortgage broker fees, assumption fees, credit reports, and other costs charged by the lender. (See "Amortization," below, for more information.)

RESOURCE

Want more information on deductions for rental property? Take a look at *Every Landlord's Tax Deduction Guide*, by Stephen Fishman (Nolo). It's full of information, strategies, and tips that will help you take full advantage of the deductions available to landlords.

Rental Income

Of course, your income from a rental includes the rent your tenants pay. But other, less obvious, items are treated as rental income, as well. For example, if your rental agreement allows tenants to pay for repairs they make to the property and then deduct the expense from their rent, you must report the entire amount (the rent they actually paid you plus the amount they deducted for expenses) as rental income. You may deduct the amount the tenant didn't pay you— that is, the cost of the repairs—as a rental expense on Schedule E.

Certain types of income might seem to qualify as rental income, but in fact they don't. Suppose, for example, that you maintain a bank account where you keep money to use for rental expenses. The interest (if any) you earn on those funds is *not* considered rental income. Instead, it is treated as personal interest, which you must report on Schedule B, *Interest and Ordinary Dividends*, along with interest and dividends from your other personal accounts.

Are Security Deposits Income?

Most landlords require tenants to pay a security deposit. If a tenant damages the rental or fails to pay rent, the landlord can use the security deposit to cover these costs.

If the security deposit (or a portion of it) is earmarked as "last-month's rent" when you first receive it from the tenant, you must report that portion as rental income for the tax year in which you initially receive the deposit.

A security deposit is not taxable income to you if it's refundable, however. Most security deposits are returned to tenants when they move out, as long as they leave the rental in good condition. If you must withhold some of the security deposit to pay for damage the tenant caused or to cover unpaid rent, then you must report the amount you withheld as income to you in the year it becomes nonrefundable to the tenant (that is, the year you make the decision to keep some or all of the deposit).

If you retain some or all of the security deposit when a tenant leaves, it generally won't result in any additional tax liability. For example, if you withhold money to pay the rent, it won't change your overall net income from the property: The total amount of rent paid remains the same, whether you received it directly from the tenant or indirectly from the security deposit. If you withhold money to make repairs, you can deduct those costs on Schedule E. In that way, you offset the additional income with additional expenses. Of course, if you use the money to make a capital improvement (instead of a repair), it's not quite a wash because you recover the cost of the capital improvement gradually through depreciation.

Deductible Rental Expenses

You can deduct almost everything you spend to maintain your rental property. This section describes the most common types of rental expenses. You will find a space for most of them on Schedule

E. If you have expenses that don't fit neatly into the categories listed on Schedule E, you may list them separately on the line labeled "Other."

Common Deductions

You may deduct many of the costs of operating and maintaining your rental property in the year you spend the money. If you start renting out property you once used as a residence, you may start claiming these deductions from the day you first make the property available to rent—that is, the day the home is "placed in service" as a rental property. If you purchase property specifically to use as a rental, some of these costs—such as insurance or prorated property taxes—might appear on your settlement papers.

Here are some of the many costs you may deduct.

Advertising. If you advertise a vacancy in order to find a tenant, the cost is deductible.

Cleaning and maintenance. You may deduct the cost of a housekeeper or janitorial service, a gardener, a chimney sweep, pest control, trash pickup, and similar services required to keep the property clean and in good order.

Commissions. If you pay a commission to a broker for helping you rent your property, you may deduct that cost. However, if the lease lasts for more than one year and you pay the entire commission up front, you will probably have to amortize the commission.

Homeowners' association dues. If you pay dues to a homeowners' association for your rental property, those dues are deductible.

Insurance. Insurance expenses might include premiums for theft, fire, or other hazard insurance.

Legal and other professional fees. Professional fees might include fees you pay an attorney to draw up a rental contract or the portion of your tax preparation fee that went toward preparing Schedule E and related forms for your tax return.

Management fees. Some people who own rental property turn over all of the management responsibilities to another person or a professional property management company. The fees you pay for that service are deductible rental expenses.

Mortgage interest. If you obtain a loan to purchase your rental, the interest on the loan is a deductible rental expense. Similarly, if you convert your own home to a rental, the interest you pay on the mortgage is still deductible, but now it's deductible as a rental expense, which you should report along with your other rental expenses on Schedule E. You should *not* report mortgage interest related to your rental on Schedule A, *Itemized Deductions*. Only mortgage interest related to your principal residence and second home is reported on Schedule A.

Other interest. If you obtain a loan to pay expenses related to your rental, you may deduct the interest as a rental expense. This is true even if the loan is not secured by the property, as long as you can show that you used the loan proceeds to pay rental expenses.

Painting and decorating. You can deduct the costs of sprucing up your rental in the year you pay them. For example, if you hire someone to repaint the interior of your house, that expense is deductible.

Supplies. Supplies that you purchase to help you manage or maintain the rental are deductible. For example, you might keep light bulbs and cleaning supplies on hand to use as needed.

Taxes. Real estate tax assessed on your rental property is deductible in the year you pay the tax. If you have to pay income tax or a business tax for the privilege of offering a property for rent in the city in which the rental is located, you may deduct those taxes, too.

Utilities. If you, rather than your tenant, pay the electric or other utility bills for the rental property, you may deduct those expenses.

Deducting the Cost of Repairs and Improvements

It can be difficult for landlords to decide how to fit their rental expenses into the categories listed on Schedule E. In most cases, it probably doesn't matter much where you list an expense. For example, if you can't decide whether an expense belongs under "supplies" or "maintenance," you can make your best guess or list it separately under "other." The tax result will be the same.

However, you must be more careful when trying to distinguish between a "repair" and an "improvement," which are treated differently for tax purposes. You are entitled to deduct the full cost of repairs in the year you pay for them. However, if the work done on your property is actually an improvement rather than a repair, you may not deduct the full cost that year. Instead, you must recover the cost a little bit at a time over the expected life of the property that was improved. Generally, you don't need to figure out for yourself how long your property will last; the IRS provides charts showing the expected life of various types of property. (See "Depreciation," below, for information about determining the amount you may deduct each year.)

The distinction between a repair and an improvement is simple enough to state: An improvement increases the value of the property or prolongs its useful life, while a repair simply keeps the property in good working order. That distinction seems clear, but gray areas abound. For example, replacing a carpet, furnace, or a hot water heater might seem like a repair. After all, those replacements are necessary from time to time to keep the property in good working order. For the most part, however, the IRS views replacements, as well as structural changes, as improvements that extend the life of the property.

In contrast, repairs simply halt the property's deterioration. For example, suppose your rental has termite damage that costs thousands of dollars to repair. Can you deduct all of it as a repair in the year you fix it? Probably so, unless repair work actually improves the property rather than returning it to its previous condition. For example, perhaps you had to tear up your linoleum to make repairs, but then decided to upgrade the flooring to hardwood. In that case, the entire job is considered an improvement.

Typical Repairs and Improvements

Although it can be tough to determine whether certain types of work qualify as repairs or improvements, there are some jobs that the IRS has already passed judgment on:

Repairs include:

- filling a hole with drywall
- replacing a broken door or window
- fixing leaks, and
- repairing a fence.

Improvements include:

- remodeling
- upgrading single-pane to double-pane windows
- replacing the roof
- installing a sprinkler system
- replacing appliances, and
- installing new flooring.

Deducting Travel Expenses

You may deduct travel expenses related to maintaining your rental. For example, you might need to travel to the property to show it to prospective tenants, collect rent, or do some maintenance or repair work. The rules for deducting these expenses differ depending on whether you travel locally or out of town.

Local Travel

If you travel by bus, cab, or train to handle work relating to your rental, you may deduct the cost of the trip. But if you drive your car (as many local landlords do), computing your deductible expense becomes quite a bit more complicated. There are two ways to calculate the amount you may deduct for using your car: (1) you may keep careful records and claim your actual expenses; or (2) you may use the standard mileage rate. Generally, you may choose the method that is most beneficial to you. However, many taxpayers use the standard rate simply to avoid the tedium of keeping track of every dollar they spend.

Option 1: Actual expenses. If you choose to keep track of your actual vehicle expenses, you may deduct only those expenses that are related to your rental, of course. No matter how much rental property you own, you probably don't have a vehicle that you use only for your work as a landlord. That's why you must allocate the cost of maintaining and operating your car between rental and personal use. To make that allocation, you must keep track of how much the car was used for each purpose (typically, by recording the number of miles traveled). For example, if you drove 10,000 miles during the year and you put 2,000 of those miles on the car while driving to and from your rental property, then the expenses of operating and maintaining the car would be allocated 20% to the rental and 80% to personal use.

In addition to keeping track of your mileage, you will need to keep track of other car-related expenses, such as:

- auto loan interest
- gasoline
- repairs
- insurance
- oil and lube or other maintenance
- tires
- license and registration fees
- lease payments (if you are leasing your car), and
- depreciation, if you own your car (see "Depreciation" and "Amortization," below, for information on the special rules that apply to depreciation deductions for your car).

All of those expenses must be allocated between rental and personal use. However, expenses that are directly related to managing your rental are fully deductible. For example, if you must pay tolls or parking fees when you travel to the rental, those expenses are fully deductible as rental-related travel expenses.

Option 2: **Standard mileage rate.** Although using the actual expense method often results in a larger deduction, it requires you to keep good records of all of your car expenses, in addition to keeping track of your mileage. Too often, "keeping good records" is something that, at tax time, you berate yourself for not having done. Or, maybe you decided that the tax savings aren't worth the additional effort. When you choose to use the standard mileage rate to compute your deduction, you need only keep a log of the miles you travel to maintain your rental property. Each year, the IRS provides the amount you may deduct for each mile traveled. For 2008, that number is 50.5 cents per mile for the first half of the year, and 58.5 cents per mile for the second (starting on July 1, 2008). (You can find the mileage rate for the current year by going to www.irs.gov and searching for "standard mileage rates.")

To use the standard mileage rate, you must meet these two conditions:

- You must have used the standard mileage rate (instead of deducting your actual expenses) in the first year you used your car in your rental business. If you used actual expenses the first year, you are stuck with that method for as long as you use that car for your rental business. On the other hand, if you used the standard mileage rate the first year, you generally may choose either method in the years that follow.

> CAUTION
>
> **Depreciation gets more complicated if you change methods.**
> If you switch back and forth between deducting actual expenses and using
> the standard mileage rate, you must make adjustments to your depreciation
> calculations each time you switch back to the actual expense method. See
> IRS Publication 463, *Travel, Entertainment, Gift, and Car Expenses,* for more
> information.

- You must not have claimed depreciation on the car in the past and used a depreciation method other than straight line. (See "Depreciation," below, for more on this and other depreciation methods.)

There are several other somewhat esoteric conditions that might disqualify you from using the standard mileage rate. For a summary of those conditions, see IRS Publication 463, *Travel, Entertainment, Gift, and Car Expenses.*

If you elect to use the standard mileage rate instead of your actual expenses, you simply multiply the number of miles you drove for rental-related business by the applicable rate (50.5 cents for the first half of 2008, and 58.5 cents for the second). The standard mileage rate has built into it most of the costs of using your car, such as gas, repairs, insurance, and depreciation. However, some expenses are *not* included in the standard mileage rate, such as parking and tolls related to your rental activity, personal property taxes you pay on the value of your car, and the business portion of your auto loan (if any). You may deduct those expenses as rental expenses, in addition to taking the standard mileage rate deduction.

Long-Distance Travel

If you must travel out of town to take care of rental business, you may be able to deduct your costs. The rules for claiming theses expenses depend on the purpose of your trip.

If the primary purpose of the trip is to manage or maintain your property and an insignificant portion of the trip is for personal pleasure, you may deduct the full cost of your travel and lodging, and 50% of what you spend on meals.

If the primary purpose is tending to your rental property but you spend more than 25% of your time on personal pursuits, you must allocate your travel expenses (including meals and lodging) between business and personal.

- If the primary purpose of your trip is personal, then you may not deduct the cost of the trip. For example, you own rental property in Tampa, Florida. You decide to go to Florida to spend two weeks hanging out on a beach on Sanibel Island. If you are thinking you can deduct the entire trip if you drive over to Tampa to take a peek at your rental property there, think again. If you had legitimate business (maybe you had to drive over there to fix the water heater), then you may deduct the cost of that trip—from Sanibel to Tampa and back.
- If the primary purpose of the trip is to make improvements to the rental property (instead of management or maintenance), the trip is not currently deductible. Instead, you must add your travel cost to the cost of the improvements themselves, then depreciate the total over the original life of the property. (See "Depreciation," below, for more information.)

Depreciation

The single largest expense you incur when you go into the rental business is the cost of the property itself. But just imagine how horrified Congress would be at the prospect of innumerable taxpayers claiming rental expense deductions in a single year for the full purchase price of their rental, to the tune of hundreds of thousands of dollars. To forestall such a nightmare, legislators created a system by which expensive items, such as real estate, and even less expensive items like appliances, landscaping, sewer systems, and the like, would be deductible, but not all in one year. The system, known as depreciation, allows the owner to recover those costs over the "expected life" of the property, deducting a bit each year until the entire cost has been deducted.

The prospect of having to compute a depreciation deduction strikes fear in the hearts of most taxpayers. There's some math involved, as well as tables and formulas. Once you understand the basics, however, depreciation isn't as daunting as it might seem at first. This section explains depreciation basics, including which property is subject to depreciation, how to calculate the value of your property for purposes of depreciation, and how much you can deduct each year.

> **RESOURCE**
>
> **For more information on depreciation.** This section provides an overview of the concept of depreciation. You will also find some detailed instructions for how to compute depreciation deductions for property (buildings, appliances, and so on) related to your rental. Although this information will help you with most issues you are likely to encounter, it isn't comprehensive. For more detailed information on depreciation, take a look at IRS Publication 946, *How to Depreciate Property*.

Property Subject to Depreciation

As explained above, you may deduct the full amount of certain rental expenses in the year you pay them. However, property that might be expected to last more than a year generally cannot be expensed. Instead, you must recover the cost through depreciation. Such property includes the rental building itself, improvements to the property, and certain types of personal property associated with the rental.

The rental property. When you claim a depreciation deduction for the rental property, you may claim a depreciation deduction only for the building, not the land on which it sits. Here's why: The depreciation deduction is based on the expected life of particular types of property, as determined by the IRS. Technically, expected life is a measure of wear and tear, exhaustion, or obsolescence. It is a bit of a murky concept, which is, according to the IRS, unrelated to the value of the asset itself. An item with an expected life—also known as it's "useful life"—of five years would be expected to have lost its usefulness and need to be replaced by the end of the fifth year. However, certain types of property clearly don't wear out— such as land. And because land doesn't wear out, it is not eligible for depreciation. Consequently, you may not recover the cost of the land while you own the rental. Instead, you must wait until you sell the property, at which time you may use the cost of the land to reduce your taxable gain, if any. (See "When You Sell Your Rental," below, for more information.)

Improvements to the rental property. As explained above, the IRS distinguishes between "repairs," for which you may deduct the full cost in the year you make them, and "improvements," which must be depreciated.

Personal property. Property that you leave in the rental for tenants to use—such as appliances, carpets, or furniture—must be depreciated. You must also depreciate certain types of property that you use in connection with the rental. For example, if you purchase a cell phone that you devote solely to your rental business or a lawn mower that you use exclusively for maintaining the rental, you must depreciate those items as well.

What Is the Depreciable Basis of Your Property?

To figure out how much depreciation you may claim each year, you must determine the depreciable basis of your property at the time you start using it in your rental business. The depreciable basis is the total amount you are permitted to recover through depreciation. You will then deduct a percentage of the depreciable basis each year, according to the depreciation method you use (discussed below).

If you buy personal property and immediately start using it in your rental, its depreciable basis is generally the purchase price. For example, if you buy a new washing machine or refrigerator for your rental, its depreciable basis is simply what you paid for it. If you start using property in your rental that you already own, its depreciable basis is the lower of the adjusted basis of the property (explained in Chapter 1) or the fair market value of the property on the date you begin using it in your rental business. This latter date is known as the date the property was "placed in service."

> EXAMPLE: The refrigerator at your rental unit conks out. Rather than buying a new one, you decide to buy yourself a stainless steel, subzero model for your home, and move your old refrigerator to the rental for your tenants. The old refrigerator's depreciable basis is either what you originally paid for it or its fair market value on the day you move it over to the rental, whichever is less.

The basis of real property can be a bit tougher to calculate. If you purchase property to use as a rental, the basis is typically the cost of the property (not including the cost of the land), plus certain amounts you pay as part of the sale, such as escrow fees, recording fees, legal fees associated with the purchase, commissions, and transfer taxes. (For more on calculating the basis of a home, see Chapter 2.)

TIP

Determining the value of land. When you purchase your rental property, a portion of the purchase price (including costs related to the purchase) must be allocated to the land. Although it might be to your advantage to allocate a relatively large amount of the purchase price to the building—because you are permitted to recover that portion of the cost through depreciation—you aren't permitted to make an arbitrary allocation. And it can be difficult to determine the value of the land. Some people rely on the assessed value of the land—the value on which your property tax is based. But if you think the assessed value is unreasonably high, you might want to confer with an expert who can help you come up with a more accurate price allocation between the land and the building.

If you start using property you already own as a rental—for example, you move to a new home and decide to rent out your old home—calculating basis is more difficult. As with a rental property you purchase, you are permitted to depreciate the cost of your newly converted rental property over a period of years. But because the property was not a rental when you first purchased it, your adjusted basis for depreciation is not necessarily the original cost of the home. Instead, it is the original cost of the property (not including the cost of the land), plus any improvements you have made, less any cost recovery you have already claimed (for example, a casualty loss or depreciation for a home office). Because you have already recovered some of the cost of your home through those deductions, you must subtract them when determining your depreciable basis.

The amount you will use to compute depreciation on the rental will be the lower of your adjusted basis, as described above, or the fair market value of the home at the time it becomes a rental.

Remember, too, that if you had made improvements to your home before converting it to a rental, the cost of those improvements increase your adjusted basis. And if you had claimed depreciation for any of those improvements (to your home office, for example), the depreciation deductions represent cost recovery that you must subtract to arrive at your depreciable basis.

How Much Can You Depreciate?

Once you know the depreciable basis of your property, you need a couple of pieces of information to figure out how much you can deduct each year. First, you need to determine the expected life of the property. Then, you must decide which depreciation method to use; you may be required to use a particular one. Using the expected life, depreciation method, and basis of the property, you can come up with the deduction amount for your tax return.

TIP

For tax year 2008 only, you might be able to claim some additional depreciation. This depreciation—sometimes called "bonus" depreciation—is available only for certain types of property. To qualify, generally the property must be new and you must be the original owner. For more information about this bonus depreciation, see IRS Publication 946.

Expected (Useful) Life

As knowledgeable as you might be about how long a dishwasher will last, you are not permitted to decide for yourself what the expected life of that or any other particular item of property is. Each type of property, whether it is the rental house itself, appliances in the house, furniture, or the car you use to visit the property, is assigned an expected life (also called "useful life" or "recovery period") by the IRS. This is the period of time over which you must depreciate the property. By the end of the property's expected life, you will have recovered the entire depreciable basis.

It would be a difficult undertaking for the IRS to prepare an exhaustive list of property and assign each a life expectancy, so there is a catch-all category, too. The following chart lists the useful lives of some of the most common assets used in rental properties.

5 years
Computers and peripheral equipment
Office equipment
Cars
Appliances
Carpet
Furniture (if used in the rental home itself)

7 years
Office furniture
Uncategorized property (this is the catch-all for property that has not been assigned to another category)

15 years
> Fences
> Shrubbery

27.5 years
> Residential rental buildings (not land)
> Improvements and additions to the home

Depreciation Methods

A depreciation method is the mathematical formula you use to determine how much you may deduct each year. Most often, you will use one of the three methods described below. Although you will be required to use a particular depreciation method for certain types of property, sometimes you have a choice.

> CAUTION
>
> **If you are subject to the alternative minimum tax (AMT), depreciation rules and methods might be different.** See Chapter 1 for more information about the AMT, or see IRS Instructions for Form 6251, *Alternative Minimum Tax.*

Method 1: Straight-Line Depreciation

When you use the straight-line method, you recover the cost of your asset by deducting the same amount each year over its expected life. Well, almost. For the first and last year of the expected life, you may deduct only half of the normal amount. For example, if you purchase a refrigerator for $1,000 that has a useful life of five years, you would think you should deduct $200 per year using the straight-line method. Instead, in the first year you may deduct only $100. Then you may deduct $200 each year, leaving a deduction of $100 for the final year (the sixth year). This is called the half-year convention.

> CAUTION
>
> **If you place property in service toward the end of the year, different rules may apply.** The half-year convention doesn't apply if more

than 40% of the value of all property placed in service during the year was purchased (or first used for rental purposes) in the last quarter of the year. In that case, you must use special (and less favorable) depreciation tables provided by the IRS. This is called the midquarter convention. However, the midquarter convention does not apply to real estate, so you need not include the cost of the rental house when applying the 40% rule. See IRS Publication 946 for more information.

Generally, you may choose whether or not to use straight-line depreciation. However, you are required to use straight-line depreciation for the following types of property:

- **Residential rental property and improvements.** You must use straight-line depreciation when depreciating your rental home and the improvements you make to the home.
- **Listed property used mostly for personal purposes.** Listed property is property that could easily be used for either business or for personal purposes. The most common types of listed property are cars, computers, and mobile phones. If you are using listed property in your rental business, and you use the property for business less than 50% of the time, then you must use straight-line depreciation. For example, if you use your computer 20% of the time for your rental property business, you must use straight-line depreciation on the cost of the computer to calculate your deduction.

To calculate straight-line depreciation using the half-year convention, simply divide the depreciable basis of property by the expected life. Under the half-year convention, the IRS assumes that you placed the property in service halfway through the first year, and that the end of its useful life of five years occurs halfway through the sixth year. So, for the first and last year, you may claim a deduction of only half of the annual amount.

EXAMPLE: You spent $850 on a new stove for your rental property. You elect to recover the cost of the stove using straight-line depreciation. According to IRS guidelines, the expected life of the stove is five years. Your depreciation deductions will be as follows:

Year 1: $ 85
Year 2: $ 170
Year 3: $ 170
Year 4: $ 170
Year 5: $ 170
Year 6: $ 85

When depreciating the building (your rental house), the computation is a little different, because the amount you may deduct in the first and last years depends on which month you began renting the home or offering it for rent. The following table lists the percentages you must use to compute your depreciation deduction for the building.

Residential Rental Real Estate Depreciation Deduction Percentages				
Month placed in service	Year 1	Years 2-27	Year 28	Year 29
January	3.485	3.636	1.970	0
February	3.182	3.636	2.273	0
March	2.879	3.636	2.576	0
April	2.576	3.636	2.879	0
May	2.273	3.636	3.182	0
June	1.970	3.636	3.485	0
July	1.667	3.636	3.636	0.152
August	1.364	3.636	3.636	0.455
September	1.061	3.636	3.636	0.758
October	0.758	3.636	3.636	1.061
November	0.455	3.636	3.636	1.364
December	0.152	3.636	3.636	1.667

EXAMPLE: In March, you purchase a rental property. The basis of the building itself (excluding the cost of the land) is $280,000. Your depreciation deduction for the first year you own the property is $280,000 x 2.879%, or $8,061. Next year (the second year), you may deduct $280,000 x 3.636%, or $10,181. By year 28, you will have recovered the entire $280,000.

Method 2: Double-Declining Balance (200%)

If you are not required to use straight-line depreciation (and you choose not to do so), then you have a choice between Methods 2 and 3. These methods still require you to claim depreciation over the useful life of the asset, but instead of claiming equal amounts each year, you may skew the cost recovery so that your deduction is larger in the earlier years and smaller in later years.

As is the case with straight-line depreciation, either the half-year or midquarter convention will apply. The following chart will help you compute the deduction if the half-year convention applies to you. (If the midquarter convention applies, see IRS Publication 946 to find out how much you can deduct.)

200% Declining Balance Depreciation Method Convention: Half-Year						
If the recovery period is:						
Year	**3-year**	**5-year**	**7-year**	**10-year**	**15-year**	**20-year**
1	33.33%	20.00%	14.29%	10.00%	5.00%	3.750%
2	44.45%	32.00%	24.49%	18.00%	9.50%	7.219%
3	14.81%	19.20%	17.49%	14.40%	8.55%	6.677%
4	7.41%	11.52%	12.49%	11.52%	7.70%	6.177%
5		11.52%	8.93%	9.22%	6.93%	5.713%
6		5.76%	8.92%	7.37%	6.23%	5.285%
7			8.93%	6.55%	5.90%	4.888%
8			4.46%	6.55%	5.90%	4.522%
9				6.56%	5.91%	4.462%
10				6.55%	5.90%	4.461%
11				3.28%	5.91%	4.462%
12					5.90%	4.461%
13					5.91%	4.462%
14					5.90%	4.461%
15					5.91%	4.462%
16					2.95%	4.461%
17						4.462%
18						4.461%
19						4.462%
20						4.461%
21						2.231%

EXAMPLE: In February of this year, you purchased a new refrigerator for your rental property at a cost of $1,200. A refrigerator has an expected life of five years. On your tax return for the year, you may claim a deduction of $1,200 x 20%, or $240. Next year, you may claim a deduction of $1,200 x 32%, or $384. You continue using the above chart through year six, after which you will have recovered the entire cost of the refrigerator.

Method 3: Declining Balance (150%)

The declining balance method is similar to the double-declining balance method, but for some classes of property, the deductions in the early years are smaller than they would be if you used double-declining balance. (And consequently, the deduction is larger in the later years.) Here is the chart to help you compute the deduction amounts using the half-year convention.

150% Declining Balance Depreciation Method							
Convention: Half-Year							
If the recovery period is:							
Year	3-year	5-year	7-year	10-year	12-year	15-year	20-year
1	25.00%	15.00%	10.71%	7.50%	6.25%	5.00%	3.750%
2	37.50%	25.50%	19.13%	13.88%	11.72%	9.50%	7.219%
3	25.00%	17.85%	15.03%	11.79%	10.25%	8.55%	6.677%
4	12.50%	16.66%	12.25%	10.02%	8.97%	7.70%	6.177%
5		16.66%	12.25%	8.74%	7.85%	6.93%	5.713%
6		8.33%	12.25%	8.74%	7.33%	6.23%	5.285%
7			12.25%	8.74%	7.33%	5.90%	4.888%
8			6.13%	8.74%	7.33%	5.90%	4.522%
9				8.74%	7.33%	5.91%	4.462%
10				4.37%	7.32%	5.90%	4.461%
11					7.33%	5.91%	4.462%
12					3.66%	5.90%	4.461%
13						5.91%	4.462%
14						5.90%	4.461%
15						5.91%	4.462%
16						2.95%	4.461%
17							4.462%
18							4.461%

EXAMPLE: In June, you paid $4,500 to have new carpet installed in the living room of your rental property. The carpet has an expected life of five years. You decide to use the declining balance method of depreciation. On your tax return for the year, you may claim a deduction of $4,500 x 15%, or $675. Next year you may claim a deduction of $4,500 x 25.5%, or $1,148 (rounded). You continue using the above chart through year six, after which you will have recovered the entire cost of the carpet.

Tax Strategy: Which Depreciation Method Should You Use?

If you have a choice of depreciation methods, don't assume that you should always use the method that gives you the fastest cost recovery. Although many taxpayers choose the double-declining balance method, that isn't always the smartest choice. A slower method of depreciation might make more sense if the deduction will be more valuable to you in later years. For example, if you expect to be in a higher tax bracket or you expect more rental income later, it might make sense to take a larger portion of your depreciation deduction then.

CAUTION

You can't use the Section 179 deduction for rental property. As explained in Chapter 3, a special rule applies in the year you purchase an asset for use in your business. That rule, called first-year expensing or a Section 179 deduction, allows you to deduct the entire cost (up to a dollar limit) of an asset in the year you buy it. A favorable rule indeed! Unfortunately, it does not apply to rentals. All depreciable property placed in service for your rental must be depreciated over its useful life.

Special Depreciation Rules for Cars

If you use your car to manage your rental, you may claim depreciation on part of the car's basis, in proportion to how much you use the car for your rental. As is true of other depreciable property (except real estate), you will generally use one of the three depreciation methods described above. But, even though you are recovering the cost slowly through depreciation, the law still puts a limit on how much depreciation you may claim for a car in any given year.

Car used less than 50% for business. Because cars are listed property, you must use straight-line depreciation if you use your car less than 50% of the time for rental business. Once you compute the amount of depreciation for the year, you must multiply it by the percentage of time the car is used for your rental. You may deduct that amount subject to the annual limits described below.

> **EXAMPLE:** You use your car 20% of the time for managing your rental property. For the current tax year, you compute depreciation on the entire car to be $600. But because you only used the car 20% of the time for business, your depreciation deduction is limited to $600 x 20%, or $120.

Car used more than 50% for business. Although it is unlikely that you use your car more than half of the time to take care of your rental property, it's possible that you have dedicated a car to such use—or mostly to such use. If so, you are not restricted to the straight-line method of depreciation but instead may use any of the three methods described above: straight-line, double-declining balance, or declining balance. Again, however, if you do not use the car entirely for your rental business, you must prorate the deduction for rental use. And, you are still subject to the limits described below.

Limit on amount of depreciation to claim in a year. Once you compute depreciation using one of the methods described above, you must allocate the depreciation between business and personal use.

The business portion is deductible, but only up to a maximum dollar amount. The limits are as follows:

Maximum Deprecation for Cars				
Year car placed in service	1st Year	2nd Year	3rd Year	4th year and later
2008*	$2,960/$10,960	$4,800	$2,850	$1,775
2007	$3,060	$4,900	$2,850	$1,775
2006	$2,960	$4,800	$2,850	$1,775
2005	$2,960	$4,700	$2,850	$1,775

* Note: For tax year 2008 only, the first-year depreciation limit has been increased by $8,000 for certain passenger autos. Your car will generally qualify for the higher limit if you purchased it new during 2008 and placed it in service in the same year.

These limits must be reduced if you use your car less than 100% of the time for business. In that case, you must reduce not only your available deduction (as calculated above), but also the limit on your deduction. For example, if you started using your car for rental business in 2006, and used it half of the time for that purpose, your maximum deduction for that first year is $1,480 (50% of $2,960), no matter which depreciation method you use.

EXAMPLE: You began using your car in your rental business in January 2007. In 2008, you used your car 15% of the time to manage your rental. The depreciable basis of your car is $25,000. Because you used the car less than 50% of the time for business, you must use straight-line depreciation. On your 2008 tax return, you compute your deduction as follows:

Step 1: Straight-line depreciation for the second year of using the car (which has an expected life of five years) is $25,000 divided by five years, or $5,000.

Step 2: Because the car was used only 15% for rental business, the amount of depreciation allocated to your rental business is $5,000 x 15%, or $750.

Step 3: The ceiling on auto depreciation for a car that was placed in service in 2007 and which is in its second year of business use is $4,900. However, because the car was used only 15% for business, the ceiling is limited to $4,900 x 15%, or $735. Therefore, the amount of auto depreciation you may claim as a rental expense for the year 2008 is limited to $735.

Amortization

Amortization is similar to depreciation in that you recover the cost of an asset over its expected life. But depreciation applies to tangible property, and amortization applies to intangible property. Intangible assets are not physical in nature—that is, you can't pick them up and throw them. Copyrights, patents, and computer software are all examples of intangible assets.

When you own rental real estate, the items you are most likely to encounter that must be amortized are loan points and other loan fees. When you purchase property, you might pay points to obtain a loan with a lower interest rate. You can recover that expense by amortizing the points. Similarly, you might have loan fees (other than points) that you incurred simply to obtain the mortgage in the first place. These fees might include a credit report, appraisal fee, mortgage insurance, and underwriting fees.

> **TIP**
>
> **You may amortize most costs of a refinance.** When you purchase rental property, fees associated with obtaining the loan itself are recovered through amortization. The other expenses are added to your basis and recovered through depreciation (except for those that are allocated to the land, which you may not depreciate). However, when you refinance your rental property, items that would typically be added to basis if your were purchasing the property are instead added to other costs of the refinance and recovered through amortization over the term of the new loan.

Loan points and loan costs are amortized over the term of the loan. So, if you acquired a 30-year mortgage to purchase rental property and paid $3,000 in points, you would amortize the points over 30 years, claiming a deduction of $100 each year. (If you purchase the property midyear, you must prorate the points for the first year.)

If you refinance a loan and pay points, the rule is the same. You recover the points over the life of the new loan. If you are still deducting a portion of the points you paid upon purchase, you may deduct all of the remaining points on the original loan in the year you refinance. However, this rule applies only if you refinance with a new lender. If you refinance with the same lender, you must continue to claim the original points in bits and pieces, but the period over which you claim the points is the term of the new loan, not the term of the old loan.

> **EXAMPLE:** Ten years ago, you bought rental property with a 30-year loan. You have been amortizing the $2,000 you paid in points at the rate of $67 per year. You have deducted $670 so far. On January 1 of this year, you refinance with a new 30-year loan to reduce your interest rate. You will pay $3,000 in points on the new loan. You refinance with the same lender, which is offering the best interest rate. You have $1,330 in points remaining from your original loan. Because you are refinancing with the same lender, you must combine the remaining $1,330 in points from the old loan with the $3,000 in points from the new loan and claim $144 per year ($1,330 plus $3,000 divided by 30 years).
>
> If you had refinanced with a new lender, you would have claimed a deduction for the remaining $1,330 plus $100 of amortized points from the new loan ($3,000 divided by 30) for a total of $1,430 in the year of purchase. Then, you would claim $100 each year for the next 29 years.

Nondeductible Expenses

Although most rental-related expenses are deductible, a few are not. Here are some of the costs you may not deduct:

- **Unpaid rent.** You may not claim a deduction without an out-of-pocket expense. In other words, you must actually spend money to deduct it. This rule can be annoying when it comes to unpaid rent. If a tenant lives in your rental home but fails to pay rent for one or more months, you certainly feel as though you have lost money. But Congress doesn't see it that way. In the eyes of the law, lost rent is not an expense, because the cash didn't come out of your pocket. That's not to say you didn't suffer a loss. But what you lost was the opportunity to rent the home to a paying tenant. That's an "opportunity cost," which might be as painful as any expenditure, but is nondeductible nonetheless. The same principle applies when you are unsuccessful at renting the home and it sits empty. You may not deduct lost rents in this case either. This makes sense because you never reported the lost rent as income.

- **Travel costs to find a rental.** You can't deduct travel (or other) expenses you incur while looking for a suitable rental property to purchase. But once you own the property and make it available for rent, you may deduct your travel costs to maintain and manage the property. If you travel to the property in order to make improvements, you treat your travel expense as part of the cost of the improvement. In other words, you must recover that cost through depreciation over the life of the improvement.

- **Home office expenses.** As you may know, the IRS allows taxpayers who have a home office they use in a business to deduct a portion of the expenses associated with their home (such as rent or mortgage payments, utilities, and so on). However, you may not claim a home office just for handling your rental property, unless you are in the business of managing rental properties.

- **Education costs.** You may not deduct as a rental expense the cost of seminars that you attend, even if they teach you about managing your rental or other rental-related issues.

Rental Losses

If your rental income is greater than your expenses (including depreciation and amortization), you must pay income tax on the remainder. If your expenses exceed your income—in other words, you have a loss—you might be able to claim as much as $25,000 of the loss in the current year, using it to reduce your taxable income from other sources. Any loss in excess of $25,000 must be carried over and used in the following year, if you are eligible to claim it then.

If your income exceeds a certain threshold, however, even the $25,000 allotment might be reduced or even eliminated. Once your income reaches $100,000, you may claim only part of the $25,000 loss. The amount of loss allowed is reduced by 50 cents for each dollar by which your income exceeds $100,000. Once your income reaches $150,000, your loss allowance is reduced to zero and you must carry over the entire loss to the following year. If you fail to claim all of your losses in the next year, you may continue to carry them over indefinitely, until you have claimed them all. If you sell the property, you may claim all remaining unclaimed losses in that year.

TIP

The usual "passive loss" rules don't apply to the first $25,000 of rental loss. Rental income and losses are considered "passive," which means, among other things, that they are subject to special rules. The general rule for passive losses is that they can be used to offset only passive income, which does not include wages, interest, or dividends. However, rental activities enjoy a special place in the passive activity world. If you own rental property, you are permitted to deduct passive losses of up to $25,000 (if you otherwise qualify). If you have passive losses from your rental property, you generally must file Form 8582, *Passive Activity Loss*

Limitations, with your tax return if you are unable to claim the entire loss in the current year or you are carrying over unused losses from earlier years.

Even if your rental loss is less than the $25,000 limit (and you aren't subject to the reduction for higher-income filers), you might not be able to claim your entire loss in a particular year. If your rental loss leaves you with negative income overall on your tax return, you might have what's called a net operating loss. Net operating losses are generated by business losses, and your rental property is considered a business for this purpose.

Net operating losses may be "carried back" two years and used to refund taxes you paid in those prior years. Alternatively (or in addition), losses can be carried forward and claimed against income in future years. Calculating a net operating loss and carrying it back to prior years can be tricky. For more information about determining whether or not you have a net operating loss and how to claim a refund for prior year taxes, see IRS Publication 536, *Net Operating Losses.*

Renting to Relatives

Nothing in the tax code says you can't rent to your family members. But that doesn't necessarily mean you may claim all the usual tax benefits. If you do rent to your son or daughter or another relative, you may claim all of the tax benefits for the rental that would be available to you if you rented to strangers, provided you don't give your relatives special treatment. As long as you charge your relatives the going rate, or "fair rent," for the property, all of the deductions and rules discussed above apply.

However, if you give your relatives a deal, charging them nominal rent or no rent at all, the rules are different. You still must report the rent as income, and you may claim expenses. However, your expenses are limited to the amount of income you reported. In other words, you may not claim a loss. And, you may not carry over any unclaimed expenses to future years. Those excess expenses—and the deductions they would otherwise generate—simply evaporate.

Renting Out Part of Your Home

If you rent out a room in your home, you report rental income and expenses on Schedule E, just as you would if you owned a separate rental property. Because you are using part of your home, however, you can't claim all of your home maintenance and other costs as rental expenses. Instead, you must allocate your expenses between personal and rental use of the home. For example, if the room you rent out constitutes 15% of the total square footage of your home, you should allocate 15% of your mortgage interest, real estate taxes, utilities, and insurance to the rental and deduct the allocated amount on Schedule E. You calculate your depreciation deduction for the rental portion of the house itself the same way: as a percentage of the deduction that would be available to you if you rented out the entire house (see "Depreciation," above, for more information).

If you incur expenses that are related only to the rental (known as "direct" expenses), you may deduct them in full; you don't have to allocate. For example, if you repaint the room that you are renting out, but not the rest of the house, you may deduct the entire painting expense on Schedule E.

If you subsequently sell your home, you may treat the entire home as your principal residence (assuming you still live there). You don't have to treat the sale as two transactions—one for the rental and one for your residence. That means you may exclude gain on the rental portion as well as the residence portion (up to the exclusion limit; see Chapter 2). This is a huge advantage for homeowners, because rental property is generally not eligible for any gain exclusion, as explained below in "When You Sell Your Rental."

Beware of the fly in the ointment, though. If you were entitled to a depreciation deduction on the rental portion of your home while you were renting it out, you must pay income tax on your gain up to the amount of depreciation to which you were entitled.

EXAMPLE: You have lived in your home for seven years. Last year, for the first time, you rented out a room to a college student. On your tax return for that year, you claimed $350 of depreciation on the rental portion of the house. You just sold your home this year for $300,000, generating a gain of $50,000. Because the home is your principal residence, you are eligible to exclude up to $250,000 of gain, which more than covers your $50,000 profit. However, because you claimed depreciation on the room you rented out last year, you must pay income tax on that $350 (the amount of depreciation you claimed). You may exclude the rest of the gain.

> **! CAUTION**
>
> **Different rules apply for a separate rental property.** If the portion of your home that you rent out is actually separate from the part you live in—for example, you rent out a cottage on the back 40 or an apartment over the garage—the rented space is treated as an entirely separate property. When you sell your home, you must report two separate transactions: the sale of the rental portion and the sale of your principal residence. If you have gain on the rental portion, you may not use part of your principal residence exclusion to avoid paying tax on that gain. You must pay income tax on all of the gain allocable to the rental, not just the amount of depreciation you claimed.

When You Sell Your Rental

If you sell your rental property, you may claim rental income and expenses (including depreciation) for that year, up to the date of sale. Then, you calculate your gain or loss as of the date of sale.

Calculating gain for a rental is much like calculating gain on a principal residence (see Chapter 2). You need to determine the "amount realized" from the sale and reduce it by your adjusted basis to come up with your gain. Once you figure out your gain, however, there are a couple of important differences in how it is treated for tax purposes:

- When you sell a rental, you are not entitled to any gain exclusion. You must pay tax on your gain.
- You might have to pay tax at a higher rate on the gain from a rental sale. Some of the gain could be taxed at a rate as high as 25%. In contrast, the taxable gain (if any) on the sale of a principal residence is taxed at a maximum rate of 15%.

Tax Strategy: Exchanging Your Rental Property for Another to Defer Tax

Believe it or not, there is a way to sell your rental property and avoid paying tax on the gain. The strategy is called a "like-kind exchange" or a "1031 exchange" (after the section of the tax code that permits it). In an exchange, you trade your rental for another rental of equal or greater value. In most cases, as long as you put all of the cash from the old rental into the new rental, you shouldn't owe any tax on the transaction. To make it work, you must also follow a long list of rules laid out by the IRS. Any misstep could mean a big tax bill.

Although you may keep trading rental properties and deferring taxes indefinitely, the day might come when you will want to get out of the rental business. And that's when you'll have to pay the piper. Once you sell the last property, you will owe tax on all the gains you have deferred over the years.

On the other hand, you could keep the last property until you die, at which point the basis of your property will be "stepped up" to its fair market value on the date of your death. In effect, the tax liability for all of the appreciation in all of your exchanged properties will evaporate. That means your heirs will not have to pay income tax on the appreciation (unless the tax laws have changed by then).

The rules for exchanging property are extremely complex. You can obtain more information by reading IRS Publication 544, *Sales and Other Dispositions of Assets*. However, if you decide you want to take advantage of this strategy, you would be wise to enlist the help of an expert. There are firms that specialize in such transactions, and you should be able to get a referral from an accountant, lawyer, or real estate broker whom you trust.

Calculating Your Amount Realized

When you sell your rental property, you and the buyer will negotiate a sales price. You will also have to pay a variety of expenses related to the transaction. The "amount realized" is your agreed sales price less all the expenses of sale.

Expenses that reduce your amount realized from the sale include most of the nondeductible closing costs that appear on your settlement statement. The largest item is usually the sales commission you pay to one or more real estate brokers. Also included are legal fees related to the transaction, title fees, and title insurance that you agree to pay. You can also subtract loan points you pay on behalf of the buyer of your property. Similarly, if you pay any real estate taxes on behalf of the buyer, those are an expense of sale.

> TIP
>
> **Don't forget your deductions.** When you sell your rental, you might pay some deductible costs through escrow. These are sometimes easy to miss. For example, you might have to pay prorated mortgage interest, transfer taxes, ad valorem taxes, and/or insurance; these expenses should appear on your settlement statement. You can also deduct unamortized points or other loan costs. If you were amortizing loan fees or points from your original purchase (or a refinance), you may deduct the remaining unamortized points and fees when you sell the rental.

Calculating Your Adjusted Basis

To come up with your adjusted basis, start with your original cost to buy the property (unless you acquired the property in a tax-deferred exchange—see above). That cost should include the cost of the land as well as any of the original costs of purchasing the property that appeared on the settlement statement.

To the above, you may add the cost of all improvements you made to the property since you purchased it. Such expenses might include the cost of the new roof you installed, your remodel of the kitchen, or the third story you added to the house. Be careful not to include repairs. Those expenses, which you deducted in the years you paid for them, have no effect on your basis.

Finally, you must subtract certain items to arrive at adjusted basis. Most important, you must subtract all of the depreciation you were entitled to claim for the building and improvements over the years. Also, if you ever claimed a casualty loss, you must subtract the amount of the loss you deducted to arrive at your basis (because you already reaped the tax benefit). And, if you acquired the property in a tax-deferred exchange, then you must subtract the amount of your deferred gain when calculating your adjusted basis.

Your Gain

Your gain is simply the amount you realized on the sale minus your adjusted basis. When you sell a rental property, none of this gain is excludable—you must pay tax on the entire amount. To add insult to injury, that gain will not necessarily be taxed at the 15% capital gain rate. That's because you have enjoyed the tax benefits of depreciation deductions while owning the rental. When you eventually sell property you have been depreciating, all gain up to the amount of depreciation you were entitled to claim is subject to a maximum tax rate of 25%. The remainder of the gain will be taxed at a maximum rate of 15%.

> **EXAMPLE:** You sell your rental property and compute a long-term gain of $30,000. Over the years, you have claimed depreciation deductions totaling $22,000. Assuming you are in a 35% tax bracket, your capital gain from the sale of your rental will be 25% of the gain attributable to depreciation, plus 15% of the remaining gain.
>
> | | |
> |---|---|
> | 25% of $22,000 | $ 5,500 |
> | 15% of $8,000 | 1,200 |
> | Total (federal) capital gains tax | $ 6,700 |

Tax Strategy: Convert Your Rental to Your Principal Residence Before Selling

When you start thinking about selling your rental and discover you might be hit with a large capital gain, you might wish that you were selling your principal residence instead. That's because the tax code permits you to exclude (not just defer) gain of up to $250,000 (if you are single) or $500,000 (if you are married and filing a joint return). (See Chapter 2 for more information.)

You can turn your rental back into your principal residence before you sell it to take partial advantage of this exclusion. As long as you live in the rental as your principal residence for at least two (any two) of the five years before you sell it, you might be able to enjoy some of the tax benefits of selling a principal residence. Because of this rule, you might be able to exclude some of your gain if you sell a rental that used to be your home within three years of converting it to rental use. You might also be able to exclude some gain if you move back into your rental house and then live there for at least two years before selling it.

Generally, however, the maximum gain exclusion must be reduced in proportion to the amount of time the property was used as a rental. For example, suppose you and your spouse owned the property for five years, used it as a rental for three years and lived in it as your principal residence for two years. When you sell it, the maximum amount of gain you may exclude is $200,000. Your maximum gain exclusion is $500,000 (for married and filing jointly), but you used it as your principal resident for only two of five years, so the maximum amount of gain you can exclude is two-fifths of $500,000, or $200,000.

There is another catch, too: Although you might be entitled to exclude most of the gain when you sell a principal residence that once was a rental, you will still have to pay tax on your depreciation deductions. The portion of your gain equal to the amount of depreciation you were entitled to deduct will always be subject to tax at a maximum rate of 25%. The exclusion does not apply to that portion of your gain. There are other nuances to this strategy, so be sure to check with a tax professional before making your move.

How to Claim Rental Income and Expenses

You must report your rental income and expenses on Schedule E, *Supplemental Income and Loss*. Also, even though there is a line on Schedule E for your depreciation expense, you must include a completed Form 4562, *Depreciation and Amortization*. If your rental property generates a loss, you might need to complete Form 8582, *Passive Activity Loss Limitations*. And if you sell your rental, you must complete Form 4797, *Sales of Business Property*.

Your Second Home

From reading Chapter 2, you already know that the tax code offers some attractive tax benefits if you own the home you live in. Most significant are deductions for mortgage interest and real estate taxes. Those deductions might also apply to a second home, depending on how you use it.

Your second home, by definition, is a residence you use for part of the year, but which is not your principal residence. If you rent out your second home for any part of the year, the tax code characterizes it as a "vacation" or "mixed-use" home, to which special rules apply (see "Your Vacation Mixed-Use Home," below, for more information). However, if your second home is just that—a place to live when you are not living in your principal residence, and which you do not rent to anyone else while you are absent—then you can deduct your mortgage interest and real estate taxes, much as you can for your principal residence, although there are limits on the total amount of mortgage interest you may deduct.

Real Estate Taxes

The real estate taxes you pay on your second home are fully deductible if you itemize your deductions on Schedule A.

> **CAUTION**
>
> **Taxes are not deductible in calculating the alternative minimum tax (AMT).** When you compute your tax for AMT purposes, you are not permitted to deduct any taxes that would otherwise be deductible on Schedule A, whether real estate taxes for a first or second home, property taxes for your car or boat, or state income taxes. Note, however, that taxes claimed on other schedules are still deductible for AMT purposes. For example, property taxes that you pay for a rental and deduct on Schedule E are allowed for both regular tax and AMT purposes. See Chapter 1 for more information about the AMT.

Mortgage Interest

You may deduct mortgage interest on loans secured by your second home, as long as your total debt—on your principal residence and your second home combined—does not exceed the acquisition and home equity limits described in Chapter 2.

Points

One important difference between a principal residence and a second home is the tax treatment of points you pay on your home loan. If you pay points when you purchase your principal residence, you may generally deduct all of those points in the year of purchase. (However, if your acquisition debt exceeds $1 million, the points allocable to the excess acquisition debt might be disallowed.) If you pay points for a second home, you must instead amortize them, deducting a portion each year over the life of the loan. For example, if you obtain a 30-year loan and pay $3,000 in points, you may deduct only $100 each year. And, unless you purchase your second home at the very beginning of the year, the first year's worth of points must be prorated for a partial year. (For example, if you obtained the loan on July 1, you may claim only $50 of points for the first year.)

> CAUTION
>
> **Third homes don't qualify.** The deduction for mortgage interest and points applies to your principal residence and second home only. If you have more than two homes, mortgage interest is considered personal interest and is not deductible. In addition, you may not deduct (or amortize) any amount for points you paid to obtain a loan on additional properties.

How to Claim Deductions for Your Second Home

You may claim deductible mortgage interest, real estate taxes, and amortized points for your second home on Schedule A, *Itemized Deductions*, the same form you use to claim these deductions for your primary residence. If you sell your second home, you must report any gain on Schedule D, *Capital Gains and Losses*. (Chapter 2 explains how to calculate your gain or loss, although no gain exclusion is available for a second home.) As is the case with your principal residence, if you have a loss when you sell your second home, you may not claim that loss on your tax return to reduce your taxable income. However arbitrary that might seem, those are the rules.

Your Vacation (Mixed-Use) Home

If you rent out your second home when you are not using it, the IRS classifies it as a "vacation home" subject to special rules. The vacation home rules kick in automatically whenever you use a second home as a personal residence for some part of the year (at least one day) and rent it out for any part of the same year.

A vacation home, as described above, generally falls into one of three categories: (1) rental, (2) personal residence, or (3) both (part personal, part rental). Unfortunately, the tax terminology for vacation homes can be confusing. Although one of the subcategories of vacation home is a "rental," the vacation home rental rules vary slightly from those that apply to a typical rental property (one that you never use as a personal residence). Just remember that by definition, a vacation home is mixed-use property. That means you use it as a residence at least one day and rent it out for at least one day, each year.

Another confusing aspect of these rules is that the category into which your vacation home falls might change from year to year, because the home's classification (for tax purposes) depends on the number of days you use the home, the number of days you rent it out, and the ratio of the two numbers. A change in classification might alter the deductions you may claim from one year to the next.

This section explains how to determine which type of vacation home you have and the rules you must follow to claim deductions for the home.

What Type of Vacation Home Do You Have?

As explained above, vacation homes fall into one of three categories for tax purposes: rental, personal residence, or mixed-use home. To determine the appropriate category for your vacation home, you need to follow these steps:

Step 1: Determine the number of days you rented out the house.

Step 2: Determine how many days during the year you or your family used the house.

Step 3: Multiply the number of days the home was rented by 10% (0.1).

Use the numbers from the steps above to select the appropriate category for your vacation home (we provide the rules for each category below):

- **Rental.** Your home is a rental if you and your family used the home either (1) 14 days or fewer, or (2) for no more than 10% of the number of days it was rented (the number from Step 3, above), whichever is greater.

  EXAMPLE: This year, you and your family used your vacation home for 18 days. You rented it out for a total of 250 days.

Follow the steps above to determine whether the property is a rental, for tax purposes:

Step 1: Total rental days = 250

Step 2: Total personal use days = 18

Step 3: 10% of rental days (250 x 10%) = 25.

Although you used the home for more than 14 days, it still qualifies as a rental for the year because your personal use of the home (18 days) does not exceed the number from Step 3 (25 days).

- **Personal residence.** Your home qualifies as a personal residence if it was rented for fewer than 15 days during the year.
- **Part personal, part rental.** Your home falls into this category if it was rented out for at least 15 days *and* you and your family used the home for more than 14 days or more than 10% of the time it was rented out, whichever is greater.

Category 1: Rental

Your vacation home falls into this category if you and your family used the home for no more than 14 days or no more than 10% of the days it was rented, whichever is greater. (Legislators put this kind of language in the tax code just to keep us sharp. It's like a tongue-twister for the brain.)

Because the home was used as a residence for only a small portion of the year, a vacation home in this category is treated as a rental property. As you might expect, if your rental income exceeds your expenses for the home, you must pay tax on the excess. But the real payoff occurs if your expenses exceed your income. In that case, you may claim a loss on your tax return, subject to the limitations described in "Rental Losses," above.

There is one hitch, however. Even though the property is considered a rental, you are still required to allocate expenses between personal use and rental use. So, for example, if you use the home for ten days and rent it out for 255 days, then you must allocate 10/265 of the expenses to personal use.

This rule requires you to treat a portion of the insurance, utilities, gardening, and similar costs of owning your vacation home as nondeductible personal expenses. That probably doesn't surprise you. But what about real estate taxes and mortgage interest? Those expenses also must be allocated between rental use and personal use. The rental portion will be deductible on Schedule E.

As for the personal portion of those expenses, you may deduct the real estate taxes on Schedule A, along with the real estate taxes for other property you own. However, you may not claim a deduction for the portion of your mortgage interest allocated to personal use of the vacation home. The tax code provides that you may deduct personal mortgage interest *only* on a principal residence and a second residence of your choosing. And therein lies the problem: If your vacation home falls into Category 1, it is deemed to be a rental and not a personal residence of any kind. That's true even though you use it as a residence for a small part of the year and must allocate expenses to your personal use. The result is that the mortgage interest allocated to your personal use is not deductible at all. (See "Tax Strategy: Which Method Should You Use to Allocate Rental and Personal Expenses?" below, to learn how to limit the damage this rule can cause.)

Category 2: Personal Residence

Category 2 is essentially the reverse of Category 1. If the home was rented for fewer than 15 days, it is treated entirely as a personal residence, even if you and your family used the home for only a single day.

Because rental use of the home is minimal, you need not report your rental income on your tax return, and you may not claim rental expenses, either. However, you may deduct your real estate taxes for the property on Schedule A. If you are treating the property as your second home, you may also deduct your mortgage interest on Schedule A. (Chapter 2 explains the rules for—and limits on—deducting mortgage interest.)

Category 3: Part Personal, Part Rental

Your vacation home falls into Category 3 if the home was rented out for at least 15 days, and you and your family used it as a residence more than 14 days or more than 10% of the time it was rented out, whichever is greater.

If your vacation home falls into Category 3, it is treated as part residence, part rental. You must report rental income and the rental portion of all expenses on Schedule E of your tax return. Expenses that are directly related to renting the property (which the IRS calls "direct expenses") are fully deductible on Schedule E. These expenses might include advertising, office supplies that you use to keep track of rent, rental commissions you pay to a broker to help you rent the property, legal fees you might incur to handle tenant issues, and perhaps licenses or taxes you must pay to the city to for the privilege of renting out your property.

Expenses related to operating and maintaining the home must be divided between rental use and personal use. Such expenses might include utilities, insurance, pest control, plumbing repairs, and similar items. When making the allocation between rental and personal use, you must allocate the expenses according to the number of days the property was used for each purpose. For purposes of this calculation, you can ignore days when the property wasn't being used by anyone. For example, if you rented your vacation home for 90 days and used it yourself for 30 days, then 25% of your operating expenses would be allocated to personal use (30 days of personal use divided by 120 days of both personal and rental use). The remaining 75% of each expense would be allocated to rental use. The rental portion of expenses is deductible on Schedule E, but the personal use portions are not deductible.

Once again, mortgage interest and real estate taxes are subject to slightly different rules. Mortgage interest and real estate taxes must also be divided between personal and rental use. The rental use portion of each is deductible on Schedule E. The personal portion of real estate taxes is deductible on Schedule A. And, if you are treating the property as a second home, you may also claim the personal portion of mortgage interest on Schedule A (subject to the mortgage interest deduction limits for a principal residence and second home).

The IRS would like you to use the same method to allocate mortgage interest and real estate taxes as you do to allocate other expenses, but the tax court gives you a second option. Under the tax court's method, you may count the days the house is vacant as personal use days and add them to the number of days you actually used the house when allocating mortgage interest and real estate taxes. Although the IRS method may be more favorable if your vacation home falls into Category 1 (that is, it qualifies as a rental), the tax court's method is usually more beneficial in other circumstances. You should do the math both ways to figure out which formula gives you a greater tax break. (See "Tax Strategy: Which Method Should You Use to Allocate Rental and Personal Expenses?" below, for more information.)

Tax Strategy: Which Method Should You Use to Allocate Rental and Personal Expenses?

In its publications, the IRS provides a single method for allocating the real estate taxes and mortgage interest between rental use and personal use: Divide the total days the house was in use by the number of days it was rented out and the number of days you used it as a personal residence. But courts have also approved an alternative method that might be more beneficial to you. Under this tax court method, you count days when the house was not being used by anyone as additional personal use days (adding them to the number of days you actually did use the home) when you allocate mortgage interest and real estate taxes. You may choose the allocation method that is most favorable.

Option 1 (IRS method): You add up the number of days the property was used for either personal or rental purposes. You then divide the personal use days by the total number of days the property was used to come up with a percentage for personal use. The rental use percentage is the number of days of rental use divided by the

Tax Strategy: Which Method Should You Use to Allocate Rental and Personal Expenses? (continued)

total number of days the property was used. Finally, you multiply those percentages by the total amount of the interest or real estate taxes to come up with the portion of the expense allocable to rental or to personal use.

EXAMPLE 1: You used your vacation home ten days during the year and rented it out for 160 days. The total amount of mortgage interest you paid during the year was $20,000. Using the IRS method, 10/170 of the mortgage interest is allocated to personal use and 160/170 is allocated to rental use. Thus $20,000 x 10/170, or $1,176, is allocated to personal use and $18,824 to rental use.

Option 2 (court-approved method): Alternatively, you may treat days when no one was using your vacation home as additional personal use days. Using this method, the rental portion of an expense is the number of rental days divided by 365 (a full year) and multiplied by the total amount of mortgage interest or taxes. The personal portion is the number of days the house was either vacant or used for personal purposes, divided by 365, and then multiplied by the expense.

EXAMPLE 2: You decide to allocate your $20,000 mortgage interest between rental and personal use using the tax court method. The rental use portion is 160/365 x $20,000, or $8,767. The personal use portion is (ten personal use days + 195 vacant days)/365 x $20,000, or $11,233.

Typically, the tax court method will yield greater benefits if the rental portion of your vacation home generates a loss and you are unable to use all of the deductions allocated to the rental. In that case, the more mortgage interest and taxes you can allocate to personal use, the better off you are likely to be, because the personal portion of those expenses is generally deductible on Schedule A whether or not the rental portion generates a loss. (See "Vacation Home (Mixed-Use) Loss Limitations," below.)

Vacation Home (Mixed-Use) Loss Limitations

After reading the rules above, you might think that you have just discovered the biggest free lunch in the tax code. You hatch a plan to buy your dreamy cabin in the mountains, rent it out for exactly 15 days, use it all summer, and then claim a bunch of expenses, generating a nice big loss for your tax return. What a great way to subsidize the upkeep on your second home, right?

Unfortunately, no. Here's the spoiler: The total loss you may claim (if any) for your vacation home is equal to your rental income reduced by any direct rental expenses you have, and reduced further by the mortgage interest, real estate taxes, and casualty losses allocated to the rental. If those items alone generate a loss, you may claim that amount of loss, but no more. All of your other expenses are disallowed and must be carried over to the next year.

> **EXAMPLE:** Your vacation home is part personal use and part rental use. Your rental income for the year is $7,000. In addition you have the following expenses:
>
> | | |
> |---|---|
> | Commission paid to a rental agent (direct expense) | $ 1,200 |
> | Rental portion of mortgage interest | 6,500 |
> | Rental portion of real estate taxes | 1,800 |
> | Rental portion of utilities | 950 |
> | Depreciation on rental portion of home | $ 4,500 |
>
> Your rental income reduced by direct expenses and by the rental portion of mortgage interest, real estate taxes, and casualty losses is as follows:
>
> | | |
> |---|---|
> | Rental income | $ 7,000 |
> | Direct expenses | (1,200) |
> | Mortgage interest | (6,500) |
> | Real estate taxes | (1,800) |
> | | $(2,500) |

You may claim a vacation home loss in the amount of $2,500. However, your remaining expenses (utilities and depreciation) are disallowed for the current year.

If you still have net rental income after deducting direct expenses and the allocable amounts of mortgage interest, real estate taxes, and any casualty losses, then you may deduct your other expenses, such as the rental portion of utilities, sewage, repairs, and depreciation. You may claim enough of those additional expenses to offset all of your rental income, but no more. In other words, you may use these expenses to reduce your net rental income to zero, but not to generate a loss that you may claim against other sources of income.

> **EXAMPLE:** Assume the same facts as in the previous example, except that your rental income is $14,500. The total of all of your rental expenses is $14,950. In that case, you would be able to claim all but $450 of your expenses in the current year.

Any expenses (other than direct expenses, mortgage interest, real estate taxes, and casualty losses) you are unable to use in a given year may be carried over to the next year. You may continue carrying over unused expenses each year until you have enough income to use them or until you sell the property. If you have not used all of your expenses by the time you sell the property, you may claim any leftover expenses then.

Ordering of Deductions for Your Vacation Home

The limit on the amount of loss you may claim for renting your vacation home is only one spoiler. Here's another: When determining which rental expenses you may deduct in the current year and which must be carried over to future years, you are required to claim your expenses in a particular order.

The reason for this restriction is simple. If it didn't exist, clever taxpayers could turn the vacation home rules into a modest tax bonanza in spite of the limit on losses. Consider this situation: You purchase a second home and rent it out for 15 days, making it a vacation home that is part personal residence and part rental. When it comes time to report the rental income and expenses on your tax return, you realize that because this property is your second home, all of the mortgage interest and taxes are deductible, regardless of how they are allocated between personal and rental use. So you decide to use other expenses that would not otherwise be deductible to offset all of the rental income. Then you claim the full amount of your mortgage interest and taxes on Schedule A, as personal deductible expenses.

Unfortunately, Congress has plugged that loophole by requiring you to claim expenses in this order:

1. Mortgage interest
2. Real estate taxes
3. Any casualty loss deduction allocable to the rental
4. Expenses directly related to the rental (office supplies, etc.)
5. Rental portion of operating expenses (utilities, insurance, etc.)
6. Depreciation.

When you carry over unused expenses to a future year, you must keep track of the type of expense, because it will be added to expenses of the same type in subsequent years. For example, if you were unable to use all of your depreciation in a given year, it is carried over and added to the depreciation for the next year.

How to Claim Deductions for Your Mixed-Use Vacation Home

You claim the rental portion of your vacation home, rental income, and expenses, on Schedule E, *Supplemental Income and Loss.* Although you report depreciation and amortization on Schedule E as well, you must also include Form 4562, *Depreciation and Amortization.* And, when you sell the property, you will need to include Form 4797, *Sales of Business Property,* with your tax return.

CHAPTER

9

Personal Loans and Purchases

Tax Benefits in This Chapter

☐ **Did you make a major purchase this year?**

- If you paid for it with a loan secured by your primary residence or second home, you might be able to deduct your interest payments.
- If you purchased a vehicle and now must pay an annual tax based on its value, you may deduct that tax payment on your federal return.
- If you bought a hybrid, alternative fuel, or electric car, you might be eligible for a tax credit.
- If you purchased a boat or RV, it might qualify as your second home—which means you might be able to deduct your interest payments.
- You may deduct all of the sales tax you paid; if you choose to claim this deduction, however, you may not deduct your state and local income taxes.

☐ **Did you borrow money or make payments on a loan?**

- You may deduct the interest you paid as mortgage interest if the loan is secured by your primary residence or second home, as long as the mortgage debt doesn't exceed certain limits.
- If the lender forgave the loan, you might owe income tax on the amount you no longer have to pay back.

☐ **Did you lend money or receive payments on a loan?**

- You might have to report the interest as income.
- If you charge little or no interest, you might have to report imputed interest on your tax return.
- If the borrower doesn't pay and you write off the loan, you might be entitled to a bad debt deduction.

A s you edge into your retirement years, you might find yourself worrying way too much about the (small) size of your nest egg. Do you have enough money to take it easy for the rest of your life, or will you be slinging hash in your eighties? Will you be able to indulge yourself, or will you have to watch every penny? These worries undoubtedly intensify when you are contemplating parting with some of your savings, whether through spending or lending.

If you're considering a major purchase, such as a car or boat, you need to decide how you will pay: Will you pay cash or finance the purchase and pay it off over time? Not surprisingly, there are tax implications to consider either way.

At the same time you are eyeing your nest egg, you might notice others eyeing it as well. Your children might want to borrow money for a down payment on a house, or the grandkids might want a loan for college. And, of course, even if your children and grandchildren haven't asked to borrow money, you might want to help them out. No matter how it comes about, if you find yourself serving as banker, whether to a friend, a relative, or even a casual acquaintance, it pays to know some of the tax benefits and pitfalls.

Purchases

After retirement, the nature of your major purchases is likely to change. After all, many of us start to downsize at this point in our lives, whether it's because the house feels too large without the kids, because our needs—for professional clothing, a commuting car, and other trappings of our work lives, for example—have diminished, or simply because we want fewer things and less responsibility.

At the same time, however, many retirees are focusing on quality of life, and are starting to do things they've only dreamed about until now. If you plan to travel more, do more entertaining, learn to be a gourmet cook, or take up a hobby, you will still have a large expenditure or two in your future: a new car, an RV, an updated workshop in the garage, or maybe a kitchen remodel.

When the time comes, you will have to decide whether to finance the purchase or pay cash. You'll also want to know about any tax benefits that might be available.

Cars

Does this sound familiar? You left the office for the last time and drove directly to the local dealership to buy a new car. Then you told your spouse, "Don't worry, this is the last car I'm ever going to buy." A few years into your idyllic retirement, you realize that the only thing you need to make your retirement even better is a new car.

Financing

If you have extra money lying around, it might well be best to pay cash for your new car. That way, you won't have to make any car payments, and you can avoid paying interest on the purchase. But if you decide to obtain a loan to buy a car, either because you don't want to spend your cash or because you have no cash to spend, then you have several options.

Secured auto loan. You can get an auto loan from the dealer (who sets up the loan with a bank of the dealership's choosing) or from another source, like a credit union or bank. Generally, the loan is secured by the car, which means that the car can be repossessed if you default on the loan. You cannot deduct the interest on this type of auto loan. Interest on a personal loan—such as a car loan—is deductible only if the loan is secured by your principal residence or second home.

Home equity loan. A better financing alternative is to pay for your car with a home equity loan. A home equity loan must be secured by your principal residence or second home, which means that you can deduct the interest (subject to the home equity debt limits described in Chapter 2). The deduction will almost certainly make the home equity loan a better deal. Only a much lower interest rate—low enough to make up for the tax deduction—would make a standard auto loan more attractive.

Unsecured loan. Unless you are borrowing from a friend or relative who is giving you a special deal, an unsecured loan is likely to cost you more than a secured loan. Because there's no collateral, the loan is much riskier for the lender. The lender will compensate for that additional risk by charging you a higher interest rate. Therefore, if you obtain an unsecured loan, not only will you forgo a tax deduction, but you will likely be paying more interest as well.

Property Taxes

Another tax benefit associated with car ownership is the deduction for property tax you might have to pay each year. Under federal law, if you pay an annual tax on your vehicle that is based on its value (also known as an "ad valorem" tax), you may deduct that amount on your federal income tax return.

Not every state or locality assesses an annual tax on vehicles; of those that do, only some impose a value-based tax. Other fees you might pay, such as a surcharge based on the weight of the vehicle or flat-rate fees (such as registration fees) are not deductible. (See "States That Assess an Annual Ad Valorem Property Tax," below, to find out whether your state imposes this type of tax.) In some states, however, the tax is assessed in some locales and not in others, so you might need to do some additional research to find out if the fees you pay include an ad valorem tax.

TIP

Look for ad valorem taxes in the bill of sale or sales contract. When you purchase a car in a state that assesses an annual ad valorem tax on vehicles, the first year's tax might be collected by the dealer when you purchase the car. Be sure to check your purchase documents to see if you paid such a tax when you bought the car. If so, you may deduct that amount on your tax return.

Tax Strategy: Should You Finance a Major Purchase or Pay Cash?

When we consider whether to finance a purchase, our personal preferences often take precedence over financial considerations. For example, even if you can afford to pay cash for your new car, you might decide to finance it so you can keep that $20,000 in your bank account, where you can get to it easily if you need it. But if you plan to base your decision primarily on financial considerations, here are some guidelines:

- If you have cash sitting in the bank that you don't need for current living expenses, it is generally better to pay cash than to finance your purchase. When you borrow money, you pay interest, which adds significantly to the cost of the item you are purchasing. This is an especially important consideration if the interest on the loan won't be deductible (because it's unsecured or secured only by the car, for example).

- Even if you finance your purchase with a loan secured by your principal residence (which makes the interest deductible), it is still usually better to pay cash. The tax deduction for the interest you pay will reduce the after-tax cost of the purchase, but it would still be cheaper not to pay any interest at all.

- Financing the purchase might make more sense if you could invest the cash and make more money than you would save by not paying interest. For example, if you plan to finance the purchase of a big-ticket item and invest your cash in securities that will provide a greater return than your financing expense (interest and other costs associated with the financing), then you might save money by financing. The tricky part will be ensuring that your investment pays off as you hope. Typically, your loan interest would be at prevailing rates, which means you would need to invest your funds in securities that produce returns greater than prevailing rates. (And if you can do that consistently, you should patent your methodology.) If you decide to finance your purchase, and you will not be using a home equity loan to do so, bear in mind that you will almost certainly get a better interest rate on a loan that is secured by the car than a loan that is not secured at all.

States that Assess an Annual Ad Valorem Property Tax

If you live in one of the states listed below, you might be paying an annual ad valorem tax on your car or other vehicle. Some states impose an ad valorem tax at the state level, which means the rate is set by the state and applied statewide. Other states let local jurisdictions set the rate, which means the tax will vary depending on where you live. Three states leave it up to local jurisdictions to decide whether or not to assess an ad valorem tax. States that aren't listed in any of the categories below do not levy an ad valorem tax on vehicles; if you live in one of these states, you cannot deduct any of your annual fees.

States That Assess Tax at the State Level		
Arizona	Michigan	Oklahoma
California	Minnesota	Utah
Colorado	Montana	Washington
Indiana	Nebraska	Wyoming
Maine	Nevada	
Massachusetts	New Hampshire	
States That Allow Jurisdictions to Determine Tax Rate		
Alabama	Kentucky	South Carolina
Arkansas	Mississippi	Virginia
Georgia	Missouri	West Virginia
Kansas	North Carolina	
States That Allow Jurisdictions to Decide Whether to Levy a Tax		
Alaska	Rhode Island	Texas

Hybrid, Alternative Fuel, and Electric Car Credits

Tax credits for buying alternative fuel vehicles have been available for quite a while. It's only now, with the proliferation of more affordable energy-efficient vehicles, that taxpayers have really begun to take notice. It pays to know whether the car you're thinking about buying qualifies for one of these credits. If it does, the credit might save you thousands of dollars in taxes (and the car could save you almost as much on gas).

Hybrid Car Credit

For a number of years, taxpayers could claim a tax deduction for buying a hybrid car, like the Toyota Prius, that met certain fuel efficiency standards. Beginning in 2006, the deduction was replaced with a credit, and the IRS added more cars to the list of those that qualify. (You can find that list on the IRS website, www.irs.gov; search for "Hybrid Cars and Alternative Motor Vehicles.") The credit will be available only for cars purchased before January 1, 2011.

If your car makes the list, you'll need to calculate the credit amount. You can find detailed instructions in the tax code, but you might need a Ph.D. in propulsion physics to figure it out. Fortunately, the IRS has saved you the time and expense of all that additional schooling. On its website, the IRS lists the credit amount you may claim next to each make and model of car.

To claim the credit, you must satisfy several additional requirements. First, if the car is for personal use only (rather than business use), you must claim the credit for the year in which you purchase the car. Second, you must be the original owner of the car. And third, the car must be primarily for use in the United States.

There's one final twist: The credit, or some portion of the credit, will be available only for a certain number of each company's hybrid vehicles. The later you buy your car in relation to other purchasers, the less your credit will be, until eventually you are no longer entitled to any credit at all for your vehicle. Here are the rules:

- The first 60,000 hybrids (all models combined) sold by a given manufacturer will qualify for the full credit.

- In addition, hybrids sold after the manufacturer reaches the 60,000 threshold, but during the same calendar quarter or the quarter immediately following, qualify for the full credit.
- For hybrids sold in the second and third calendar quarters after the quarter in which the manufacturer sold its 60,000th hybrid, the credit is 50% of the original amount.
- For hybrids sold in the fourth and fifth quarters after the quarter in which the 60,000th hybrid was sold, the credit is 25% of the original amount.
- For hybrids sold in later quarters, there's no credit at all.

EXAMPLE: Ford Motor Company sold its 60,000th hybrid vehicle in April 2008. In October 2008, you purchased a Mercury Mariner 2WD Hybrid. According to the website, the full credit amount for that particular model is $3,000. Because you purchased the vehicle in the second quarter after Ford sold its 60,000th hybrid, you are entitled to 50% of the credit or $1,500.

As mentioned above, the IRS posts on its website the amount of the credit that is available for each vehicle, based on your date of purchase. The website is updated periodically to reflect reductions in the credit amount as sales of the vehicles increase. Go to www.irs. gov and search for "Hybrid Cars" in the search window in the upper right corner of the screen. When the search results come up, click on the link "Hybrid Cars and Alternative Fuel Vehicles."

Your credit could be limited further by other laws. For example, if you are eligible for other personal credits (such as the child tax credit or the dependent care credit), you must use those first. If they reduce your tax liability to zero, you may not claim a credit for the purchase of your hybrid vehicle. The credit amount also might be reduced or eliminated if you are subject to the alternative minimum tax, or if your tax liability is so low that you are unable to use the full amount of the credit (your credit amount cannot be more than your tax liability).

Alternative Fuel Motor Vehicle Credit

In addition to certain hybrid cars, other vehicles that use alternative fuels have received a Congressional blessing in the form of a sizable tax credit for their owners. Alternative fuels include compressed natural gas, liquefied natural gas or petroleum gas, hydrogen, or a liquid that is at least 85% methanol. (The Honda Civic GX qualifies for this credit.)

Again, you don't have to chemically analyze the fuel mix of your car to qualify for the credit. You can simply check the IRS website to find out whether your car is on the approved list and, if so, how much of a credit you may claim. For a complete list, go to www.irs. gov and search for "Alternative Fuel Motor Vehicles" in the search window in the upper right corner of the screen. When the search results come up, click on the link "Qualified Alternative Fuel Motor Vehicles (QAFMV) and Heavy Hybrid Vehicles."

The maximum credit for a car in this category is $4,000. Other types of vehicles have different credit limits. This credit is not subject to the phase-out rule that applies to hybrid vehicles (once the manufacturer sells 60,000 hybrid cars). However, under current law, the alternative fuel motor vehicle credit will expire on December 31, 2010.

> **TIP**
>
> **Other alternative fuel vehicles might also qualify.** In addition to the hybrid car and the alternative fuel motor vehicle, there are two other types of alternative fuel vehicles that qualify for special credits. One is a vehicle propelled by fuel cell; the other is called an "advanced lean burn technology motor vehicle." If you purchased either vehicle, you probably received a manufacturer's certificate notifying you that the vehicle qualifies for a special tax credit. You will need both the manufacturer's certificate and the information on the IRS website to help you determine your credit amount. These credits also expire at the end of 2010.

Electric Vehicle Credit

As we go to press, Congress has passed a new law allowing taxpayers to claim a credit for a portion of the cost of a qualified plug-in electric vehicle. The details, including how to claim the credit, should be worked out by the time the law takes effect in 2009.

How to Claim the Credit for Hybrid and Alternative Fuel Vehicles

To claim a hybrid or alternative fuel vehicle credit, you must first complete Form 8910, *Alternative Motor Vehicle Credit*. Then, carry the allowable amount to the second page of Form 1040, and enter it on the line marked "Other Credits" in the "Tax and Credits" section.

Boats and RVs

While some retirees rush to the car dealership, others will be looking at boats or RVs—or both. Either of these could easily cost more than a car, but they also generate some tax benefits that might ease the financial burden.

Personal Property Tax Deduction

If you live in a state that levies a personal property tax on cars, chances are good you'll be paying such a tax on your boat or RV as well. (See "Property Taxes," above, for more information on personal property taxes.) If you pay this tax on any vehicle, you may deduct it on your tax return.

Second Home

It's entirely possible that your boat or RV will qualify as your second home. As explained in Chapter 8, you may designate any home (other than your principal residence) as your second home. But you may have only one second home for tax purposes.

To qualify as a second home, your boat, RV, or other structure must have cooking, toilet, and sleeping facilities. And, as long as you don't rent it out when you are not using it, the home will qualify as your second home whether or not you actually use it during the year.

If you designate your boat or RV as your second home, you might be able to treat the interest on the loan you obtained to purchase the vehicle as mortgage interest, if the loan is secured by the vehicle. This can result in significant tax savings. (Note however, that your mortgage interest deduction is subject to certain limits. See Chapter 2 for more information.)

Sales Tax

Way back in the old days, sales tax on purchases was deductible. That particular tax benefit disappeared for about two decades, but has now been resurrected, albeit in a slightly different form.

You may claim a deduction for sales tax you pay during the year, including use taxes on out-of-state purchases, as long as you itemize deductions on Schedule A. The new twist is that you must choose between a sales tax deduction or a deduction for your state and local income taxes. You may not claim both, but you may claim whichever amount is larger.

If you live in a high-tax state like California or New York, you likely will be better off claiming the income tax deduction. That's not always the case, however, especially if you made some expensive purchases during the year. (Remember that boat you bought when you retired in June?) If you live in a state that has no income tax (Florida, Nevada, South Dakota, Texas, Washington, or Wyoming), the resurrection of the sales tax deduction is a savings bonanza for you.

There are two ways to calculate your sales tax deduction:

Method 1: Look it up. The IRS has prepared tables of average expenditures for each state. You will find those tables in IRS Publication 600, *Optional State Sales Tax Tables*. Instead of keeping track of all of your own purchases and the sales tax you paid, you may use the number from the IRS table. You may add to that number:

- **Any additional sales tax assessed by the local government where you live.** For example, if your county charges 2% sales tax over and above the amount assessed by the state, you may increase the table amount accordingly. Publication 600 helps with this calculation.
- **Any sales tax you paid for a motor vehicle, aircraft, boat, home, or home-building materials.** However, if the sales tax rate you paid for those items was greater than the general sales tax rate for your state and locality, then you may deduct only what you would have paid according to the lower general rate (not what you actually paid).

Method 2: **Add it up.** Alternatively, you may keep the receipts from all of your purchases and total the sales tax at the end of the year. For most people, the prospect of pawing through piles of tiny pieces of paper at tax time will bring on the vapors. However, if you have an inkling that your actual sales tax total will significantly exceed the number from the IRS table (which is based on average consumer spending in your area)—and if you're good with a calculator—you might want to use this alternative method.

How to Claim the Deduction for Sales Tax

You report your sales tax deduction on Schedule A, in the "Taxes You Paid" section. Remember, you may claim either the sales tax deduction or the state and local income tax deduction, not both.

Personal Loans

Loans are a fairly simple transaction: One person lends money to another, who then pays back the lender, with interest, until the loan is paid off. From a tax standpoint, however, loans can be a bit more complicated. Can you deduct the interest you pay on a loan? If your feckless brother-in-law fails to pay you back, can you write off the debt? What happens if a debt is forgiven? The answer to many of these questions can be found right in the tax code.

Loans to You

It's hard to make it all the way through life without borrowing money at some point. Many people want to own their own homes; most of us feel that we need a car to make our lives work efficiently; and a few feel that life isn't worth living without a yacht. If we can't come up with the cash to pay for such expensive items, we have to borrow the funds.

But when you borrow money to buy something, you must pay it back with interest, which in turn increases the cost of the initial purchase. Interest on personal loans generally is not deductible, unless the loan is secured by your home.

> **CROSS REFERENCE**
>
> **Interest on other types of loans might be deductible.** This chapter covers personal loans used to purchase items for personal use. If you use loan proceeds for a different purpose, however, you might be able to deduct the interest as, for example, a business expense (see Chapter 3), a rental expense (see Chapter 8), or an investment expense (see Chapter 7).

Loans Secured by Your Home

For the most part, you may not deduct the interest you pay on a personal loan. However, there is an exception to this rule: If the personal loan is secured by your principal residence or second home, and the loan qualifies as acquisition debt or home equity debt, you can deduct the interest as mortgage interest (subject to certain limits).

What Is a Secured Loan?

A loan is secured when you pledge to turn over an asset (the security, or collateral, for the loan) to the lender if you default on the loan.

If the loan is secured by your home, the lender has the right to fore-close: to force a sale of the home to satisfy the debt or cure the default. If your home is worth more than you owe, you might or might not receive the remaining proceeds from the sale (if any) once the lender has been paid. It depends on the state in which you live. In some states, all of the proceeds go to the lender regardless of the amount.

Although most of us think of secured loans as coming from a bank or credit union, you can enter into a secured loan agreement with anyone. As long as you agree to give the lender the right to foreclose if you don't repay the loan according to the terms of the loan agreement, you have created a loan secured by your home. The pledge to back the loan with your home should not be a gentleman's (or woman's) agreement, though. You and the lender should take the necessary steps to formalize the agreement:

- Prepare and sign a promissory note, which is a written commit-ment to pay a certain amount by a certain date. The promissory note might be part of a more comprehensive loan agreement that contains all of the terms of the loan, including your agreement to pledge the home as collateral.
- You might also need a document that conveys title of the property to the lender (until the loan is paid off) or places a lien on the property. Depending on the laws of the state in which you live, the appropriate document might be a deed of trust or a mortgage. Once executed, the document should be recorded with the appropriate city, county, or state recorder.

SEE AN EXPERT

Get help drafting a secured loan agreement. Each state has different rules that apply to secured loans between individuals. Consult an attorney to learn about the rules that apply in your state and to get assistance drafting your loan agreement.

Deducting Interest on a Secured Loan

If a loan is secured by your principal residence or second home, the interest you pay on that loan is generally deductible mortgage interest. As described in Chapter 2, there are different types of mortgage interest and different deduction limits, depending on the type of mortgage you have. You may deduct the interest on up to $1 million of acquisition debt (which must be used to construct, purchase, or improve the home) and $100,000 of home equity debt (which may be used for any other purpose).

These limits apply to the combined debt on your primary and second homes. For example, if you have a $75,000 home equity loan on your primary residence, then take out a $50,000 home equity loan on your second home, you may deduct the interest on only $100,000 of the total home equity debt (assuming the loan proceeds were not used to purchase or improve the home); your interest on $25,000 of the second loan won't be deductible.

The rule that allows you to use home equity loan proceeds for any purpose (other than acquiring or improving your residence) can benefit you considerably if you need to finance a personal purchase, like a boat, vacation, or car. In most areas of the tax code, whether or not interest can be deducted is determined by how the money is used. But home equity debt is different: For loans of up to $100,000 that are secured by your residence, you may deduct the interest regardless of what you do with the money. Of course, if you use it to purchase or improve your first or second home, the loan is considered acquisition debt, not home equity debt. You may still deduct the interest, as long as your total acquisition debt is less than the $1 million limit (see Chapter 2).

You may also enter into a secured loan agreement, as described above, with anyone who's willing to lend you money. A home equity loan from a bank or savings and loan qualifies, but so does a loan from your sister-in-law or friend, as long as the lender has the right to foreclose if you default on the loan.

How to Claim Deductible Interest on a Secured Loan

If your interest is deductible because your loan is secured by your principal residence or second home, you claim the deduction as mortgage interest on Schedule A, in the "Interest You Paid" section. If you borrow the money from another person (for example, a friend), you must also supply the name, address, and Social Security number of the person who loaned you the money. You enter this information next to the dollar amount of the interest on Schedule A.

Unsecured Loans

If you obtain an unsecured loan (a loan for which you put up no collateral) to purchase items for personal use, the interest on the loan is not deductible.

Forgiven Loans

If you owe someone money and can't pay it back, your lender may one day decide to forgive the debt. Although you might feel justifiably thrilled to know that you don't have to repay the loan, you can count on the IRS to temper your celebration a bit. Because you no longer have to pay the money back, you must report it as taxable income to you. So, for example, if you owe the bank $20,000 and that debt is forgiven, you won't have to pay back the $20,000, but you must report $20,000 of income on your tax return.

Debt forgiveness is complicated. Determining whether you have taxable income when a debt is forgiven—and how to characterize that income for tax purposes—can be extremely complex. For example:

- If you are insolvent even after a debt is forgiven, the income is generally not taxable.
- Whether the debt is recourse debt (meaning the lender has the right to force you to find resources—even personal assets—to make good on the debt) or nonrecourse debt (meaning secured debt that gives the lender the right to take the collateral, but none of your other assets, if you default) might determine whether you must report the income on your tax return, and if

so, whether you should treat the income as ordinary or capital gain.

- A law that applies only for years 2007 through 2012 waives the federal income tax on a limited amount of debt forgiveness for certain types of mortgage debt on your principal residence.

For more information about these issues, see IRS Publication 508, *Bankruptcy Tax Guide,* or *Solve Your Money Troubles*, by Robin Leonard and John Lamb (Nolo).

If a financial institution forgives a debt, it will issue you a Form 1099-C, *Cancellation of Debt*, and send a copy to the IRS. When debt forgiveness occurs between friends or relatives, however, it is usually intended as a favor—a gift to the person who owed the money. In that case, you don't need to include the forgiven amount as income, and the person forgiving the debt need not file a Form 1099-C. However, the person who forgives the debt may have to pay gift tax if the forgiven amount is more than the gift tax limit. For more on gift taxes, see Chapter 11.

Loans You Make to Others

If you are the lender rather than the borrower, you will have different concerns. Rather than worrying about whether you can deduct interest you pay, you'll want to know whether you must report the interest you earn on the loan. And, if the borrower doesn't pay you back, can you write off the loan and claim a deduction on your tax return?

Reporting Interest You Receive

If you lend money to someone, and the borrower pays you interest on the loan amount, you must report that interest as income. This rule applies whether the loan is secured or not. The advantage of making a secured loan, of course, is that you have a remedy if the borrower defaults. If the loan is secured by the borrower's house, for example, you can force the sale of the house to recover the amount owed to you.

If you charge interest on a loan, you must report the interest you receive as income on Schedule B, *Interest and Ordinary Dividends*, along with interest you receive from other sources, like a bank or brokerage account.

> **CAUTION**
> **You might not be first in line to recover your money.** If the borrower also owes money to other people or institutions, you might not be fully repaid. The law dictates the order in which creditors receive proceeds from the sale of collateral. If the house or other collateral isn't worth enough to pay back all of the creditors, you might not get all—or any—of your money back.

Needless to say, making an unsecured loan can be risky. Without collateral, you might have difficulty recovering your money if the borrower defaults. Even a court fight might prove unproductive if the borrower has no assets. Whether or not the borrower puts up collateral, you should have a written loan agreement that gives you a way to recover on a defaulted loan.

No-Interest or Low-Interest Loans

Remember the adage "neither a borrower nor a lender be"? Although Shakespeare warned of deepening debt and lost friendships, he could easily have added another item to the list of potential problems: "Beware the tax man!" When you lend money, even to a friend or family member, there might be tax consequences. As explained above, you must report any interest you receive as income. But what if you don't charge interest, or don't charge the going rate? Believe it or not, you still might have to report your friendly transaction on your tax return.

Many a dollar has changed hands on a handshake, with the understanding that the money will be repaid when the borrower is able to do so (or when the lender asks for it). More often than not, the loan is made to a friend or relative, to help with a house purchase, pay for an emergency expenditure (a new roof or unexpected medical bills, for example), or to underwrite a much-needed vacation. If you have made a loan like this to someone close to you, you might be charging no interest at all, or just a nominal amount.

You might think the IRS would have little interest in loans between friends and family members. And for the most part, you would be right—unless the IRS sees your no- or low-interest loan as a scheme to transfer wealth without paying gift or estate taxes. Although gifts and inheritances are not subject to income tax, they are potentially subject to gift tax (if you make the transfer during your lifetime) or estate tax (if you make the transfer after your death).

> **TIP**
>
> **Smaller gifts don't have to be reported.** Gifts you receive are not taxable as income regardless of the amount of the gift. If you are the donor, your gifts are not deductible. In fact, there are no tax consequences to you at all, as long as your gifts to any one person do not add up to more than $12,000 for the year. (This is the limit for 2008; it's scheduled to increase for 2009.) If your gifts to any person exceed the limit, you must file a gift tax return and you might have to pay gift taxes. The gift will not be subject to income tax, but the gift might have estate and gift tax consequences. For more information about gifts, see Chapter 11.

For example, consider the parent who decides to bypass gift tax rules by making a large interest-free "loan" to a child, with no intention of asking for the money back. By categorizing the transfer of funds as a loan rather than a gift, the parent could give away significant wealth without tax consequences. To forestall such abuses, Congress constructed a set of rules for low-interest and interest-free loans, intended to permit legitimate loans while curbing tax-avoidance ploys.

The Minimum Interest Rate

The cornerstone of this effort by Congress is the "minimum interest rate" rule, which requires lenders to charge at least a certain rate of interest, called the "applicable federal rate." As long as the minimum interest rate requirement is met, the usual rules apply: If you are the lender, you must report the interest you receive as income. The borrower may deduct interest paid on the loan if it is secured by his or her principal residence or second home (assuming the mortgage debt does not exceed the limits), or if it is deductible because of the way the funds are used (for example, as a business or rental expense).

If you fail to charge the prescribed minimum rate of interest, but your transaction is in fact a loan, then you must report "imputed" interest. When interest is "imputed," no interest payments actually change hands. Instead, you are deemed to have given the borrower the money to make the interest payments to you. More specifically, here's how the IRS will view the transaction:

You, the lender, should have charged interest, but you didn't. The interest you didn't charge is considered a gift to the borrower, and it is subject to gift tax if it exceeds the limit ($12,000 for 2008). (See Chapter 11 for more information about gift tax.) If the borrower and lender have a business relationship (e.g. the borrower is your employee), the interest is not treated as a gift, but as compensation.

The borrower used that gift of interest to pay you the interest you should have charged.

The tax consequences of this presumed transaction are:

- You must report the imputed interest as income.
- The borrower may deduct the interest if the loan is secured by his or her principal residence or second home.
- You must file a gift tax return (and perhaps pay gift tax) if the imputed interest you should have charged is more than the gift tax limit ($12,000 for 2008) in a year.

SEE AN EXPERT

Get some help if you have to figure out imputed interest.
The imputed interest rules are extremely complex. The IRS's prescribed
interest rate varies according to the type of loan transaction you have
structured and the terms of repayment. If you find yourself in the midst of a
transaction that requires imputing interest, consult with an expert who can
help you structure a legally sound loan agreement.

Exceptions for Loans to Family and Friends

Although the minimum interest rule requires that lenders charge
a minimum rate of interest, some exceptions have been carved out
primarily to accommodate loan transactions among family members
and friends. The rules vary according to how much money changes
hands.

Loans of $10,000 or less. You may lend $10,000 or less to anyone,
relative or stranger, without any tax consequences. However, the
borrower may *not* use the loan to purchase income-producing
assets, such as a rental property or securities (stocks and bonds, for
example). If the loan exceeds $10,000 at any point during the year,
interest will be imputed for each day the loan exceeds the limit.

Loans of more than $10,000 but no more than $100,000. For loans
within these limits, the following rules apply:

- As long as the borrower has investment income of no more
  than $1,000, there will be no imputed interest. (Investment
  income includes interest and ordinary dividends earned from
  investments; if the borrower has elected, on his or her tax
  return, to include capital gains and qualified dividends as
  investment income, those count as well. See Chapter 7 for
  more information on investment income and tax issues.) The
  lender need not report interest income, and the borrower may
  not deduct it, either.

- If the borrower's investment income exceeds $1,000 for the
  year, then interest must be imputed. However, the imputed
  interest is limited to the amount of investment income the

borrower has earned during the year. The lender must report imputed interest, as limited, as income, and the borrower may deduct it if the loan qualifies (for example, the loan is secured by the borrower's home or the funds from the loan are used to repair rental property).

- The forgone interest—the difference between the interest actually charged (and paid annually) and the imputed interest—is considered a gift from the lender to the borrower. This rule applies whether or not the imputed interest must be reported as income.

- If the $100,000 limit is exceeded at any time during the year, the imputed interest rules will apply for each of those days. This means the lender must compute the imputed interest for those days and report that amount on his or her tax return, regardless of the amount of the borrower's investment income.

CAUTION

Spouses are treated as one person. For purposes of the rules regarding interest-free and below-market loans, a husband and wife are considered one person. The loans you make will be combined with the loans your spouse makes to determine whether you have loaned someone more than $10,000, for example.

Loans to a Continuing Care Facility

In the world of retirement living, a continuing care facility is one that allows you to live independently for as long as you can and then provides increasing care as you need it. Increased care might mean moving from a self-contained apartment to an assisted living unit or perhaps into a skilled nursing unit if and when you need more care.

Although continuing care facilities provide very valuable services, many of them charge an "entrance fee" for which you could reasonably expect to be living in Windsor Castle rather than a retirement home. To ease the pain of the large initial fee, some continuing care facilities promise to refund a portion of the fee to you if you move out, or to your heirs when you die.

The refundable portion of the fee is generally treated as a "loan" you make to the facility. Now that you know something about imputed interest, alarm bells are surely ringing in your head. Does that mean you must report imputed interest on your tax return? And pay tax on it? Paying tax on imputed (dare we say phantom?) interest when you've already forked over a huge chunk of your nest egg probably doesn't sound all that good. Happily, Congress recognized the problem, and created an exception to the usual rules.

Your loan to a continuing care facility is completely exempt from the imputed interest rules as long as all of the following are true:

- Either you or your spouse (if you are married) is at least 62 years old as of December 31 of the year you move into the facility.
- The entrance fee is part of a contract you must sign before you move in.
- The facility has all of the following characteristics:
  - It allows you to live there for life.
  - Housing is provided.
  - Meals and personal care are available outside of your particular housing unit.
  - You are permitted to move into the assisted living or skilled nursing area of the facility when and if you require such additional care.

How to Report Imputed Interest on a Personal Loan

To report imputed interest, you must attach a statement to your tax return indicating how you calculated the imputed interest. You must also provide the name and Social Security number of the borrower. The interest income itself is reported on Schedule B, *Interest and Ordinary Dividends*, along with interest you receive from other sources, like a bank or brokerage account.

Bad Debts

Suppose you lend money to someone and the unthinkable happens: The borrower never pays you back. Can you deduct the loss?

If the loan was valid when you made it and is now truly uncollectible, then you should be able to deduct it. However, proving this to the IRS's satisfaction is sometimes difficult. This is especially true if the loan was a personal loan rather than a business loan.

What Is a Bad Debt?

To qualify as a bad debt, a loan must meet these requirements:

- **The loan must be valid.** In other words, you and the borrower must have a legitimate debtor-creditor relationship in which the borrower promises to pay the debt and you have a right to enforce that promise to recover your money. If you didn't expect to be repaid when you made the loan, it won't be considered valid.
- **Money must have actually changed hands.** Without a cash outlay on your part, you cannot incur a deductible tax loss. For example, if someone agrees to give you money but never makes good on the promise, you do not have a bad debt and may not claim a deduction.
- **The debt must have become worthless in the year for which you claim the loss.** To satisfy this condition, all of the following must be true:
    - The debt was collectible in the previous year.
    - An identifiable event occurred in the current year that made the debt totally worthless (for example, the borrower filed for bankruptcy).
    - You have no reasonable hope of recovery in a future year. (This is difficult to prove, but you must offer a reasonable explanation why you believe recovery is not in the cards.)

If you are making a loan to a family member, keep in mind that the government may presume the loan is a gift. It will be up to you to prove otherwise. The best way to do so is to create a written loan agreement or promissory note that sets the loan interest at prevailing rates and requires payment on a specific date or dates. If the borrower defaults on the loan, you should exhaust your remedies in your effort to collect your money. If you don't, the loan looks more like a gift.

> **CAUTION**
>
> **You may not claim a bad debt deduction if you cosigned the loan.** When you voluntarily take over a debt (by cosigning for it in the first place), you may not claim a bad debt deduction if and when you are left holding the bag. For example, you might cosign a loan to help your child purchase a first home. Once you guarantee the loan, you must take over the obligation if your child defaults—and you may not claim a bad debt deduction for the amount of the loan on which your child defaulted.

How to Deduct a Bad Debt

If you qualify to claim a bad debt on your tax return, you claim it as a short-term capital loss on Schedule D, *Capital Gains and Losses*. You must also attach a statement to your tax return, which:

- describes the loan and its terms, including the amount and the payment due date
- indicates your relationship to the borrower
- indicates how you tried to collect the money owed to you, and
- explains why you think the loan is now worthless (totally uncollectible).

Your deduction will be treated like other capital losses, which means that the bad debt, when combined with other capital gains and losses, cannot exceed $3,000 for the year. If your net capital loss (including the bad debt) exceeds $3,000, then you must carry over the remaining loss to the following year.

Your Family

Tax Benefits in This Chapter

☐ **Are you supporting a child or other relative who is living with you?**
- You might be able to claim that person as a dependent on your tax return.
- You may be eligible to claim a Child Tax Credit.

☐ **Did you pay someone else's medical expenses?**
- You might be able to claim a deduction for those expenses even if the person is not your dependent.

☐ **Did you pay someone else's mortgage or property tax?**
- You might be able to deduct the interest if you are a part owner of the property.

☐ **Did you pay someone else's education expenses?**
- If you paid expenses for a dependent, you may be eligible for a Hope Credit, Lifetime Learning Credit, or a higher education expense deduction.
- If you obtained a student loan for someone else and are responsible for repaying it, you may be able to deduct some of the interest you pay.

☐ **Did you make contributions to a Coverdell ESA or 529 plan for someone else?**
- Although you can't deduct your contributions, the beneficiary of the account may be able to take distributions tax free.

☐ **Are you making support payments to a former spouse?**
- Some or all of those payments might be deductible.

R elatives! You can't live with them and you can't live without them. But what about doing business with them, lending them money, claiming them as dependents on your tax return, or paying their expenses? We can't help you with the emotional issues that might come up if you decide to combine family and money, but we can at least help you find some tax benefits to take out of the mix.

If you engage in a financial transaction with someone to whom you are related, it's quite possible that special tax laws will apply. Suppose you take someone into your home and support him or her during a financial rough patch or through college. Can you deduct the expenses you pay on your lodger's behalf? Do you know which tax benefits are available to you and which are off limits? The answer could well depend on whether or not you are related to the person you are helping.

This chapter covers the tax rules that apply to some common family situations and to transactions that occur between family members.

Claiming an Exemption for Dependents

Everyone is entitled to claim a personal exemption on his or her income tax return. If you file a joint return with your spouse, you may each claim an exemption on the return. Each exemption is worth a specific dollar amount ($3,500 in 2008), which you may deduct from your adjusted gross income (AGI). Through the personal exemption, Congress ensures that you will owe little or no tax if you don't have much income. If you earn more than the exemption, at least you don't have to pay tax on the exempt amount.

Exemptions vs. Deductions

The terms "exemption" and "deduction" are sometimes used inter-changeably because both can help reduce your tax liability. Technically, however, a deduction is available primarily for expenses you actually paid, such as mortgage interest, medical bills, and business expenses. In contrast, you don't have to spend any money to claim a personal exemption: This benefit is available to you simply because you exist.

CAUTION

The higher your income, the lower your exemption. If your income exceeds a certain amount, the personal exemptions you may claim on your tax return are phased out. The effect of this phase-out is to require high-income taxpayers to pay more tax by gradually reducing to zero the amount of income that is exempt from tax. For more information, see "Exemption Phase-Out," below.

In addition to your own personal exemption (as well as your spouse's, if you are married and filing a joint return), you may claim an exemption in the same amount for each of your dependents. From a public policy perspective, this is no surprise. The tax code has long reflected the government's belief that those who are supporting large families should be able to shelter more income than those who are supporting smaller families.

By the time you're ready to retire, you might think that you're through claiming others as dependents. Once your kids are grown and filing their own tax returns, dependency exemptions should be a distant memory, right? Not necessarily. What if one of your kids needs to move back home, has a disability, or asks you to take care of the grandchildren for a while? What if another relative—perhaps a sibling or parent—is no longer able to live alone? What if you need to take in a friend? In each of these situations, you might be able to claim a dependency exemption.

Who Qualifies as a Dependent

You may claim a dependency exemption for someone you support only if that person meets the tax code's technical definition of a dependent. A dependent must be either a "qualifying child" or a "qualifying relative." Although these categories sound fairly straightforward, there are a few twists. For example, a qualifying child need not be a child of yours and in fact need not be a child. Similarly, a qualifying relative need not actually be a blood relative. Here are the rules for each type of dependent.

Qualifying Child

A qualifying child must meet all of the following conditions:

- The person must be your child, stepchild, sibling, stepsibling, half-sibling, foster child, or a descendant of one of these relatives.
- The person must have lived with you for more than half the year.
- The person must not have provided more than half of his or her own support during the year.
- As of December 31 of the current tax year, the person must be younger than 19; younger than 24 and a full-time student for at least five months during the year; or disabled (no age limits apply in this situation).

> TIP
> **You don't have to be the child's sole provider.** To meet the definition of a qualifying child, a dependent must not pay more than half of his or her own support, as noted above. However, this does not mean that you have to pay the rest.

Disputes sometimes arise over who may claim the exemption for a qualifying child. For example, if a disabled adult's parents are divorced, and both contribute to their child's support, both might believe they are entitled to claim the exemption. And often, that's just what happens: Each parent claims the exemption on his or her own return. That's not kosher, however. Only one taxpayer may claim an exemption for a given child, even if both individuals technically qualify to claim the exemption.

Congress fearlessly waded into the realm of dispute resolution by providing solutions to this problem in the tax code. If two people are eligible for a deduction and both attempt to claim it, the issue will be resolved as follows:

- If the dispute is between a parent and a nonparent, the parent may claim the exemption.
- If two parents are involved, the parent who has the child for the most time during the year may claim the exemption.
- If two parents have the child equal amounts of time, the parent with the highest adjusted gross income may claim the exemption.
- If the dispute is between two nonparents, the individual with the highest adjusted gross income may claim the exemption.

EXAMPLE: Your daughter is a single mother. She and her eight-year-old son, (your grandchild) both live with you. Although your daughter pays her own way, you have paid most of your grandchild's expenses for the entire year. Technically, you are both eligible to claim your grandson as a dependent—and that's what both of you do. If the IRS catches on, only your daughter will be allowed to claim the exemption because she is the child's parent. Your exemption deduction will be denied.

Qualifying Relative

If the person you want to claim as a dependent doesn't meet the requirements for a qualifying child, you might still be able to claim that person as a qualifying relative. Believe it or not, your qualifying "relative" doesn't actually have to be related to you, and you might even be able to claim this exemption for someone who doesn't live with you for any part of the year. You may claim a dependency exemption if all of the following criteria are met:

- Your qualifying relative must be your child, stepchild, adopted child, foster child, or a descendant of any of these relatives; your sibling, stepsibling, or half-sibling; your parent or an ancestor of your parent; your stepparent; your niece or nephew; your aunt or uncle; your child, parent, or sibling by marriage; or any person, other than your spouse, who lived with you for the entire tax year (except for temporary absences).

> TIP
>
> **Your spouse is not a dependent (to the IRS).** You might consider your spouse a dependent (although perhaps you had better not say so), but the IRS does not. This is true even if you support your spouse financially. Just as you are entitled to a personal exemption (as opposed to a dependency exemption) for yourself, your spouse is entitled to his or her own personal exemption. If you file a joint return, you will each claim a personal exemption on that return.

- The relative's gross income must be less than the exemption amount ($3,500 for 2008).
- You must provide more than half of the qualifying relative's support. When tallying up how much support you are providing, you should include food, clothing, health care, education, transportation, recreation, and the fair rental value of the portion of your home used by the person, including utilities and furnishings, if he or she lives with you.
- The person is not being claimed as a qualifying child (as described above) by you or anyone else.

When You Support a Nursing Home Resident

Because your qualifying relative need not live with you, you may claim an exemption even for a relative who lives in a nursing home or assisted living facility—but only if you provide more than half of his or her support for the year.

Suppose you have been taking care of your elderly mother and claiming a dependency exemption for her on your tax return, but you are no longer able to care for her yourself. The long-term care facility you have found requires you to make a lump-sum payment to cover her future care. In order to determine whether or not you are providing more than half of her support, you must prorate the lump-sum payment over your mother's life expectancy, then include the prorated amount in your support figures for the current year.

If your dependent dies during the year, you may still claim a dependency exemption for that year. Similarly, if your spouse dies during the year, you may claim your spouse's personal exemption on a jointly filed return for the year of death. For more information about tax issues when a spouse dies, see Chapter 11.

When You May Not Claim a Dependency Exemption

Even if you meet all of the criteria to claim a dependent as either a qualifying child or qualifying relative, you might not be allowed to take the exemption. You are automatically disqualified from claiming a dependency exemption if:

- you are claimed as a dependent on another taxpayer's return
- the person you want to claim as a dependent files a joint tax return, or
- the person you want to claim is not a U.S. citizen or national (someone who owes allegiance to the United States, such as a citizen of American Samoa or the Commonwealth of the Northern Mariana Islands), unless:

- the person resides in the United States
- the person resides in a country contiguous to the United States or
- you are a U.S. citizen or national, and the person you want to claim is your adopted child or stepchild who lives with you.

TIP

Exception to the joint tax return rule. If your dependent files a joint return simply to claim a refund (in other words, your dependent and his or her spouse have income below the filing threshold and are not required to file a return, but do so anyway to claim a refund), you can still claim a dependency exemption. You are prohibited from claiming a dependency exemption only if your dependent is required to file a return and files one jointly with a spouse.

Exemption Phase-Out

Once you determine that you qualify to claim a dependency exemption, you have one more hurdle to clear before you can actually claim a tax benefit. Every exemption on your tax return, whether it is a personal exemption (like yours and your spouse's) or a dependency exemption, must be reduced if your adjusted gross income exceeds a given threshold. You must reduce the total exemption amount by a fixed percentage for every $2,500 (or part of $2,500) by which your income exceeds the threshold. The percentage reduction for each tax year is shown in the chart below. Calculating the reduced exemption is a bit complicated; see the example, below, to get a sense of how it works.

Married Filing Jointly			
Year	Phase-Out Threshold	Reduction for Each $2,500 Over Threshold	No Exemption Income Levels
2007	$234,600	1.3333%	No exemption for incomes at or over $357,100
2008	$239,950	0.6667%	No exemption for incomes at or over $362,450
2009	$250,200	0.6667%	No exemption for incomes at or over $372,700
2010	None (full exemption)	0%	N/A
2011	To be determined	2%	To be determined

Single			
Year	Phase-Out Threshold	Reduction for Each $2,500 Over Threshold	No Exemption Income Levels
2007	$156,400	1.3333%	No exemption for incomes at or over $278,900
2008	$159,950	0.6667%	No exemption for incomes at or over $282,450
2009	$166,800	0.6667%	No exemption for incomes at or over $289,300
2010	None (full exemption)	0%	N/A
2011	To be determined	2%	To be determined

EXAMPLE: You are married and filing a joint return with your spouse. Your eight-year-old grandson has lived with you all year, and you will claim him as your dependent in the year 2007. The total of your three exemptions (for yourself, your spouse, and your grandson) is $10,200 (3 x $3,400). But because your adjusted gross income is $250,000, you must reduce the amount you may claim on your tax return. You calculate your exemption amount as follows:

Step 1: Subtract the phase-out threshold amount of $234,600 from your income of $250,000. The result is $15,400.

Step 2: You must reduce the exemption amount for each $2,500 by which your income exceeds the threshold. You divide $15,400 by $2,500. The result is 6.16. You must round up, so the result becomes 7.

Step 3: Multiply 7 (the result from Step 2) by the reduction percentage of 1.3333 (for tax year 2007). The result is 9.3331%.

Step 4: Multiply 9.3331% (or 0.093331) by your total exemption amount of $10,200. The result is $952 (rounded). That is the amount by which you must reduce your total exemption amount.

Step 5: Subtract $952 from $10,200 to arrive at the final exemption amount you may claim on your return: $9,248.

How to Claim Exemptions

Claim your dependency exemptions along with your personal exemptions on Form 1040. First, complete the "Exemptions" section of the return on the first page. If your adjusted gross income is in the phase-out range, you will need to use the IRS's "Deduction for Exemptions Worksheet" (found in the instruction booklet for Form 1040) to calculate your reduced exemption amount. Enter the total amount of your allowable exemption deduction on the second page of Form 1040, in the "Tax and Credits" section.

Child Tax Credit

If you are caring for a grandchild or other qualifying child, you might be able to take advantage of another tax benefit in addition to the dependency exemption described above. If the child meets the definition of a "qualifying child" (described above) and is 16 or younger at the end of the tax year, you might be able to claim a child tax credit.

Calculating Your Credit

The full credit amount is $1,000 per qualifying child. However, like the dependency exemption, the tax credit is gradually phased out once your adjusted gross income exceeds a threshold amount. You must reduce your credit by $50 for each $1,000 (or fraction thereof) by which your income exceeds $110,000 (for married filing jointly) or $75,000 (for single filers). (For help figuring out how to reduce your credit, see "Exemption Phase-Out," above.)

Additional Child Tax Credit

If the child tax credit to which you are entitled is greater than your tax liability, you won't be able to use the full credit amount. However, you might qualify for a special refund, the "Additional Child Tax Credit." You may claim this special refund only if one of the following is true:

- You have earned at least $8,500 from employment or self-employment during the year (for 2008).
- You have three or more "qualifying children" for whom you are eligible to claim a child tax credit *and* you paid Social Security taxes during the year (through an employer or as self-employment taxes).

The amount of the refund cannot exceed your unused child tax credit, but the actual refund amount is based on your earned income (income from employment or self-employment). If you don't have earned income, you are not entitled to the special refund. Complete IRS Form 8812, *Additional Child Tax Credit*, to calculate the amount (if any) you may claim.

How to Claim the Child Tax Credit

Claim the child tax credit on the second page of Form 1040, in the "Tax and Credits" section. If your child tax credit exceeds the amount of tax you owe, complete Form 8812 to see if you are entitled to an Additional Child Tax Credit. If you are, you should enter the additional amount on the second page of Form 1040, in the "Payments" section, and attach Form 8812 to your tax return.

Deducting Expenses You Pay for Someone Else

Even if your home hasn't become a way station for refugee family members, you still might be giving them some financial help here and there. If you pay someone else's expenses, your payment is usually treated as a gift to that person. Gifts to friends and relatives are not income to the recipient, nor are they deductible by you. (Although you might have to worry about the gift tax if you give more than $12,000 (for 2008) to one person in a year; for more information about gifts and gift tax, see Chapter 11.)

There are some exceptions, however: situations in which you may claim a deduction for payments you make on behalf of others. And even if you aren't permitted to claim a deduction, other tax benefits might be available, depending on the type of expenses you pay.

Medical Expenses

If you pay medical expenses for a dependent (as defined by the IRS; see "Claiming an Exemption for Dependents," above), you may claim those expenses as though they were your own. You report them on Schedule A, and they will be deductible to the extent that the total of all medical expenses claimed on your tax return (yours, your spouse's, and your dependents') exceed 7.5% of your adjusted gross income. (See Chapter 4 for more information about calculating your medical expense deduction.)

You may deduct someone else's medical expenses in the year you pay the bill as long as the person was your dependent either when he or she received medical treatment *or* when you paid the bill. For example, suppose your granddaughter lived with you last year and was your dependent. She broke her leg and had to go to the hospital. You didn't settle the medical bills until this year, after your granddaughter went back to live with her mother and was no longer your dependent. You may still claim the medical expenses you paid on her behalf because she was your dependent when she received treatment.

In some situations, you may even deduct medical expenses you pay for someone who isn't your dependent. However, the person whose expenses you pay must fit into one of these categories:

- The person would qualify as your dependent except for the fact that his or her income exceeds the exemption amount ($3,500 for 2008).
- The person would qualify as your dependent except for the fact that he or she filed a joint return with a spouse.
- The person would qualify as your dependent except for the fact that you are claimed as a dependent on someone else's return (and therefore can't claim any exemptions yourself).

Tax Strategy: Should You Use Retirement Account Funds to Pay Medical Bills?

Do you remember reading somewhere that there's a tax benefit available if you pay medical expenses with money from your IRA? Well, it's true—but the benefit doesn't really help most retirees.

If you have not yet reached age 59½ and are subject to "early distribution" penalties when you withdraw money from your IRA or other retirement plan, you are permitted to withdraw retirement funds to pay medical expenses without incurring penalties on the full amount of your distribution. You must still pay some penalties, though. And you will owe regular income tax on the entire distribution.

Once you reach age 59½, however, this particular tax benefit doesn't apply to you, because you are not subject to penalties on any withdrawal from your retirement plan. In this situation, there's no advantage to using your retirement money for medical bills. Unless you are short of cash and have no other resources, it is usually best to leave your retirement funds alone to grow for as long as possible.

Mortgage Payments

Family members often find themselves helping a child or grandchild pay the mortgage. You might think that if you make a mortgage payment out of your own pocket, you should be able to claim a deduction on your own tax return for the interest you paid. That's certainly a logical interpretation, but it's not correct.

If you are not liable for the debt and therefore have no real obligation to make the mortgage payment, then you are not permitted to claim a deduction for any mortgage interest you pay. Instead, the payment is viewed as a gift to the person whose name is on the loan and who is liable for the debt.

If, on the other hand, your name is also on the loan (because you cosigned, for example), then you may deduct the interest you pay.

If you make all of the mortgage payments, you may claim all of the interest, assuming you are liable for the entire debt if the cosigner defaults. This deduction is available whether or not the person whose mortgage you are paying is your dependent. As long as your name also appears on the loan agreement and you are liable for the debt, you may claim a deduction for the interest you pay.

> **CAUTION**
>
> **Don't use your retirement funds.** It's usually not wise to pull money from a retirement account to help a child or grandchild buy a home. Although you can withdraw $10,000 from an IRA for a first-home purchase without paying any early distribution penalty, you don't have to worry about the penalty if you have already reached the age of 59½—all of your distributions are penalty-free, no matter what you spend them on. And you will still have to pay regular income tax on the entire distribution.

Property Taxes

Instead of helping out with mortgage payments, perhaps you agreed to pay some or all of a needy relative's real estate taxes. As is true of mortgage interest, you may not deduct real property taxes that you pay for someone else, whether or not that person is your dependent. You may deduct only those taxes for which you are liable—those that you are legally required to pay. Otherwise, your payment is treated as a gift to the person who is liable for the tax.

If you and another person are both named on a single deed for real property, then you are liable for the property taxes in proportion to your ownership interest. For example, if you and your grandson each own half of a home, you are responsible for half of the property taxes and he is responsible for the other half. If you pay all of the property taxes, you still may deduct only half. The other half of your payment is treated as a gift to your grandson.

As you might expect, there is an exception to this rule. If you have an interest in property and your investment is at risk because your co-owner is not paying his or her share of property taxes, you may pay—and deduct—the entire amount. In this situation, paying all of the taxes is necessary to protect your investment, which is what makes it fully deductible.

> ### TIP
> **The same rules apply to vehicle taxes.** If you pay someone else's vehicle registration fees, the same principles apply. The *ad valorem* taxes (taxes based on the value of the car) are deductible, but only by the person who is responsible for the tax: the car's owner. If you are a co-owner, then you may deduct the taxes you pay only to the limit of your liability. If you own half the car, you may claim only half of the *ad valorem* taxes, even if you pay the whole bill. For more information on deducting ad valorem taxes, see Chapter 9.

Education Expenses

Many people prefer to help family members with education expenses rather than daily living expenses. If you are among them, you will be pleased to know that the tax code is a bit more generous with deductions and credits for education than for other types of financial assistance you might provide.

If you search, you will find a cornucopia of tax benefits to help you cope with education expenses. Most of the benefits can be divided into two large categories: (1) benefits available when you pay expenses for yourself, your spouse, and your dependents; and (2) benefits available when you pay the education expenses of anyone else. (For information on paying your own or your spouse's education expenses, see Chapter 6.)

Education Expenses You Pay for a Dependent

If you are paying education expenses for yourself, your spouse, and your dependents, the big benefits come in the form of tax credits. But don't overlook the occasional deduction, which might be a better choice, depending on your situation.

Tuition and Fees

If you pay tuition and fees for a spouse or dependent, you may claim the same benefits that are available for your own education expenses. These benefits—the Hope Credit, the Lifetime Learning Credit, and the higher education expense deduction—are covered in Chapter 6, which provides information on funding your own education. Here, we explain the special rules that apply when you use these benefits for a dependent's education expenses.

> **TIP**
>
> **You may claim a tax benefit for prepaid tuition.** To claim a credit or deduction for education expenses, your payment must generally be for an academic program that begins during the current tax year. However, you have a little leeway. You may also include payments you make in the current year for a term that begins within the first three months of the next tax year. If you know you will qualify for the credit or deduction this year but are unlikely to qualify next year because of income limitations, you might want to prepay tuition for the academic term that begins within the first three months of the next year.

Hope Credit

If you pay tuition and required fees for a student who is your dependent and is in the first or second year of postsecondary education, then you might qualify to claim a credit of up to $1,800 (in tax year 2008) for the expenses you pay. And, if you happen to be paying those expenses for two or more of your dependents, then you may claim the credit for each of them. You are eligible to claim the credit for an individual student if all of the following apply:

- The student must be your dependent.
- The student must be in his or her first or second year of postsecondary education.
- The student must be enrolled in a degree, certificate, or credential program.
- The student must be enrolled at least half-time.

Not only is this credit restricted to freshmen and sophomores, but you may claim the credit only twice per student. If it takes your granddaughter three years to finish her freshman year, you may claim a Hope Credit for her expenses in two of those years, but never again. (However, you might be able to claim a different education credit or deduction for her expenses, as explained in the sections that follow.)

Although the maximum Hope Credit you may claim for each qualifying student is $1,800 per year, you are not automatically entitled to the full amount. See Chapter 6 for information on how to calculate and claim your Hope Credit, including the phase-out that applies to higher-income filers.

Tax Strategy: Should You or the Student Claim the Credit?

Typically, you will claim the Hope Credit when you pay a dependent's education expenses. Even after you've retired, your income is likely to be higher than your dependent student's, which means the credit will probably be more valuable to you. And, it's only fair: You're footing the bill, so why shouldn't you get the benefit?

You may find, however, that you are unable to claim the credit because your income is too high and you are subject to the credit phase-out. In this situation, the tax benefit doesn't go away entirely: The student whose expenses you pay may claim the credit on his or her own tax return, as long as you forgo the dependency exemption. If the credit is only partly phased out for you, you might need to make some calculations to determine which of you will benefit more from claiming the credit.

When totaling the tuition and fees on which the credit is based, you may include all eligible expenses paid by you and by your dependent (the student). That same rule applies to your dependent. If you decide to let your dependent claim the credit, he or she may include tuition and fees paid by both of you.

Lifetime Learning Credit

As an alternative to the Hope Credit, you may claim a Lifetime Learning Credit for the tuition and fees you pay on behalf of a dependent. You may claim either the Hope Credit or the Lifetime Learning Credit for a given student, but not both.

The Lifetime Learning Credit differs from the Hope Credit in the following ways:

- The Lifetime Learning Credit is not limited to the first two years of postsecondary education (hence the moniker "Lifetime Learning"). If you otherwise qualify, you may claim the credit every year for the same student.
- The student need not be enrolled in a degree program.
- The student need not be enrolled at least half-time.
- The Lifetime Learning Credit has a higher limit—$2,000, instead of $1,800 for the Hope Credit—but the Lifetime Learning Credit limit is a family limit. The maximum Lifetime Learning Credit you may claim on your return for any year is $2,000, regardless of how many students you are helping out. In contrast, the Hope Credit is a per-student limit.

TIP

You may claim both the Hope and Lifetime Learning Credits in the same year for different students. If you are paying the education expenses of several dependents, your best strategy may be to claim the Lifetime Learning Credit for one of the students and the Hope Credit for the others, if you qualify to do so. Although you can't claim both of these credits for the same student in the same year, you can claim a credit for each student whose expenses you pay.

Although you may claim a maximum Lifetime Learning Credit of $2,000 for any given tax year, the credit you claim may not exceed 20% of your expenses (tuition and fees for those individuals for whom you are claiming the credit). In other words, the limit is actually the lesser of $2,000 or 20% of your expenses.

You must claim the Lifetime Learning Credit instead of the Hope Credit for any student who has already completed two years of postsecondary schooling. But if the student's circumstances qualify you to claim either credit, you should do some calculations before making a decision.

> **EXAMPLE:** Your grandson is living with you and you claim him as your dependent each year. This year he is a freshman at a private college. You have paid $10,000 in tuition and fees for the year. Your income is low enough that you will not be subject to a credit phase-out for either the Hope or the Lifetime Learning Credit.
>
> If you claim the Hope Credit, you will be eligible for the maximum credit of $1,800 (100% of the first $1,200 plus 50% of the next $1,200).
>
> However, if you claim the Lifetime Learning Credit, your credit amount is the lesser of $2,000 or 20% of the education expenses. Because 20% of $10,000 is $2,000 (which is more than the Hope Credit of $1,800), you are better off claiming the Lifetime Learning Credit.

Both credits are subject to the same income phase-out. And, as is the case with the Hope Credit, you may forgo the dependency exemption to let your dependent claim the Lifetime Learning Credit if you find that results in greater net tax savings. To find out how to calculate and claim your Lifetime Learning Credit, see Chapter 6.

Deduction for Higher Education Expenses

As an alternative to claiming either a Hope or a Lifetime Learning Credit, you may claim a deduction for college tuition and fees you pay on behalf of a dependent. Again, you must choose among the education benefits: You may not claim two benefits in the same year for the same student.

Although this benefit is a deduction rather than a credit, it can be quite valuable. You claim this deduction above the line, which means it reduces your adjusted gross income (AGI). And, even if you aren't eligible for either of the education credits, you may still be eligible for the higher education expense deduction because the income restrictions are less stringent:

- If you are single and your modified AGI is no more than $65,000 ($130,000 if you are married and filing a joint return), you may claim a deduction of up to $4,000 of tuition and fees that you pay on behalf of your dependent.
- If you are single and your modified AGI is greater than $65,000 but no more than $80,000 (or greater than $130,000 but no more than $160,000 if you are married filing a joint return), you may claim a deduction of up to $2,000 of tuition and fees that you pay on behalf of your dependent.
- If you are single and your modified AGI is more than $80,000 (or more than $160,000 if you are married and filing a joint return), you may not claim the deduction.

Like the limit on the Lifetime Learning Credit, the deduction limits are per family, not per student. No matter how many dependents you are helping out, the total deduction you may claim on your return is $4,000 (assuming the income restrictions discussed above don't apply).

You may claim a deduction only for expenses you actually pay. Unlike the Hope and Lifetime Learning Credits, you may not include expenses paid by your dependent. Similarly, the student may not claim a deduction for expenses you pay on his or her behalf, even if you forgo the dependency exemption. The student may claim only those expenses that he or she actually paid.

For more information on the higher education expense deduction, including which expenses qualify and how to calculate and claim your deduction, see Chapter 6.

Student Loan Interest

If you take out a loan to pay the higher education expenses of your dependent, you might qualify for another education tax benefit.

The loan interest might be deductible, up to a maximum annual deduction of $2,500. Like the higher education expense deduction, the student loan interest deduction is claimed above the line.

You can find information on eligibility requirements, qualified expenses, and how to calculate and claim your deduction for student loan interest in Chapter 6. One of the eligibility requirements is especially important if you are using a loan to pay a dependent's education expenses: You may deduct interest on the loan only if you are liable for the loan. If the loan is in your dependent's name, you may not deduct the interest. Your dependent may not deduct the interest, either, even if he or she is liable for the loan: The deduction is not available to someone who can be claimed as a dependent on another person's tax return.

Education Expenses You Pay for Someone Who Is Not a Dependent

Most retirees who are paying someone else's education expenses are not helping a dependent. More often, that help is going to a student who still lives at home with his or her parents, such as a grandchild, niece, or nephew.

There are even some generous retirees who are paying the education expenses of a more distant relative, or (gasp!) an in-law or a friend. If the target of your generosity is not your dependent, you won't find any education credits or deductions in the tax code to help you out. However, you can leverage the help you provide by choosing an investment vehicle that offers tax benefits to the person you are assisting: a Coverdell Education Savings Account (ESA) or a Qualified Tuition Program (also known as a 529 Plan).

Coverdell ESA

A Coverdell ESA is a special type of savings account, which can be established in the name of any person (the "beneficiary") who is under the age of 18. Once the account is established, you may make contributions to the account for as long as the child is younger than 18. Other people and entities (such as trusts and estates) may also make contributions to the account, but the total of all contributions to one or more Coverdell accounts for a given beneficiary may not exceed $2,000 per year.

When the beneficiary turns 18, control of the account transfers to the beneficiary. Although no additional contributions can be made to the account after the beneficiary's 18th birthday, the beneficiary may continue to use the funds for education expenses until he or she turns 30. At that time, the entire remaining balance of the account must be distributed to the beneficiary.

The advantage of a Coverdell ESA goes not to the contributor, but to the child for whom the account is established. As long as the funds are used for qualified education expenses, distributions from the account—both the contributions and the investment earnings—will be completely tax free to the beneficiary.

> **CAUTION**
>
> **Some states tax distributions.** Although distributions from a Coverdell ESA are free of federal tax, some states tax a portion of the distributions for state income tax purposes. Be sure to check the rules of your state.

The student can use account funds to pay tuition, fees, tutors, books, supplies, equipment, uniforms, computers, and even room and board if the student is enrolled at least half-time, whether at an elementary, a secondary, or a college institution. If the funds are not used to pay qualified education expenses, the earnings portion of the distribution will be subject to both income tax and penalties. This rule also applies to the final distribution of funds, when the beneficiary turns 30, unless they are used for qualified education expenses.

As noted above, your contribution to a Coverdell ESA is not deductible. Furthermore, the contribution is treated as a gift to the account beneficiary, which means you might have to file a gift tax return or even pay gift tax if your contribution, along with other gifts to the same person in the same year, come to more than $12,000 (for 2008). (See Chapter 11 for more on gifts and gift tax.)

Contribution Phase-Out for Higher-Income Filers

The contribution ceiling of $2,000 is gradually reduced when your income exceeds certain limits. Your maximum contribution is phased out if your modified adjusted gross income is between $95,000 and $110,000 (if you are single) or between $190,000 and $220,000 (if you are married filing a joint return). The $2,000 limit is reduced in direct proportion to the amount by which your income exceeds the lower phase-out threshold.

> **EXAMPLE:** You are married and your modified adjusted gross income is $205,000. Because your income exceeds the lower phase-out threshold of $190,000, you must compute your new contribution limit, as follows:
>
> **Step 1:** Calculate the total phase-out range for your marital status.
> $220,000 – $190,000 = $30,000
>
> **Step 2:** Calculate the amount by which your income exceeds the lower threshold amount.
> $205,000 – $190,000 = $15,000
>
> **Step 3:** Determine the ratio of Step 2 to Step 3.
> $15,000 ÷ $30,000 = ½
>
> **Step 4:** Multiply the ratio from Step 3 by $2,000 to determine your new contribution limit.
> ½ x $2,000 = $1,000.
>
> Your contribution limit for the tax year is $1,000.

CAUTION

The rules will soon be stricter. Under current law, the rules for Coverdell ESAs are scheduled to tighten up considerably beginning in 2011. Among other things, contribution limits will be reduced and fewer expenses will qualify for tax-free treatment.

Claiming a Loss

Suppose the investments in the Coverdell ESA you set up didn't do very well. You have spent all the funds in the account for the beneficiary's education, and the beneficiary is still under the age of 18. If the total amount that you distributed from the account over the years was less than your total contributions, you may claim a loss in the year of the final distribution from the account.

You must claim the loss as a miscellaneous itemized deduction on Schedule A. The loss will be deductible only if you itemize deductions and only to the extent that all of your miscellaneous itemized deductions exceed 2% of your adjusted gross income.

How to Report Your Coverdell ESA Contribution

Because your contribution to a Coverdell ESA is not deductible, you are not required to report the contribution on your tax return. However, the student who uses the funds for education might be required to report the distribution on his or her income tax return, if taxes or penalties apply.

Section 529 Plans

A more flexible alternative to the Coverdell ESA is the Qualified Tuition Program, usually referred to as a 529 plan (after the section of the tax code that gave it life). Like a Coverdell ESA, a 529 plan allows you to make nondeductible contributions on behalf of a named recipient—any person, not just a dependent. Distributions from the account that are used for certain college expenses are tax free. Such expenses include tuition and fees, books, supplies, equipment, and room and board if the student attends at least half time.

TIP

State rules may vary. For example, although contributions to a 529 plan are not deductible for federal purposes, many states allow you to deduct contributions on your state income tax return if you contribute to the 529 plan sponsored by the state in which you reside. For more information about which states allow deductions for contributions by residents, see the Saving for College website, www.savingforcollege.com. Some states also impose additional restrictions on 529 plans, such as limits on how long they can exist.

If the funds are distributed to the beneficiary and the beneficiary does not use the funds for qualified education expenses, the beneficiary must pay the taxes and penalties.

Unlike a Coverdell ESA, which goes to the student once he or she turns 18, you own the 529 plan and control distribution of the assets. When the beneficiary needs funds for education, you notify the administrator of the plan to distribute the funds to you, the beneficiary, or the institution. If you die before all the funds are distributed, the terms of the plan determine who takes over as owner. Some plans allow you to name a successor, others pass ownership to the beneficiary, and, in some states, ownership passes under the terms of your will.

If the account is distributed because of the beneficiary's death or disability, no penalties will apply. However, the person who receives the remaining funds must pay income tax on the earnings portion— the investment returns. If the beneficiary dies, the remaining funds are included in the beneficiary's estate, and the estate (or the beneficiary's heirs) will be liable for the income tax on the distributed funds.

One advantage of a Coverdell ESA over a 529 plan is that qualified educational expenses include elementary and secondary education expenses as well as college expenses. Funds in a 529 plan may be used for postsecondary education only. However, 529 plans offer some important advantages over Coverdell ESAs:

- There are no age restrictions on the beneficiary of the account (the student). An account may be established for a beneficiary of any age.
- There are no income restrictions on you, the contributor. You may make the maximum contribution regardless of how high your adjusted gross income is.
- Although contribution limits vary from state to state, some states allow you to contribute several hundred thousand dollars to a 529 plan. However, that amount is a lifetime limit (per beneficiary), not an annual limit.

One caution, however: Any contribution you make to such an account for someone other than yourself is considered a gift. If you contribute more than $12,000 (for 2008), you must file a gift tax return. (This rule doesn't apply to your spouse, to whom you may make unlimited gifts without filing a gift tax return.) And if you contribute a very large sum, you might actually be required to pay gift tax, as well. If you plan to make a large contribution to a 529 plan for someone other than yourself or your spouse, you should confer with an estate planning expert before doing so.

For more information about 529 plans, including eligibility requirements, types of plans, and changing beneficiaries, see Chapter 6.

Tax Strategy: Should You Make Advance Gifts to a 529 Plan?

To encourage taxpayers to put money into 529 plans, Congress has provided an incentive for front-loading the plans. Generally, gifts of more than $12,000 (for 2008) that you make to one person in a single year are subject to gift tax and could affect the amount of estate tax due (if any) upon your death.

However, the tax code provides an exception for contributions to 529 plans. When you make a lump sum contribution to a 529 plan, you may elect on your gift tax return to treat the gift as allocable equally to the current year and each of the four succeeding years for gift tax purposes. For example, if you contribute $60,000 in the current year, you may elect to treat it as a $12,000 annual contribution for the current year and each of the next four years. Because gifts of $12,000 or less are not taxable, your contribution will not use any of your lifetime exemption or be subject to gift tax, as long as you make no other gifts to the beneficiary of the 529 plan during the year. Of course, if you make additional contributions to the 529 plan account on behalf of the same beneficiary during any of those years, the additional contributions might bring your total contribution for the year to more than $12,000. For more information about gifts, see Chapter 11.

How to Report Your Contribution to a 529 Plan

As is the case with your contribution to a Coverdell ESA, you are not required to report a contribution to a 529 plan on your income tax return because it is not deductible for federal purposes. (If your state permits a deduction for state income tax purposes, you will need to review the instructions for completing your state form to determine how to claim the deduction.) However, your contribution to a 529 plan is considered a gift to the beneficiary of the account. If the amount of your contribution exceeds $12,000 (for 2008), you must file a gift tax return. See Chapter 11 for more information about gifts.

Alimony

Nowadays, we look for tax benefits wherever we can find them. If you are paying alimony to a former spouse (or fear you soon will be), the tax code offers you a bit of a silver lining, in the form of a tax deduction. And the news gets a little better: The deduction, if you are entitled to it, is an above-the-line deduction, which means you may claim it even if you don't itemize your deductions on Schedule A. It also reduces your AGI, which leads to other tax benefits. (See Chapter 1 for more information about the benefits of above-the-line deductions.)

Which Payments Count as Alimony?

Your divorce decree or separation agreement might require you to make payments to your former spouse that don't technically qualify as alimony—and, therefore, are not deductible.

To be deductible, your payments must satisfy all of the following requirements:

- There must be a written divorce decree, legal separation agreement, or decree of support that requires you to make the payments.
- You cannot be living with the person to whom you are making the payments.
- You must make your payments in cash, rather than other types of property (like stock or real estate).
- Your written agreement or divorce decree must explicitly state that payments will terminate upon the death of your former spouse (or sooner). If your agreement does not include this language, then the laws of your state must require that payments terminate when your former spouse dies. If your agreement or state law allows or requires payments to continue after the death of your former spouse, none of your alimony payments will be deductible—even those made before your former spouse dies.

Tax Strategy: Should You Claim an Alimony Deduction?

You are not required to claim a deduction for the alimony you pay. And, although you might think that any deduction is a good deduction, there is a downside—for your former spouse. If you claim an alimony deduction, your former spouse is required to report that amount as income. If you do not claim the deduction, your former spouse won't have to report (or pay tax on) the alimony income.

Maybe you aren't on speaking terms with your former spouse, and you have no interest in coordinating your efforts to save taxes. But just for the sake of argument, let's assume that you are willing to consider it. If the money you save by claiming the deduction is insignificant relative to the additional tax liability your spouse would incur by reporting the income, perhaps you can come to some agreement. For example, perhaps your former spouse could make a gift to you of the amount of tax savings you lost as a result of not claiming the alimony deduction. You both might come out ahead.

If you decide to forgo the deduction, you must make it official. Your agreement to do so (as well as your former spouse's intent to exclude—that is, to not report—the income) must be part of your divorce decree or written separation or support agreement. Your former spouse must attach a copy of that portion of your agreement to his or her tax return for each year that the agreement is in place.

Payments That Are Not Alimony

You may deduct only payments that meet the requirements described above, regardless of the agreement between you and your former spouse. For example, you may not deduct any of the following:

- **Child support payments.** If you have minor children, your divorce decree (or separation or support agreement) might require child support payments. If the payments are specifically designated as child support, you may not deduct them. Even if your agreement does not designate the required payments as child support, they will be deemed child support payments if they are tied to your children in some well-defined way. For example, payments that continue until your children reach a certain age or until the children leave home will be treated as child support rather than as deductible alimony.

- **Voluntary payments.** Payments you make to your former spouse out of the goodness of your heart are not alimony, and you may not deduct them.

- **Property settlement payments.** Payments you make to your spouse as part of dividing up your assets are not alimony. For example, if you give your spouse the house as part of your divorce agreement, or you pay your spouse half the value of the family car you are keeping after the divorce, that is a property settlement, not alimony.

Because alimony payments are deductible and other payments to a former spouse are not, the IRS is on the alert for taxpayers who try to disguise certain nondeductible payments as alimony. Most often, the IRS decides that the payments should have been classified as part of a nondeductible property settlement. Here are the rules the IRS uses to help distinguish between property settlements and alimony payments.

As long as your payments add up to $15,000 a year or less, and you meet the requirements listed under "Which Payments Count as

Alimony?" above, the payments will qualify as deductible alimony regardless of how many payments you make.

If your payments decline in the second or third year after they began, you might be required to report as income ("recapture"), in the third year, the alimony deductions you claimed in the first or second year. The specific requirements are:

- You must recapture the deduction you claimed in the first year if your total first-year payments exceed the average of your total second-year and total third-year payments by more than $15,000.

- You must recapture your deduction for the second year if your total second-year payments exceed your total third-year payments by more than $15,000.

> **CAUTION**
>
> **Older agreements might be treated differently.** If you are paying alimony under an agreement that was put in place before 1985, different rules might apply. If you have an older agreement, talk to a tax professional.

> **RESOURCE**
>
> For more information about alimony, see IRS Publication 504, *Divorced or Separated Individuals*.

How to Deduct Alimony

Claim the deduction for alimony payments on the first page of Form 1040, in the "Adjusted Gross Income" section. You must also enter the Social Security number of your former spouse.

CHAPTER 11

Gifts, Inheritances, and Surviving Your Spouse

Tax Benefits in This Chapter

☐ **Did you receive a gift from someone?**

- Generally, you don't have to pay income tax on gifts you receive.

☐ **Did you give someone a gift?**

- You may not deduct the value of gifts you make to another person.
- If the value of the gift is more than $12,000 (for 2008), however, you might have to file a gift tax return and pay gift tax.

☐ **Did you inherit cash or other property?**

- You do not have to pay income tax on the value of most types of assets you inherit.
- If you inherit property that generates income, you will have to report and pay tax on income it generates after you inherit it.
- If you inherit money that was owed to the decedent at the time of death (such as a final paycheck), you generally must pay income tax on it when you receive it.

☐ **Did your spouse pass away in the last year or two?**

- You may file a joint return for the year in which your spouse died, and claim the exemptions and tax rates that would have been available if your spouse were still alive.
- You may deduct, on your tax return for the year your spouse dies, medical expenses you pay on behalf of your spouse in the 12 months following your spouse's death
- You might be able to exclude up to $500,000 of gain from the sale of your home if you sell the house after 2007 and within two years after your spouse dies.
- You may not deduct the cost of a funeral, memorial service, or grave marker on your personal tax return, but those costs may be deductible on your spouse's estate tax return.

I f you are confused about the tax rules for gifts and inheritances, you aren't alone. Many an accountant has fielded questions like, "Where do I deduct the $10,000 I gave to my daughter?" and "How do I report the inheritance I received?" For the most part, the answer to those questions is: You don't. Most gifts and inheritances are not subject to income tax, and you may not claim a deduction on your income tax return for gifts you make to individuals.

Many retirees increase their gift-giving in later years. They often make gifts of cash—or perhaps other types of assets, such as stock—to help out children or grandchildren or simply to reduce the size of their estates before they die. But there's a catch when making gifts: Although the recipient won't have to pay regular income tax on the gift, the person making the gift might have to pay gift taxes.

Inheritances also take on more importance as we get older, whether we're on the receiving end of someone else's generosity or planning for the eventual distribution of our own estates. Plenty of retirees find themselves the recipient of an inheritance at the same time they are coping with the death of a parent, sibling, or spouse. The influx of cash or property is often welcome even though it means learning new financial strategies during a time of grief. For many people, it's a nice surprise to learn that the inheritance is not subject to income tax. However, if the deceased person's estate was large, the inherited assets might be subject to estate tax.

Gifts

In general, a gift is a transfer of cash or other property to another person or entity. When you make a gift, the asset you give away is no longer yours: It becomes the property of the recipient. Making lifetime gifts to children and grandchildren is a strategy that many wealthy individuals use to reduce the size of their estates, thereby reducing the amount of estate tax due when they die.

CROSS REFERENCE

Information on charitable gifts. This chapter covers gifts you might make to an individual or to an entity that does not qualify as a charity for tax deduction purposes. For information about gifts made to charitable organizations (for which you might be entitled to a deduction on your income tax return), see Chapter 5.

Different Rules Might Apply If Your Gift Has Strings Attached

When you make a completed gift, generally the asset you give away is removed from your estate and becomes the property of the recipient of the gift. But if you haven't made a completed gift, you have not successfully removed the asset from your estate and different tax rules might apply.

To make a completed gift, you generally must give up control of the asset, or more specifically, you must give up the ability to control the recipient's interest in the gift. If your gift has strings attached—for example, if you give your stock portfolio away with the proviso that you can receive some or all of the income when and if you need it during your lifetime—then you probably haven't made a completed gift. If you're considering making a gift in this manner, you should talk to an estate planning attorney or other tax professional to determine the best way to accomplish your goals while achieving the best possible estate or gift tax result.

Gifts typically do not result in taxable income or deductions for either the donor or the recipient. If a gift exceeds a certain limit, however, the giver (the donor) must file a special return—a gift tax return—and might be required to pay gift tax.

> ⚠ **CAUTION**
>
> **Gift tax rules can get complicated in a hurry.** The rules described in this chapter apply to many of the most common types of gifts. However, people often become creative with their gifts, structuring them in ways that might lead to different results than those described in this chapter. For example, you might give a "net gift": a gift conditioned on the recipient paying the gift tax. In that case, although you must still file the gift tax return, the recipient must pay the gift taxes. If the gift tax on a net gift exceeds your basis in the property, you might even have to pay some income tax. You might also have to pay income tax if your adjusted basis in a gift is less than any debt (such as a mortgage) that might be attached to the gift. If you plan to be creative in your gift giving, you should first speak with a tax professional to make sure you understand the laws that might apply to your particular transaction.

Gifts You Make

As you get older, you might be in a position to provide some financial assistance to a child or grandchild or perhaps a needy friend or relative. Even if your relatives aren't facing financial problems, you might want to give them some of your assets, to reduce the size of your estate. No matter why you've decided to be generous, any gift you make, whether cash or property, will not be deductible on your income tax return. And, it isn't treated as income to the recipient of the gift.

After you make the gift, however, any income the gifted asset generates will be taxable to the recipient. The new owner might also have to pay income tax, if he or she decides to sell the gifted asset. (See "Gifts You Receive," below.) And, you may have to worry about the gift tax.

Gift Tax

Although gifts you make will not generally affect your (or the recipient's) income tax, you will need to pay attention to potential gift tax issues and reporting requirements. Gift taxes are calculated whenever you make a gift, although exclusions, deductions, and credits often eliminate any current liability.

The person making the gift (the donor) is the one who might have to pay gift tax, not the recipient. This might seem counter-intuitive: After all, it's usually the person who receives money who has to pay tax, while the person who gives it away gets a deduction. Making the donor foot the bill makes more sense if you consider the primary purpose of the gift tax rules: to prevent wealthy individuals from avoiding estate tax at their death by giving away assets during their lifetime. If taxpayers were allowed to give away their property and other assets without tax liability during their lifetime, they could pass on their wealth, depleting their estate to the point where no estate tax would be due when they died. Imposing a gift tax is simply a way to make sure that large transfers of assets are taxed at some point, whether during life or after death.

Unless you are making an extremely large gift, you probably won't have to pony up any cash. The general rule is that gifts that don't exceed the annual exclusion amount, which is $12,000 for 2008 (the amount is scheduled to increase to $13,000 in 2009) are not subject to gift tax. And this limit applies per recipient. You can give away cash or property worth up to $12,000 each to as many different people as you like in a single year without incurring any gift tax.

 CAUTION

The value of a gift is determined on the day you make the gift. To figure out whether your gift exceeds the $12,000 exclusion, you must determine its fair market value on the day you make the gift. Although your basis in an asset—what you paid for it, plus certain adjustments—determines whether the recipient must pay income tax when it's sold, the gift's value for gift tax purposes is determined on the day of the gift.

For example, if you have seven children, you may give $12,000 to each of them during 2008 without incurring any gift tax. And, as long as nobody receives more than $12,000 from you during the year, you won't have to file a gift tax return (IRS Form 709, *United States Gift and Generation-Skipping Transfer Tax Return*).

> ! **CAUTION**
>
> **Gifts of a future interest are not eligible for the $12,000 exclusion.** A future interest is the right to possess or enjoy the gift only in the future, not currently (in the "present"). For example, suppose you give your fishing buddy the exclusive right to use your boat for the rest of his life. When he dies, the boat will go to your daughter. The gift to your daughter is a future interest. You might need the help of a tax professional to determine the value of that future interest, but regardless of the value, the gift will be subject to gift tax and you will be required to report the gift on Form 709.

The $12,000 limit applies separately to each person making a gift. If you are married, your spouse may also give away $12,000 to any number of people without gift tax consequences. For example, you and your spouse could give $12,000 each—$24,000 total—to your child in one year without having to pay gift tax.

But everything changes if you give more than $12,000 to one person during the year. Once you exceed the limit, you incur gift tax and have to file a gift tax return. That doesn't necessarily mean you have to send money to the IRS, however. Each person is entitled to claim a lifetime credit against gift tax in the amount of $345,800. That credit amount is the equivalent of tax on a $1 million gift. If you use up the entire amount of the credit during your lifetime, you must actually start sending real dollars to the IRS when you make gifts that exceed the exclusion amount. The use of both the annual exclusion and the lifetime gift tax exemption is automatic. You may not elect to "save" the exclusion or exemption for future gifts.

> **EXAMPLE:** In 2007, you gave $262,000 to each of your four children so that each could buy a house. You filed a gift tax return claiming a $12,000 exclusion for each child. The "taxable gift" to each child would be $250,000—a total of

$1,000,000 for all gifts. The tax (before the use of your credit) would be $345,800. Applying the credit ($345,800) against the tax, the balance due to the IRS is zero.

In 2008, you gave your grandson $10,000 for a car and gave your granddaughter $20,000. The gift to your grandson is not subject to gift tax because it's less than the $12,000 annual exclusion amount. However, the gift to your granddaughter is subject to gift tax because it exceeds the annual exclusion amount. You must file a gift tax return reporting both gifts, and you must pay gift tax on $8,000— the amount by which the gift to your granddaughter exceeds $12,000.

The lifetime credit amount is shared between gift taxes and estate taxes. When you die, your estate is eligible for a credit against estate taxes. But any amount of the gift tax credit you have used up during your lifetime will reduce the amount of estate tax credit available upon your death. If you use up your entire gift tax credit during your lifetime, you must pay gift tax on all future gifts that exceed the exclusion amount and, after you die, more of your assets will be subject to estate taxes.

Generation-Skipping Transfer Tax

If you make a gift during your lifetime—or a bequest after your death—to someone who is more than one generation younger than you (such as a grandchild), then you have made a generation-skipping transfer. Such transfers are subject to additional tax over and above any gift or estate tax you might owe. However, there are sizable exclusion amounts that can reduce or eliminate the tax liability. If you plan to make a large gift or bequest to someone who falls into this category, be sure to confer with a tax professional first.

Gifts That Aren't Taxed

Certain gifts that you make to, or on behalf of, another person are entirely exempt from gift tax, regardless of the size of the gift.

Medical Expenses

If you pay someone else's medical expenses, the payments are not subject to gift tax as long as you make them directly to the medical care provider. To qualify for this exclusion, the medical expenses you pay must be expenses that you could deduct if you paid them for your own health care. (For a detailed list of these expenses, see Chapter 4.)

If you give cash to someone who then uses it to pay his or her own medical expenses, the gift is not exempt from gift tax. (However, you may use the annual gift tax exclusion to avoid gift tax liability on at least $12,000 (for 2008).)

The unlimited exclusion for medical expenses paid directly to a medical care provider applies regardless of the relationship between you and the person whose expenses you pay. That person need not be your dependent, nor even related to you in any way.

Education Expenses

There is also an unlimited gift tax exclusion for certain education expenses you pay for someone else. You must make the payments directly to a "qualified educational organization," which is defined quite broadly. To qualify, the organization must have a regular faculty, curriculum, and student body; and it must conduct educational activities on a regular basis.

Only tuition payments are covered. Payments for room and board, books, supplies, and equipment do not qualify for the unlimited exclusion.

Your relationship to the person whose tuition you pay is irrelevant; that person need not be your relative or your dependent.

CAUTION

Payments to qualified tuition programs can't be excluded.
Contributions that you make to a qualified tuition program (also known as a 529 plan) do not qualify for the unlimited gift tax exclusion. For more information about using a 529 plan to fund someone else's education, see Chapter 10.

Gifts to Your Spouse

Gifts to your spouse are generally excluded from gift tax under gift and estate tax laws that provide an unlimited gift tax "marital deduction." There is some fine print, however.

Although most gifts to a spouse qualify for the marital deduction, gifts of a "terminable interest" do not. A terminable interest is one that is contingent on another event or expires after a certain period of time. For example, suppose you inherit a vacation property from your father. You decide to give your spouse the right to use the property for five years, after which you plan to give the property to your brother. Because your spouse's interest in the property (the right to use it) expires after five years, it is a terminable interest and might not qualify for the marital deduction. (For more information about gifts, estate planning and the marital deduction, see *Plan Your Estate,* by Denis Clifford (Nolo).)

Gifts you make to a spouse who is a U.S. citizen qualify for an unlimited marital deduction. If your spouse is not a citizen when you make the gift, the gift is subject to gift tax if it exceeds the annual exclusion amount. But a noncitizen spouse is allowed a much higher annual exclusion amount. For 2008, the annual exclusion for a noncitizen spouse is $125,000. However, your spouse may claim this higher exclusion only if your gift otherwise qualifies for the marital deduction; if it does not, your spouse may claim only the $12,000 exclusion amount.

Custodial Accounts

Many donors make gifts to minors through a custodial account. The custodian manages the account and makes financial decisions about the assets until the minor reaches the age of majority. The income generated by the account is taxable to the minor (who is usually in a lower income tax bracket). When the minor reaches legal age, he or she takes full control of the account.

When you contribute funds to a custodial account for a minor—perhaps a grandchild, niece, or nephew—the transaction is considered a gift by you to the child. If the amount of your gift exceeds $12,000 (for 2008), you must file a gift tax return.

But watch out for this quirky feature: If you serve as custodian of the account you funded and you happen to die before the minor reaches legal age, the value of the account will be included in your estate for estate tax purposes. That is true even though you are deemed to have made a completed gift at the time you funded the account. You can avoid this problem by naming someone else as custodian of the account.

> ## CAUTION
> **State laws may differ.** Rules for custodial accounts vary from state to state. For example, some states do not turn over control of the account to the beneficiary until age 21. Other states set the legal age at 18. If you're planning to set up a custodial account, read through the custodial agreement to make sure you understand the rules that apply.

Gifts You Receive

In the happy event that you are on the receiving end of a gift, the tax laws aren't going to rain on your parade. The gift you receive is not taxable to you under either the income tax laws or the gift tax laws. You also have no reporting requirements.

Your sole obligation is to report any income the property generates after you receive it. For example, if you receive a gift of savings bonds, you must report—and pay income tax on—the interest that accrues once ownership transfers to you. The donor must report on his own tax return the income that accrued before the date of the gift. This is true even if the accrued interest is delivered to you. However, in that case, the value of the gift for gift tax purposes would include the accrued interest.

You might also have to pay tax when you sell property you received as a gift. If the property has appreciated in value since the person who gave it to you first acquired it, you might owe income tax. Your taxable gain is typically the difference between your basis and the amount you receive when you sell it. When you receive a gift of appreciated property, your basis is the same as the donor's basis, not the fair market value of the gift at the time you received it. (See Chapter 1 for more information about determining basis.)

> **EXAMPLE:** Ten years ago, your brother bought 100 shares of GFX common stock for $25 per share. Your brother gave you 80 of his shares for your 80th birthday. You decide to sell the stock when it's selling for $60 a share. Your basis (for purposes of calculating your capital gain) will be what your brother paid for the stock—$25 per share—which means you will have a capital gain of $35 per share ($60 minus $25).

On the other hand, if you receive a gift of an asset that did not appreciate while the donor owned it, your basis depends on whether you will recognize a gain or a loss when you eventually sell it. If you will have a loss when you sell, your basis is the asset's fair market value on the date you received it. But, if you will have a gain when you sell, your basis is the same as the donor's basis at the time of the gift. If your proceeds from selling the asset fall somewhere between the fair market value on the date of the gift and the donor's adjusted basis at the time of the gift, then you recognize no gain and no loss.

EXAMPLE: Your uncle gave you 100 shares of XYZ stock for which he originally paid $5,000. When he gave you the stock, it was worth $4,000. You later sell the stock for $6,000. Because you have a gain from the sale, you use your uncle's basis of $5,000 to calculate your gain, which is $1,000.

On the other hand, if you had sold the stock for $3,000 (a loss), you would use the fair market value of the stock on the date of the gift ($4,000), and you would have a loss of $1,000.

If you sell the stock for an amount that is between your uncle's basis and the fair market value at the date of the gift (for example, you sell it for $4,500), you are deemed to have no gain and no loss.

Inheritances

As is the case with gifts that you receive, inherited property is generally not subject to income tax when you receive it. The primary exception to this rule is for certain types of income that the deceased person was entitled to, but had not yet received, at the time of death. Such income falls into the category of "income in respect of a decedent" (IRD), discussed below.

For the most part, however, your only obligation upon receiving an inheritance is to report (and pay income tax on) income the property generates after you inherit it. There is, however, a significant difference between gifts you receive during the donor's lifetime and property you inherit after the donor dies. Your basis in property that you inherit is generally the fair market value of the property when the donor dies. (IRD is an exception to this rule also, as explained below.) In tax terms, your basis is "stepped up" to the property's value on the date of death. As explained above, your basis in gifts that you receive during the donor's lifetime is the same as the donor's basis. Consequently, when you sell the property, you must pay income tax on the gain from the date the donor first acquired the property until you sell it. But when you inherit appreciated property, your basis is deemed to be the fair market value on the date of the donor's death. The tax on the property's appreciation is effectively eliminated if you sell the property immediately after inheriting it.

> **EXAMPLE:** Rather than receiving stock as a gift on your birthday, as in the example above, you inherit it. Your brother died when the stock hit $60 per share. He left all of the stock to you in his will. Your basis in the stock is deemed to be $60 per share, the fair market value of the stock at the time of your brother's death. If you sell the stock immediately, you will have no gain or loss and will owe no income tax on the proceeds of the sale.

Income in Respect of a Decedent

If someone dies before receiving certain taxable income to which he or she was entitled, such as salary or deferred compensation, the heir or beneficiary who receives the income must report it on his or her income tax return. This income is known as "income in respect of a decedent" (IRD). It might include wages that the decedent earned but had not yet been paid, as well as interest or dividends that had accrued but had not yet been paid. IRD also includes distributions of pretax money from the decedent's IRA or other retirement plan. In this latter case, the IRD doesn't have to be reported on the beneficiary's income tax return until funds are actually distributed from the account.

IRD is taxable income that eventually would have been included on the income tax return of the decedent, had he or she survived. Unfortunately, but perhaps logically, the income tax liability does not evaporate upon the death of the person to whom the income belonged. Instead, it transfers, along with the assets themselves, to the heirs and beneficiaries.

No Stepped-Up Basis for IRD

IRD has some unique qualities. Not only is there always built-in income tax liability, but the assets themselves do not acquire a new basis upon the death of the owner as other assets do. For example, if you inherit stock that is held in a regular, taxable brokerage account, your basis in the stock is "stepped up" to its value on the date of the decedent's death. But stock that is held in an IRA is not entitled to a step-up. If you take shares of stock out of your pretax IRA, you generally will owe regular income tax on the fair market value of the stock on the date of distribution. When your beneficiaries inherit the IRA assets, the same rules will apply. The beneficiaries must pay income tax on the fair market value of any property (including cash) that they withdraw from the inherited IRA.

Perhaps what pains a beneficiary most about IRD is the prospect of a double tax. IRD is included in the estate of a decedent and subject to estate tax (if the estate is large enough to be subject to estate tax). In addition, the beneficiary must pay income tax on IRD. However, there is some pain relief available, in the form of an IRD deduction.

IRD Deduction

The deduction for "estate tax attributable to IRD," better known as the IRD deduction, was introduced to relieve the double tax problem.

If an estate actually paid some estate taxes, then a beneficiary who receives IRD may deduct, on his or her own income tax return, the amount of estate tax that was attributable to the IRD. To figure out how much you can deduct, you must calculate the estate tax liability twice: once with the IRD included, and a second time without the IRD. The difference is the amount of your IRD deduction.

Which Estates Must Pay Estate Tax?

The law allows each person to leave a certain amount, called an "exclusion amount," to his or her heirs free of estate taxes. The exclusion amount is scheduled to increase from $2 million in 2008 to $3.5 million in 2009. The estate tax is a perennial tinkering target for politicians on both sides of the Congressional aisle, however, so only time will tell how large the exclusion will be in future years. Your estate generally will not be subject to estate tax if the value of the estate is less than the exclusion amount.

You may claim the IRD deduction only in the year you report the IRD on your income tax return. The deduction is a miscellaneous itemized deduction, so you may claim the deduction only if you are itemizing your deductions (instead of claiming the standard deduction). However, the IRD deduction is not subject to the 2% floor, as many other itemized deductions are. (The 2% floor means you may deduct certain itemized deductions only to the extent they exceed 2% of your adjusted gross income; some of these itemized deductions are covered in Chapter 7.)

There is a gray area of the IRD deduction rules dealing with IRD property that has appreciated between the date of death and the date the IRD must be reported for income tax purposes. Suppose you inherit a $50,000 IRA, which you now know to be IRD. You (or perhaps your accountant) have determined that the IRD deduction is $20,000. If you take a distribution of the entire IRA and report it on your income tax return, you are entitled to claim an IRD deduction of $20,000.

But suppose you withdraw only $10,000 in the current year, rather than cleaning out the account. Because you withdrew only one-fifth of the assets, you may claim only one-fifth of the total deduction, or $4,000. The following year, the IRA grows to $60,000. But only $40,000 of that is IRD. If you take another distribution of $10,000, can you assume that all of it is IRD, or must you assume part of it is attributable to earnings that accrued after the date of death? If the distribution is deemed to include some earnings, then your IRD deduction for the year will be something less than $4,000.

Unfortunately, the tax code and regulations have not provided a clear answer. Some tax professionals believe that you may treat all distributions as 100% IRD until the entire amount of the allocable estate tax has been deducted. Others feel that approach is too aggressive, as that it is not supported by the tax code or the regulations. You will want to discuss how to handle this situation with a tax professional before you take the plunge.

How to Claim an IRD Deduction

You may claim a deduction for IRD only if you itemize your deductions. Claim the deduction on Schedule A, in the "Other Miscellaneous Itemized Deductions" section. Identify the deduction as "Income in respect of a decedent" next to the amount of the deduction.

Beneficiary of an Estate or Trust

When you inherit assets, you rarely receive those assets immediately. The delay often results from all of the administrative tasks that need attention, as well as legal red tape that must be cut before distributions can be made. Sometimes, an inheritance is held in trust, which by its terms might delay the distribution of the assets. If assets are being held for you in a trust, the trust is a separate taxpayer for as long as it holds any of those assets. The trust owns the assets and is responsible for paying tax on the income they generate. Similarly, if an estate must go through probate, the estate itself becomes a separate taxpayer and must pay tax on income generated by the assets of the estate until those assets are distributed to the beneficiaries.

While the trust or estate is in existence (that is, before it has distributed all of its assets), it might occasionally make distributions to beneficiaries—distributions of assets and the income those assets generate. If so, you (if you are a beneficiary) might be required to report your share of the taxable income on your own tax return and pay income tax on it. You might also be able to claim some deductions related to the trust or estate on your own tax return.

Your share of the income and expenses of an estate is typically reported to you on a Schedule K-1, *Beneficiary's Share of Income, Deductions, Credits, etc.* For example, if your assets earn interest, the interest will be reported on the K-1. You take the number from the K-1 and report it on Schedule B of your individual income tax return, just as you would if interest income were reported by your bank or brokerage firm on a Form 1099. The K-1 will also report deductions to which you are entitled, such as investment expenses associated with your assets. You report those expenses on Schedule A of your individual income tax return, and they will be deductible if you itemize your deductions.

The same rules apply if you are the beneficiary of a trust. For example, suppose your mother left certain assets in a trust. You are to receive income from the trust for your lifetime; when you die, the trust assets go to your children. Because you are a beneficiary of the trust, you will receive a Schedule K-1 each year indicating the amount and character of the income you must report on your own tax return, as well as any deductions you might be entitled to claim.

If You Survive Your Spouse

Of course, there are additional considerations—both emotional and financial—if the person from whom you inherit assets is your spouse. Immediately after the death of a spouse, grief and sorrow often run roughshod over the ability to make decisions. Fortunately, many big decisions can wait, and tasks that need immediate attention can often be handled by someone else. Eventually, the survivor will feel able to tackle some business and financial matters and might even welcome the distraction. Here is an overview of some of the tax issues that might come up, with a particular emphasis on deductions and exemptions.

Filing Status and Exemptions

If you and your spouse were filing a joint return, you claimed a personal exemption for each of you. For the year of your spouse's death, you may still file a joint return. You may also claim a personal exemption for your deceased spouse (as well as for yourself), as long as you did not remarry during the year. Starting in the year after your spouse's death, you will file as a single individual and you will claim only your own personal exemption. But of course, if you remarry, you may once again decide to file as married filing jointly (or married filing separately, but not single).

Qualified Widow or Widower With Dependent May Use Joint Tax Rates

If you are caring for a dependent child in one or both of the two years following your spouse's death, you may use the married filing jointly income tax rates to compute your tax if all of the following are true:

- You did not remarry during either tax year.
- You were entitled to file a joint return with your spouse (even if you elected to file separately).
- You are eligible to claim as a dependent a child, stepchild, or adopted child, and
  - you paid more than half of the cost of maintaining your home
  - the child lived with you for the entire year (except for temporary absences), and
  - the child is not your foster child.

Standard Deduction

If you will be claiming the standard deduction instead of itemizing your deductions for the year of your spouse's death, you may claim the standard deduction amount for a married couple ($10,900 for 2008).

You may claim the additional standard deduction of $1,050 for yourself if you are at least age 65. In addition, you may claim the additional standard deduction for your spouse if your spouse was at least age 65 at the time of his or her death. To claim the additional amount, you (the survivor) must turn 65 by the end of the year. However, your spouse must have turned 65 before death. If you both qualify, the total additional amount is $2,100.

Similarly, if you are blind on December 31 of the tax year or your spouse was blind at the time of death, you may claim an additional standard deduction amount of $1,050 for one or both of you. If you both qualify, the total additional deduction amount is $2,100. For more about these deductions, see Chapter 2.

Itemized Deductions

A deceased person's tax year ends when he or she dies. Consequently, reporting income and deductions for the year a spouse dies is a little more complex. If you file a joint return, typically you report your own income and deductions for the entire year, and your spouse's income and deductions through the date of death. Your spouse's income and deductions for the period after death are reported on the income tax return of your spouse's estate or trust.

Medical Expenses

The most significant exception to the above rule is for medical expenses. It's not uncommon for someone to incur large medical expenses before death. Ordinarily, expenses are deductible for the tax year in which you actually pay them. But in this case, even if your spouse dies in the middle of the year, you may claim all of the medical expenses paid during the year, before or after the date of death.

> ⚠ **CAUTION**
> **Not all expenses that are deductible on an individual tax return would be deductible on an estate or trust income tax return.** Medical expenses are one example of this rule. However, although medical expenses are not deductible on an estate or trust income tax return, they are deductible on an estate tax return if paid after the date of death. See "Estate Tax Return vs. Estate Fiduciary Income Tax Return," below, for more information about the difference between these types of tax returns.

Medical Expenses Paid in the Year After Death

In some situations, you might pay a spouse's medical expenses the year after a spouse dies. Fortunately, a special rule allows the executor or administrator of the estate to elect to treat medical expenses as though they were paid in the year the services were provided, rather than the year they were actually paid. The election is valid only for expenses paid within 12 months after death. If the election is made, the additional medical expenses are claimed on the decedent's final income tax return. If the return has already been filed, you may file an amended return to claim the additional amounts, as long as you file it within the requisite period (generally, within three years of the original due date of the return).

> **EXAMPLE:** Your wife died in September 2008. You are the executor of her estate. The medical expenses for your wife's final illness totaled $12,000. You paid $7,500 of those expenses before December 31. You paid the remaining $4,500 in February 2009. If you make an election to deduct the amounts paid in 2009 on your spouse's final income tax return, you may deduct the entire $12,000 on your joint 2008 income tax return.

> ## Tax Strategy: Should You Claim Medical Expenses on an Individual Income Tax Return or an Estate Tax Return?
>
> You may claim medical expenses paid in the year after death on your spouse's final income tax return, if you elect to do so. Alternatively, you may deduct those expenses on the decedent's estate tax return. The choice is yours. You may deduct the expenses on the return that provides the most tax relief.
>
> If, as is often the case, a decedent's estate is not large enough to require the filing of an estate tax return, you will want to claim the medical expenses on the decedent's income tax return to avoid losing the deduction altogether.
>
> But if the estate is subject to estate tax, chances are good that you will want to claim the medical expense deduction on the estate tax return. For one thing, medical expenses may be claimed on an individual income tax return only to the extent they exceed 7½% of adjusted gross income. (See Chapter 4 for more information.) And estate tax rates are generally higher than income tax rates, so you'll save more by claiming the deduction on the estate tax return.
>
> You may also divide the deduction—that is, make an election to claim some medical expenses on the final return of the decedent and the remainder on the estate tax return. But again, expenses you elect to deduct on an income tax return will be subject to the 7½% floor. Amounts you are not able to deduct because of this limitation are not deductible for estate tax purposes, either.

How to Claim a Deduction for Medical Expenses of Decedent

If you would like to claim some or all of the medical expenses paid for your spouse after death, the executor must sign a statement (which you must attach to the income tax return for the year of death) that: (1) the medical expenses you are deducting on the income tax return have not been claimed as a deduction on an estate tax return; and (2) the executor waives the right to claim the expenses on an estate tax return in the future.

Gain Exclusion on Sale of Principal Residence

As described in Chapter 2, married couples who satisfy certain requirements may exclude up to $500,000 of gain when they sell their principal residence. If you are single, the gain exclusion is only $250,000.

When your spouse dies, you are single in the eyes of the law (although you are permitted to file a joint return in the year of death). However, it seems unreasonable that you should have to rush to sell your home before your ill spouse dies so that you can take advantage of the larger exclusion amount.

Fortunately, Congress agreed with this logic. Beginning in 2008, if you sell your principal residence within two years after the date your spouse dies, you may still claim the $500,000 gain exclusion. This law applies to home sales that occur after 2007. Even if your spouse died before 2008, as long as you sell the home in 2008 or later and within two years of the date of death, you may claim the $500,000 gain exclusion if you and your spouse would have qualified for the exclusion immediately before your spouse's death.

> **CAUTION**
>
> **If your home goes into trust.** The above rule applies if your principal residence goes directly to you when your spouse dies. However, if the residence goes into a trust or a subtrust, different rules might apply. If your principal residence is held in a trust or will be transferred to a trust when you or your spouse die, check with a tax professional to find out if the $500,000 exclusion will apply to the sale of the residence after one of you dies.

Nondeductible Expenses

Some of the most significant postmortem expenses are for funerals, memorial services, grave markers, and related items. Those expenses can be deducted on an estate tax return (if the estate is required to file one), but not on an individual income tax return.

Also, expenses incurred by the estate (or trust, if your deceased spouse's assets are held in trust) must be deducted on the estate's or trust's own income tax return, not yours. For example, if you pay an accountant to prepare an income tax return for your spouse's estate or trust, you can't deduct those fees on your individual income tax return. The fees are an expense of the estate or trust, which should be paid with assets of the estate or trust and then deducted on its income tax return.

Estate Tax Return vs. Estate Fiduciary Income Tax Return

When someone dies, a new tax entity comes into being, which generally takes ownership of many of the deceased person's assets. Most often the new entity is the "estate" of the decedent, although it might be a "trust" if the decedent directed that some or all assets be held in trust after his or her death. The new entity is a taxpayer in the eyes of the IRS, just as the deceased person was. Some of the assets will generate income while they are held in the estate or the trust (before they are distributed to other beneficiaries). That income must be reported on an income tax return. Income tax returns of estates and trusts are called fiduciary returns.

In addition to taxing income generated by a deceased person's assets, the U.S. government levies a tax on the assets themselves at the time of death. That tax is not an income tax, but an estate tax.

Distinguishing between these two types of tax can be confusing, especially for those who do not deal with such matters on a daily basis. Here's a distinction that should help: Although it is not uncommon for an estate to owe income taxes, it is quite rare for an estate to owe estate taxes. That's because there is a large estate tax exemption. For the year 2008, an individual may pass an estate of $2 million without incurring any estate tax liability.

Index

A

Get the Latest in the Law

 Nolo's Legal Updater
We'll send you an email whenever a new edition of your book is published!
Sign up at **www.nolo.com/legalupdater**.

 Updates at Nolo.com
Check **www.nolo.com/update** to find recent changes in the law that
affect the current edition of your book.

Nolo Customer Service
To make sure that this edition of the book is the most recent one, call us at
800-728-3555 and ask one of our friendly customer service representatives
(7:00 am to 6:00 pm PST, weekdays only). Or find out at **www.nolo.com**.

 Complete the Registration & Comment Card ...
... and we'll do the work for you! Just indicate your preferences below:

Registration & Comment Card

NAME _____ DATE _____

ADDRESS _____

CITY _____ STATE _____ ZIP _____

PHONE _____ EMAIL _____

COMMENTS _____

WAS THIS BOOK EASY TO USE?   (VERY EASY)   5   4   3   2   1   (VERY DIFFICULT)

☐ Yes, you can quote me in future Nolo promotional materials. *Please include phone number above.*

☐ Yes, send me **Nolo's Legal Updater** via email when a new edition of this book is available.

Yes, I want to sign up for the following email newsletters:

   ☐ **NoloBriefs** (monthly)
   ☐ **Nolo's Special Offer** (monthly)
   ☐ **Nolo's BizBriefs** (monthly)
   ☐ **Every Landlord's Quarterly** (four times a year)

☐ Yes, you can give my contact info to carefully selected
partners whose products may be of interest to me.

RTAX1

Send to: **Nolo** 950 Parker Street Berkeley, CA 94710-9867, Fax: (800) 645-0895, or include all of
the above information in an email to regcard@nolo.com with the subject line "RATX1."

more from

NOLO *and* USA TODAY

Cutting-Edge Content, Unparalleled Expertise

The Busy Family's Guide to Money

by Sandra Block, Kathy Chu & John Waggoner

The Busy Family's Guide to Money will help you make the most of your income, handle major one-time expenses, figure children into the budget—and much more. **$19.99**

The Work From Home Handbook

Flex Your Time, Improve Your Life

by Diana Fitzpatrick & Stephen Fishman

If you're one of those people who need to (or simply want to) work from home, let this book help you come up with a plan that both you and your boss can embrace! **$19.99**

Retire Happy

What You Can Do NOW to Guarantee a Great Retirement

by Richard Stim & Ralph Warner

You don't need a million dollars to retire well, but you do need friends, hobbies and an active lifestyle. This book shows how to make retirement the best time of your life. **$19.99**

The Essential Guide for First-Time Homeowners

Maximize Your Investment & Enjoy Your New Home

by Ilona Bray & Alayna Schroeder

This reassuring resource is filled with crucial financial advice, real solutions and easy-to-implement ideas that can save you thousands of dollars. **$19.99**

Easy Ways to Lower Your Taxes

Simple Strategies Every Taxpayer Should Know

by Sandra Block & Stephen Fishman

Provides useful insights and tactics to help lower your taxes. Learn how to boost tax-free income, get a lower tax rate, defer paying taxes, make the most of deductions—and more! **$19.99**

Prices subject to change.

800-728-3555 or www.nolo.com

NOLO More Help from **Nolo.com**

ONLINE LEGAL DOCUMENTS *NOW*

Preparing legal documents used to be time consuming and expensive. Not anymore. Created by Nolo's experienced legal staff, these documents can now be prepared in a matter of minutes at:
www.nolo.com

BUSINESS FORMATION

Form your business right now with our easy-to-use online service. Simply follow our detailed, step-by-step instructions and leave the rest to us.

Online LLC Formation	from $149
Online Corporation Formation	from $149

ESTATE PLANNING

Plan your estate, and save on legal fees at the same time with Nolo's comprehensive online forms. Don't delay—get your affairs in order now!

Online Will	from $69.95
Online Living Trust	from $169.99

INTELLECTUAL PROPERTY

Got a terrific idea? The fastest and safest way to establish proof of creation is a Provisional Patent Application. File a PPA now!

Online PPA	from $169.99

100s more business and consumer legal forms available at www.nolo.com—from $4.99 to $16.99

Related Books

Get It Together
Organize Your Records So Your Family Won't Have To
$21.99

IRAs, 401(k)s, & Other Retirement Plans
Taking Your Money Out
$34.99

Retire—And Start Your Own Business
Simple Strategies Every Taxpayer Should Know
$19.99

Long Term Care
How to Plan & Pay for It
$24.99

All titles are also available in downloadable format at nolo.com.

Find a Tax Attorney

- *Qualified lawyers*
- *In-depth profiles*
- *Respectful service*

If you're facing an IRS audit or unexpected tax bill, you don't need just any lawyer. You need a knowledgeable tax professional who can answer your questions on tax exemptions and deductions, and can provide up-to-the-minute legal advice and strategic help.

Nolo's Lawyer Directory is designed to help you search for the right attorney. Lawyers in our program are in good standing with their State Bar Associations and have created extensive profiles that feature their professional histories, credentials, legal philosophies, fees and more.

Check out **Nolo's Lawyer Directory** to find a tax lawyer who is right for you.

www.lawyers.nolo.com

The attorneys shown above are fictitious. Any resemblance to an actual attorney is purely coincidental.